THE GRAIL - TWO STUDIES

LEOPOLD VON SCHROEDER, ALEXANDER JACOB

Published in Australia
BIC Classification:
HRKP (Ancient Religions & Mythologies), DSBB (Literary Studies: Medieval), HRLK2 (Mysticism), HRAX (History of Religion).
978-0-9875598-9-0

NUMEN BOOKS
WWW.NUMENBOOKS.COM

The Grail

TWO STUDIES

THE ROOTS OF THE SAGA OF THE HOLY GRAIL

by

LEOPOLD VON SCHROEDER

THE INDO-EUROPEAN ORIGINS OF THE GRAIL

by

ALEXANDER JACOB

Was er auch sprach, doch hielt ihn noch
Der Knapp für Gott: so malt' Ihn doch
Die Königin Frau Herzeleid,
Die vom lichten Schein ihm gab Bescheid.
Da rief er laut sonder Spott:
"Nun hilf mir, hilfreicher Gott."
Niederwarf sich zum Gebet
Le Fils dü Roi Gahmuret.

Wolfram von Eschenbach, *Parzival*, Bk.III
(tr. Karl Simrock, 1842)

CONTENTS

LEOPOLD VON SCHROEDER:
THE ROOTS OF THE SAGA OF THE HOLY GRAIL

Preface: Leopold von Schroeder and the Grail Romances   *11*
Alexander Jacob

I. INTRODUCTION   23

II. SUN AND MOON AS HEAVENLY VESSELS AMONG THE INDIANS   30

III. RAIN-PRODUCTION. THE STORM-WEAPON   88

IV. LAND OF SOULS, LAND OF THE SWAN-ELVES,   105
      SOMA-PROTECTORS AND GRAIL-PROTECTORS

V. SUMMARY AND CONCLUSION   118
Bibliography   *125*

ALEXANDER JACOB:
THE INDO-EUROPEAN ORIGINS OF THE GRAIL

I. THE INDO-EUROPEANS   135

II. THE SOLAR COSMOLOGY OF THE INDO-EUROPEANS   178

III. THE SOLAR RITUALS OF THE INDO-EUROPEANS   243
IV. THE GRAIL   264
Bibliography   *279*

PREFACE

LEOPOLD VON SCHROEDER AND THE GRAIL ROMANCES

Alexander Jacob

Leopold von Schroeder (1851-1920) was born in Dorpat (Tartu) in Estonia and began his studies in Comparative Linguistics at the University of Dorpat in 1870. Further studies at the Universities of Leipzig, Jena and Tübingen led him to concentrate on Indology, in which he obtained a master's degree from the University of Dorpat in 1877. After his post-doctoral work at the same university, he became lecturer in Indology there in 1882. In 1896, he was appointed professor of Indology at the University of Innsbruck in Austria and, in 1899, professor of Indology at the University of Vienna. Apart from his several Indological studies, Schroeder also made significant contributions to the understanding of ancient Indo-European myths and sagas. His close friendship with Houston Stewart Chamberlain[1] brought him into contact with the circle of Richard Wagner and he contributed several articles to the *Bayreuther*

---

[1] Schroeder wrote a biography of Chamberlain, *Houston Stewart Chamberlain. Ein Abriß seines Lebens, auf Grund eigener Mitteilungen* which was published in Munich in 1918.

Blätter edited by Richard Wagner's friend, Hans von Wolzogen. He also wrote a major study of Wagner's music dramas, *Die Vollendung des arischen Mysteriums in Bayreuth* (Munich, 1910), which, like his work on the Grail, was an elaborate exercise in comparative Indo-European mythology.

Schroeder's work on the mediaeval Grail saga is extremely significant for its pioneering connection of the Grail story to the mythology of the ancient Indians. Before Schroeder, Grail scholars had concentrated mostly on the Celtic or Christian origins of the Grail story. This focus was not false since the popular stories of the Grail that served as the subjects of the mediaeval romances indeed originated in the Celtic lands and were eventually transferred to the German. All these romances were centred on the mysterious cultic object called the Grail but the conception of the Grail varied considerably among the different authors of the mediaeval romances.

The original meaning of the "grail" was perhaps that identified by the Cistercian chronicler Helinand de Froidmont,[2] who recorded that, around 717, a vision appeared to a hermit concerning the dish used by Our Lord at the Last Supper, and about which the hermit then wrote a Latin book called "Gradale." As Helinand explained,

> Now in French, *Gradalis* or *Gradale* means a dish (scutella), wide and somewhat deep, in which costly viands are wont to be served to the rich in degrees (*gradatim*), one morsel after another in different rows. In popular speech it is also called "greal" because it is pleasant (*grata*) and acceptable to him eating therein.[3]

The transformation of "San Greal" or the Holy Greal (Holy Dish) into Sang Real (Royal Blood) did not occur until the late Middle Ages.

The first major literary work on the Grail was the unfinished romance by Chrétien de Troyes, *Perceval, le Conte du Graal*, written

---

[2] Helinand de Froidmont (ca.1160-1230) was a Flemish Cistercian monk at the monastery of Froidmont in Beauvais. His explanation of the word, "Graal" is found in his chronicle of world history, Chronicon (1211-1123).

[3] See Remy, Arthur F.J., "The Holy Grail" in *The Catholic Encyclopedia*. Vol. 6. New York: Robert Appleton Company, 1909.

in the 12th century.[4] It depicts the grail as a dish that is presented in a procession along with a candelabra and a lance. The story is set in Wales and the lance and the grail are first observed by Perceval in the castle of the Fisher King, who is gravely wounded. There, during a meal, a young man bears a bleeding lance followed by two boys with a candelabra and, finally, a young woman enters with a dish that serves food at every course. Perceval fails to ask the king the meaning of these objects and is reprimanded the following day by an ugly woman for not inquiring about the identity of the Fisher King and the reason why the lance bled, for this would have healed the wounded King. Later he learns from a hermit that the Grail contains a holy wafer that sustains the Fisher King's father, who is also wounded.

In the First Continuation of the unfinished Perceval romance attributed to Pseudo-Wauchier[5] de Denain, Gawain visits the Grail castle with a broken sword that can only be mended by a hero who can cure the Fisher King of his ailment. In the Second Continuation, attributed to Wauchier, Perceval attempts to mend the sword but fails since the sword still has a thin fissure in it. In the Continuation provided by Manessier, the Fisher King's death is described as well as Perceval's ascension to his throne. After seven years as Lord of the Grail, Perceval retires to a forest as a hermit and Manessier supposes that he took the lance, Grail and a silver dish with him to heaven. Another continuation was provided by a "Gerbert", probably Gerbert de Montreuil, around the same time as the Manessier, and this seems to have been composed under the influence of Robert de Boron.

Robert de Boron (late 12th-early 13th century) was indeed the first major poet to provide a specifically Christian context for the Perceval story in his Grail poem, *Le petit Saint Graal, ou Joseph d'Arimathie*, and its fragmentary supplement, Merlin. Boron's narrative is apparently based on the 4th century apocryphal 'Gospel of Nicodemus'. According to Boron, the Grail was the vessel in which Joseph of Arimathea collected the blood of Christ as he lay on the

---

[4] For a good overview of the Grail romances, see A.E. Waite, *The Hidden Church of the Holy Graal*.

[5] This is the same as the Pseudo-Gautier referred to by Schroeder (see below p.62).

cross. Joseph is imprisoned but sustained in his imprisonment by the Grail. Joseph and his friends then bring the Grail to Avalon in Britain, where they guard it until the reign of Arthur and the arrival of Perceval. The Fisher King is in this poem called the Rich Fisher, though the first Fisher King is called Bron, a personage we shall meet again later in the Celtic literature.

The most detailed history of the Grail is to be found in the prose romance of the first half of the 13th century called *Grand St. Graal* which declares that this book was presented by Christ himself to a hermit. Other prose romances of the 13th century include the *Queste del St. Graal*, the so-called *Didot Perceval*,[6] also known as *La petite Queste*, and *Perceval le Gallois*, also known as *Perlesvaus* or *Li Hauz Livres du Graal*. The anonymous author of *Perlesvaus* makes the Fisher King an uncle of Perlesvaus (Perceval), who is the nephew of Joseph of Arimathea. Perlesvaus does not succeed in saving the Fisher King, and the Grail and the bleeding lance are lost. However, Perlesvaus does win a Ring of Gold representing the Christian 'crown of thorns', instead, and after reconquering the Grail castle from another evil uncle, the King of Castle Mortal, he becomes the lord of the Grail castle, when the holy relics are returned to the Grail chapel.

One of the most important romances relating to the Grail is the 13th century Middle High German poem of Wolfram von Eschenbach, *Parzival*, which, like Chrétien's poem, starts with Parsifal, the son of the dead king Gamuret and his wife Herzeleide, going to Arthur's castle and setting off on a quest for the Grail. Wolfram indeed states his dependence on Chrétien as his major source though he mentions also a certain Kyot of Provence who provided him with additional Arabic and Angevin sources.[7] After some adventures in the court of King Arthur, Parzival meets (in Book III) the knight Gurnemanz,[8] who teaches him about knighthood and tells him of the Castle of the Grail. He cautions him about asking too much regarding the Grail or its guardian, Amfortas, who is wounded. During the evening

---

[6] See below p. 94.

[7] The Frankish house of Anjou ruled the Kingdom of Jerusalem from 1131 to 1205.

[8] Gurnemantz represents the knightly, or kshatriya, virtues.

meal at the castle, Parzival observes that the knights are all mournful on account of the languishing Amfortas. A squire enters bearing a bleeding lance. The queen enters bearing the Grail, which is a stone that is laid upon a table of "garnet hyacinth" and provides abundant food and drink as well as life, since the mortally wounded Amfortas is indeed sustained by it. In an inner room Parzival sees the older Fisher King, Titurel, who is also wounded. Parzival leaves the castle amazed by the events and objects he has seen in it and soon meets his cousin, Sigune, who tells him that he should have asked the king a certain crucial question.

After further adventures, Parzival is tormented by his lack of faith and eventually (in Book IX) encounters, on Good Friday, a hermit, Trevrizent,[9] who instructs him on the meaning of the Grail. Amfortas, who is Trevrizent's brother, was wounded – in his testicles – by a heathen during his pursuit of amorous adventures. He is sustained by a holy wafer that is brought to the Grail every Good Friday by a heavenly dove. The knights who guard the Grail have renounced the love of women, although the lord of the Grail may himself be married. Trevrizent also informs Parzival that the knight who would heal Amfortas must thrust the lance that caused the wound into the wound itself in order to heal it. Later (in the second last book, XV), Cundrie, a messenger of the Grail, comes to him and reveals that his name has appeared on the Grail as its next guardian. Parzival returns to the Grail castle, asks his uncle (since Amfortas is his mother's brother) what it is that ails him and he is now made the Grail King.

The romance ends with the story of Parzival's son by his wife Conwiramur called Loherangrin, who is taken in a swan-boat to Antwerp, where he marries the princess of Brabant on the condition that she never ask him his name. She breaks her pledge and so he is forced to return to the Grail castle in his swan-boat.

The story of Perceval appears in a more pristine form in Celtic Brittany in the folk tale of *Peronnik l'idiot*. Peronnik succeeds in entering the magic castle Kerglas of the wicked giant Rogéar and retrieves the diamond lance and golden bowl (grail) that had been

---

[9] Trevrizent represents the priestly, or brāhmanical, virtues.

stolen from the King of Brittany and returns them to the latter, whereupon the wasting land begins to flourish again. The bowl that represents the Grail is said to provide an inexhaustible supply of food and heal all illnesses while the lance is capable of killing all enemies. One of the ordeals Peronnik has to undergo before entering the Grail castle is to withstand the temptations of the Valley of Delights where the flowers sing and beautiful maidens dance alluringly on the grass. When Nantes is besieged by the French, Peronnik succeeds in killing the French with the lance and in healing the wounded with the bowl. The name of the hero itself is related to the Breton 'per' meaning bowl. So we may assume that Perceval is derived from the same word.

The word "graal", used in Boron's *Joseph d'Arimathie*, however translates the Welsh "dyscyl" or "dysgyl", which denotes the platter of the Fisher King. The latter also owns a "cors" or horn that provides him with drink. Since the platter contains a mass-wafer "oiste" (host) for the father of the Fisher King, it is possible that a corruption of the two words "cors" and "oiste" into "corpus christi" was partly responsible for the gradual transformation of an originally pagan Welsh legend into a Christian one.[10]

A couple of Welsh tales that are related to the Grail contain a curious conception of the Grail which the French and German romances do not. The 14th century Welsh romance *Peredur son of Efrawg* included in the collection of stories entitled *Mabinogion*, for instance, does not even mention the Grail. As in *Perceval*, Peredur's father dies when he is young and his mother raises him in the woods. He meets an uncle, who, like Chrétien's Gornemant and Wolfram's Gurnemanz, trains him in fighting and warns him not to ask for explanations of what he sees. Another uncle, who plays the part of the Fisher King, shows him not a grail but a plate bearing a decapitated head. After many unrelated adventures, Peredur learns that the head belonged to a cousin of his who had been murdered by the "nine witches of Gloucester". Peredur then avenges the murder.

---

[10] This is suggested in the edition of *Parzival. A Romance of the Middle Ages*, tr. H.M. Mustard and C.E. Passage, N.Y.: Vintage Books, 1961.

The motif of the decapitated head is found also in the second section of the Welsh *Mabinogian* tales called *Branwen ferch Llŷr* dealing with Bran the Blessed, King of the Island of the Mighty and his sister Branwen. Matholwch, King of Ireland, marries Branwen but her half-brother Efnisien mutilates the king's horses during the wedding celebrations. Bran offers him as compensation a magic cauldron that can restore the dead to life. The insult however rankles among the Irish and Branwen is maltreated, whereupon Bran decides to attack Ireland along with his half-brother Efnisien. Seeing that the Irish are reviving their dead with the aid of the cauldron, Efnisien jumps into it and breaks the cauldron, sacrificing himself in doing so. Only seven men survive the battle and Bran himself is mortally wounded. His comrades advise him to cut off his head and return it to Britain, where it is guarded by his friends for several years during which the head continues to speak as if alive. It finally falls silent and is buried in Gwynfryn, "the White Hill", facing France in order that it may ward off invasion from the mainland.[11]

Given the bewildering metamorphoses that the originally Celtic story of the cultic object called the Grail underwent in the various romances of the Middle Ages, it is not surprising that a proper understanding of the significance of this cultic object eluded most scholars who had confined their researches to western European literary and cultural sources. It was Leopold von Schroeder's reading of the Grail story in the light of his knowledge of Indic mythology that first achieved a dramatic expansion of the field of Grail scholarship. The only other scholar who developed a comprehensive comparative mythological study of the Grail was perhaps Julius Evola in his *Il Mistero del Graal e la Tradizione Ghibellina dell'Impero* (1937), which was a reworking of an appendix to his *Rivolta contro il mondo moderno* (1934).[12]

The text of Schroeder's *Die Wurzeln der Sage vom heiligen Gral* was first presented at a meeting of the Imperial Academy of Sciences

---

[11] The practice of head-hunting among Celtic warriors is reported also by Diodorus Siculus (*Bibliotheca Historica* V,29,4-5; XIV,115,5) and Strabo (*Geographica* IV,4,5).

[12] See below p. 264f.

in Vienna on 6 July 1910. It was then published as a monograph (Sitzungsbericht) by Alfred Hölder (Vienna, 1910), and a second edition of it was issued in 1911.

THE ROOTS OF THE SAGA
OF THE HOLY GRAIL

by

LEOPOLD VON SCHROEDER

MEMBER OF THE IMPERIAL ACADEMY OF SCIENCES

Translated by

ALEXANDER JACOB

I.   INTRODUCTION

II.   SUN AND MOON AS HEAVENLY VESSELS AMONG THE INDIANS

III.   RAIN-PRODUCTION. THE STORM-WEAPON

IV.   LAND OF SOULS, LAND OF THE SWAN-ELVES, SOMA-PROTECTORS AND GRAIL-PROTECTORS

V.   SUMMARY AND CONCLUSION

I. INTRODUCTION

𝕿he wonderful saga of the Holy Grail has been brought to life again in our days by the brilliant dramas of Richard Wagner. If *Lohengrin* already allowed us to glimpse the sublime wonder of the Grail from a distance, the consecratory festival drama, *Parsifal*, led us directly into the centre of the sanctuary of the Grail Mountain and directed the eyes and hearts of the entire cultured world to it. In this way art fulfilled its duty completely with regard to this most awe-inspiring saga literature of the Middle Ages through creations that will hardly ever be surpassed. It seems to me that nothing nearly similar can yet be said of the sciences. To be sure, there is no lack of big and small essays and books on the subject and indeed the most recent times have gifted us many of these. Alongside works of profound scholarship such as Richard Heinzel's essay, *On the French Grail romances*,[13] we meet spirited stimulants like Burdach's reference to the Byzantine mass as the model of the Grail procession in Crestien de Troyes' *Perceval*.[14] But, on the other hand, there came about an unfortunate tendency in our age to quite deliberately

---

[13] *Denkschriften der kaiserlichen Akademie der Wissenschaften in Wien*, philosoph-histor. Klasse, Bd.40, Wien, 1892.

[14] Cf. *Deutsche Literaturzeitung*, 1903, No.46; 1904, No.50. See also [Wolfgang] Golther, *Parzival und der Gral in deutscher Sage des Mittelalters und der Neuzeit*, p.4 and 5; 38 and 39 (Ulrich Schmid's *Walhalla* [: *Bücherei für vaterländische Geschichte, Kunst und Kulturgeschichte*], Bk.IV).

obscure and obstruct other and extremely important sources for the understanding of this subject.

One can hardly fail to recognise that the Middle Ages saw in the Holy Grail a relic of the Passion endowed with wonderful powers, the cup of the last supper of Christ or the cup in which Joseph of Arimathea collected the blood of the Saviour or both at the same time; that the wonder of the Grail was connected in some way to the secrets of the sacrifice of the Christian mass – and only a few have gone so far as Gottfried Baist, who denies the Grail procession in Crestien's *Perceval* any religious mystical character in general and very seriously considers it possible "that the Grail in its first form was without any wonderful quality and only helped to exemplify the rule that in certain circumstances even speeches are gold".[15] But that there could survive in the well-nigh undeniable abundance of miraculous stories and miraculous traits that surround the Grail and its environment extremely ancient pre-Christian, pagan myths and sagas in a Christian adaptation, this very high possibility has now for a long time been denied almost stubbornly since Birch-Hirschfeld tried to provide the evidence, in an industriously researched but in no way wide-ranging or deep book, that the saga of the Holy Grail has nothing to do with the different magical cauldrons and beakers of the Celtic sagas that one earlier connected to it but has its roots solely in the Christian legend of the cup of the last supper or the cup of Joseph of Arimathea.[16]

To be sure, all researchers have not followed him in his negative direction denying the influence of the mysterious world of saga. Thus Eduard Wechssler, in his excellent book on *The Saga of the Holy Grail* maintains quite firmly that, in the Grail poem, a mixture has taken place of mysterious sagas and fairy-tales with the Christian legend.[17]

[15] Cf. Dr. Gottfried Baist, *Parzival und der Gral*, Freiburg im Breisgau, 1909, p.17 and 19 of the offprint, p.41 and 43 of the official edition.

[16] Cf. Adolf Birch-Hirschfeld, *Die Sage vom Gral, ihre Entwicklung und dichterische Ausbildung in Frankreich und Deutschland im 12. u. 13. Jahrhundert. Eine literarhistorische Untersuchung*, Leipzig, 1877.

[17] Cf. Eduard Wechssler, *Die Sage vom heiligen Gral und ihre Entwicklung bis auf Wagners Parsifal*, Halle a.S., Max Niemeyer, 1898.

However, in general, Birch-Hirschfeld succeeded. How his view gradually rose to power is, for example, to be observed in R. Heinzel, who in an essay that appeared in 1872, *A French romance of the 13th century*, indeed considers a connection between the magical vessels of certain Celtic sagas and the Grail as probable and comes to the, in my opinion, right conclusion: "As regards the Grail, the bowl has clearly entered into the legend of Joseph of Arimathea in the place of pagan symbols".[18] On the other hand, he explains on p.97 of the earlier mentioned comprehensive essay which appeared twenty years later (1892) that most of the Celtic magical pots and vessels had nothing in common with the Grail bowl. Of course some of them are expressly excepted since they possess the miraculous power of producing nourishment, such as the pan of Diwrnah, which leaves no one unsatisfied, the basket of Gwyddneus, the pan with plates of Rhegynydd Ysgolhaig; however, this track is not followed further and therefore seems not to have been considered as important by the author. It cannot surprise us if Gottfried Baist similarly denies the connection between the Grail and the Celtic magical vessels and remarks: "There is lacking any definite characteristic which would permit us to identify our bowl with any of the magical pots that are to be found in the Celtic mythology as in every other".[19] That this is not at all right I hope to be able to show in the following essay. There is evident not only one characteristic but an entire series of very definite and special characteristics which – as I believe – quite irrefutably suggest a connection of the saga of the Holy Grail with ancient Aryan (i.e. Indo-European) myths and sagas of miraculous vessels. If these agreements and connections have up to now been almost never remarked upon, that is explained partly by the still prevalent and irresponsible neglect of comparative mythological studies which are indispensable for the settling of the present question. This condition of things certainly serves to excuse the excellent researchers who, in their handling of mediaeval sagas, were not in a position to look very

---

[18] Cf. p.86 in R. Heinzel, *Kleine Schriften*, ed. M.H. Jellinek and C.v. Kraus, Heidelberg, 1907.

[19] Cf. G. Baist, *op.cit.*, pp.17,18 (offprint).

far beyond them. However it constitutes at the same time a powerful incentive to fill in the present gaps as far as possible.

We should not naturally restrict ourselves to the Celtic sagas but must rather seek to ascertain which sagas about such vessels and heroes that accomplish the same things may indeed be considered as ancient Aryan. Then it will be shown if these sagas possess characteristics that make it probable that they are at the basis of the Grail saga or may have influenced the same in essential points. In order to come closer to a solution of this question it is certainly recommendable to research therefore the oldest mythical-historical monument of the Aryans, the hymns of the Rigveda, and the Vedic literature connected to them. If the mythical vessels play a role even in the ritual and cult, in the sacrificial services, then it will naturally be so much more significant. To approach the problem from this angle is not only favoured by me personally but is certainly demanded also by scholarship. We therefore wish to consider the Rigveda and the accompanying literature in order to then proceed to a comparison.

Recently Ludwig Emil Iselin has tried to demonstrate an entirely different source of the Grail saga.[20] He places a special importance on the early Christian literature of the east, especially on the so-called "Cave of Treasures", a popular saga book of Syrian or Nestorian Christianity that belongs to the numerous group of so-called Adam books.[21] The essential content of the "Cave of Treasures" is found also in the Ethiopian and Arabic Christian Adam books whose foundations go back to the 6th century[22] as well as to the so-called "Apocalypse" of the apostle Peter whose older version belongs to

---

[20] Cf. Ludwig Emil Iselin, *Der morgenländische Ursprung der Grallegende, aus orientalischen Quellen erschlossen*, Halle a.S., 1909.

[21] [*The Book of the Cave of Treasures or The Book of the order of the succession of Generations (or Families)*, the Families being those of the Patriarchs and Kings of Israel and Judah, was a Syriac work originally written perhaps in the 4th century whose aim was to demonstrate that Christ was descended from Adam.]

[22] [Much of the *Cave of Treasures* is borrowed from an Arabic book on the *Conflict of Adam and Eve with Satan* that is extant in an Ethiopic translation dating from the 5th/6th century.]

the 8th century.[23] Iselin seems to me to have made it probable that the representation emerging many times in these and related books of a wonderful precious stone working miracles has influenced the special conception of the Grail in Wolfram von Eschenbach, in whom the Grail is not a cup but an expensive stone on which the host is placed. The pictorial representations of Christ as the rock, the stone that construction workers have discarded but which then became a corner-stone, were connected in that eastern literature with the Jewish narratives of a precious stone in Paradise, the foundation stone of Earth, the tombstone of Adam and Christ, the rock that provided water to the Israelites in the desert, the sacrificial altar of Melchisedek, etc. This stone as an altar stone becomes also the bearer of the host and may well lie at the basis of the miraculous things in Wolfram von Eschenbach, whereas the narrative of the Holy Cup again goes back to other sources. That the many and partly really essential divergences that we observe in Wolfram's narrative in comparison to Crestien de Troyes have only him as a source, that the Provencal Kyot, or Guiot, which in turn employed the Arabic book of the heathen Flegetanis, is a mere fiction, an invention of Wolfram's – these opinions repeated often nowadays and with all too great certainty[24] I consider as in no way proved but as very doubtful. I see no sufficient reason to blame Wolfram for simply fabricating those so definitely cited sources

---

[23] [*The Apocalypse of Peter* is an early Christian text dating from the 2nd century A.D. that was originally written in Greek but is extant in two later versions, in Koine Greek and Ethiopic respectively]. Cf. Iselin, *op.cit.*, pp.17ff-26,27ff.

[24] Cf. Birch-Hirschfeld, *op.cit.*, pp.285ff. *et passim*; Baist, *op.cit.*, p.14.15; earlier W. Golther, following Wolfram's own statement, accepted as the sole model of Wolfram the poet Kyot, who revised and elaborated Crestien's work (cf. Golther, Lohengrin, *Romanische Forschungen V*, pp.115-122; E. Wechssler, *op.cit.*, p.165); recently (1908) he too has preferred to consider the poet Kyot as well as his Arabic and Latin sources as an invention of Wolfram's (cf. Golther, *Parzival und der Gral in deutscher Sage des Mittelalters und der Neuzeit*, p.17). E. Wechssler, on the other hand, rightly continues to maintain the credibility of Wolfram's statement of source, sees in Wolfram's Kyot an actual source and remarks quite rightly, *op.cit.*, p.165: "Even granted that Wolfram wanted to claim another model along with Crestien, namely Kyot, he certainly had no reason to state also the different sources of the invented Kyot". Cf. his instructive explanations, pp.163-178.

even if the Provencal Kyot and the heathen Flegetanis cannot either now or ever be proven but, like other sources, are forever lost (cf., in this context, E. Wechssler, *op.cit.*, p.177). In the course of our representation I shall have further opportunity many times to prove that precisely such characteristics of the saga as are said to be Wolfram's invention are ancient characteristics of the underlying saga realm. And so it is also quite possible that Wolfram may have derived his conception of the Grail as a wonderful stone indirectly – as Iselin supposes – from the literature of the Cave of Treasures, and directly from the source cited by him.[25] With much less probability Iselin traces also other characteristics of the saga to that eastern Christian literature. The guardians of the Grail, the motif of the forbidden question,[26] etc. find only very weak counterparts there. That the latter very important motif of the Lohengrin saga is rooted in the ancient saga of the swan-elf may now indeed be, nay has already for a long time been considered as certain.[27] Iselin, as may be easily understood, has overvalued the significance of his sources for the Grail saga in many aspects, but its partial significance for the same should for that reason in no way be contested.

I am convinced that the saga source of the Holy Grail that has been richly spun out, ramified and endlessly varied has absorbed into itself an abundance of sagas and legends of the most different origins. It is a powerful current whose water is fed by many other streams. One of these streams, and indeed one of the most important, I think is to be recognised in the ancient Aryan saga, in the mythology of Aryan antiquity. In order to be able to observe this stream as close to its source as possible let us take into consideration first the oldest monument of the Aryans, the Vedas.

---

[25] It is also perhaps remarkable that Wagner, in the letters to Mathilde Wesendonck, p.146, p.147 speaks angrily about the fact that Wolfram sees in the Grail a stone and expresses the opinion that this should be of heathen-Arabic origin, pointing to the Kaaba of Mecca.

[26] Cf. Iselin, *op.cit.*, pp.88ff,102ff.

[27] Cf. my book *Mysterium und Mimus im Rigveda*, pp.232-274; *Griechische Götter und Heroen* I, p.52ff.

II. SUN AND MOON AS HEAVENLY VESSELS
AMONG THE INDIANS

Both in the ritual and in the mythology of the Vedic age it clearly emerges that the two big round luminous bodies of heaven, the sun and the moon, were thought of as heavenly vessels whose contents were enjoyed, sipped, drunk by the gods or the blessed dead or by both. Gods and demons fight for the possession of these wonderful vessels and men are glad when the divine hero defeats the demon in such a battle for the god – unlike the envious demons – allows men too to, at least indirectly, participate in the rich blessing that streams down from above as heavenly light and rain. But to directly approach those wonderful vessels and enjoy their contents is naturally forbidden to men. "Unapproachable to their steps", they stream and grant blessings in a remote land of the holy. Only when a man dies may he hope to arrive there like the other dead – through the mercy of the god Soma, the Moon-god, who is the heavenly drink itself, or even through other corresponding deeds, especially certain offerings, at least according to the later conception. It is true that an old saga narrates that once a higher semi-divine being from that host of elves and swan-elves who live there guarding the heavenly fire and heavenly drink condescended to a matrimonial alliance with a man.[28] But that did not last for a long time and ended tragically for the man. Hopelessly tragically according

---

[28] [See *RV* X,95 for the story of the Apsara, Urvasi, and the legendary king, Pururavas].

to the oldest version of the saga, whereas a later age was able even here to find a way and means to transform the tragedy of the old saga into a conclusion of happiness and bliss.[29]

But men seek to approach and appropriate that heavenly vessel and its wonderful contents in another celebratory cultish manner. A milk-pot, a porridge-pot, represents the sun in the sacrificial feasts, and the soma in the most diverse vessels the heavenly Soma, that is, the moon. And when the priests enjoy milk and porridge and soma they appropriate in a primitive sacramental manner the divine food, the divine drink, indeed the godhead itself.

Let us observe in detail what the Veda has to report of the sun and the moon as heavenly vessels, occasionally drawing upon the representations of related peoples also in comparison.

THE SUN

Let us first take into consideration the relevant representations of the sun. They are more varied, but for that reason also more fluctuating and less uniform, than those related to the moon. In some instances it will also remain doubtful whether it is the sun or the moon that is being spoken of, or whether perhaps originally moon-mythological representations were later transferred to the sun. In the main, however, there prevails perfect clarity both in the hymns and myths of the Veda and in the ritual, and the latter as the preferentially sanctified and to a certain extent canonised element indeed deserves special consideration.

The sun is thought of as a heavenly milk-pot, a cooking pot, a porridge-pot. Indeed in it is also to be found the heavenly mead which is normally connected to the moon even if it is not precisely designated as a vessel with mead.

The sun appears as an earthen pot with hot milk in the ritual of the so-called Pravargya sacrifice which is offered to the two Ashwins. Originally perhaps an independent sacrifice, it was then accepted

---

[29] Cf. my book *Mysterium und Mimus im Rigveda*, Leipzig, 1908, pp.232-274.

among the introductory ceremonies of the great Soma sacrifice and firmly absorbed into it already in its simplest form, the Agnishtoma. R. Garbe devoted a valuable monograph to this sacrifice already in 1890.[30] Following him, H. Oldenberg and A. Hillebrandt have contributed substantially to the illumination of its nature.[31]

The Pravargya sacrifice bears a highly simple, primitive character and Garbe was certainly right when he wished to see in it a very ancient Aryan sacrifice. "The offering of milk", as he says, "is even as old as, if not older than, the soma cult and both go back to the age of the unseparated habitation of the two Aryan peoples".[32] He means thereby the Indians and the Persians. But we may indeed go farther and consider milk-sacrifices in any form from the oldest Aryan period. The milk-sacrifice is thus rightly a sacrifice such as suits a people of cattle-breeders, a pastoral people, whose pride and wealth is constituted by cattle herds. Even in the Avesta the hot milk-drink is a consecrated food. Between the pure soma and the pure milk of the Pravargya sacrifice stands the common mixing of milk and soma in the Indian ritual and even this mixture of intoxicating drink and milk must be of the greatest antiquity.[33]

But let us stay for now with the Pravargya. For the understanding of it, Garbe thought it necessary to place a special weight on *Ait. Br.*I,22. According to it, "the Pravargya" is "to be seen as a symbol of the mating of the gods, from which there emerges for the sacrificer a

---

[30] Cf. R. Garbe, *Die Pravargya-Zeremonie nach dem Âpastamba-Çrâutasûtra, mit einer Einleitung über die Bedeutung desselben, Zeitschrift der deutschen Morgenländischen Gesellschaft*, Vol.34, pp.319-370.

[31] H. Oldenberg, [*Die*] *Religion des Veda*, pp.447-451; A. Hillebrandt, *Vedische Mythologie*, Vol.I, p.299, fn.4; Vol.II, p.217ff; *id., Ritual-literatur* [: *Vedische Opfer und Zauber*], p.136.

[32] Cf. R. Garbe, *op.cit.*, p.322.

[33] Cf. R. Garbe, *op.cit.*, p.321,322. The native ritual milk-dance that is traditional on Johannis day in Klein-Gschwenda in Thuringia (Schwarzburg-Rudolstadt) perhaps points back to an ancient milk sacrifice; cf. on this, Reinsberg-Düringsfeld, *Das festliche Jahr*, 2. ed., p.298,299. During the Roman Palilia [a Roman festival held in honour of Pales, the guardian of shepherds and their flocks] a mixture of milk and fruit wine was drunk while milk appears as the accompaniment of the food sacrifice. Cf. [Ludwig] *Preller, Römische Mythologie*, 3rd ed., I, p.417.

new body consisting of Rk, Yajus, Saman and the Vedas in general, of Brahman and immortality, suitable for taking his place among the gods; or, as Haug expresses it in the note to p. 42 of the translation, "It (the Pravargya) is intended for providing the sacrificer with a heavenly body with which alone he is permitted to enter the residence of the gods."[34]

This power of the Pravargya sacrifice of providing the sacrificer a heavenly immaterial body with which he can enter the land of the blessed, the divine world, is certainly of great significance and agrees, as we shall see, with an analogous significance of the offering of a porridge-pot signifying the sun (odana) which helps towards a blessed community with Yama, the gods and the gandharvas, with whom the dead person is supposed to feast after his death. It agrees also with an analogous function of soma (cf. especially, *RV* IX,113,6-11). The high significance of the Pravargya is also expressed in the fact that the earthen sacrificial pot that contains the hot milk is called the Mahāvira, i.e. "the great hero". But most important of all was the evidence of Oldenberg that this Mahāvira or Gharma[35] with its content of hot milk represents and signifies the sun.

The sacrificial verses of the Yajurveda indicate this or express it quite directly and clearly: "You are the sun! Give me the sun!" And in the Brāhmanas it is often said that the Gharma feast, or the boiling kettle used for it, is the sun. The heat of the boiling drink represents the heat of the sun.[36] If there follows directly upon the repeated ceremony with this hot milk-pot the soma sacrifice, which is at the same time a lunar sacrifice and a rain magic, then precisely through this sequence is indicated symbolically, in a manner that cannot be ignored, the immediate succession of the highest fervour of the sun of summer by the rainy season. And here also the ritual image of the natural relations influences it, as so often, magically, in a magical-cultic manner, and holds Nature in its right course. First the heat

---

[34] Cf. R. Garbe, *op.cit.*, p.320.

[35] [Gharma is life-producing heat. It is also an epithet of Kumāra/Muruga, the son of Shiva, since he is an embodiment of his father's divine semen.]

[36] See Oldenberg, *Religion des Veda*, p.448,449. Compare further references there.

of the sun, then the moisture of the rain – in the ritual process as in Nature. The famous frog-hymn[37] signifies the same. The frogs, who later provide rain, are first described as officiating priests who, sweating, take care of the hot pot or kettle of the Ashwins (*adhvaryávo gharminah sishvidánáh RV* VII,103,8).

A. Hillebrandt has confirmed Oldenberg's evidence and thereby further strengthened it essentially in that in his – doubtless correct – identification of Soma with the moon the cool and cooling Soma, which signifies the moon and produces rain, now stands very illuminatingly as a counterpart to the hot milk vessel, which signifies the sun and its heat.[38] The parallelism is as clear and convincing as possible.

This conception of the Mahāvira – or Gharma vessel in the Pravargya as a solar symbol is not contradicted but can only be confirmed by the fact that the Pravargya vessel is also called the head of Makha – *makhasya çirah*. For even the head of Makha, of a god or a demon, who occasionally sacrifices along with the gods, but then gets into conflict with them and is killed by them, is nothing but the sun, just as the moon is in turn considered as the decapitated head of the demon Vrtra.[39] Just as the cultic legend lets the decapitated head of Makha become the Pravargya vessel, so also the decapitated head of Vrtra the Soma vessel, Dronakalaça. If the gods drink out of the sun and the moon, or in the ritual out of the Pravargya vessel and the Dronakalaça, then they drink out of the heads, or the skulls of their murdered enemies, as it was the well-known barbaric custom.[40] I do

---

[37] [*RV* VII,103.]

[38] A. Hillebrandt, *Vedische Mythologie*, Vol.I, p.229n; Vol.II, p.217ff.

[39] [See p. 223f.]

[40] Cf. H. Brunnhofer, *Arische Urzeit*, Bern, 1910, p.321; Hillebrandt, *Vedische Mythologie*, Vol.III, p.427,428n; Oldenberg, *Religion des Veda*, p.89 fn.7. According to the *Çatapata Brâhmana*, XIV,1,2,17, "the rough features of a human face were given to the Mahâvira or Gharma pot" (Oldenberg, *op.cit.*, p.89). It seems thus to have been something like a face-urn. That is perhaps explained by the fact that this pot, or the sun which it represents, is considered as the decapitated head of a demon. Cf, in this context, the idea among the North American Prairie tribes, according to whom the moon is a skull, or the sun and moon the two halves of a broken skull, as it is narrated of the Panis; see P. Ehenreich, *Die allgemeine Mythologie, und*

not wish to go more closely into this parallel view of the sun and the moon as head - and skull - vessels since this could lead us too far from our path.

The *gharma*, the pot or kettle belonging to the Ashwins with hot milk, is often mentioned under this name already in the hymns of the Rigveda. And the name already indicates that here it is a question of something hot or at least warm, in contrast to the cool Soma beaker. For *gharma* comes from the root *ghar* which means "to glow, be warm"; *gharma* also means directly "warmth of the sun, glow of the sun, glow of the fire"; then later it signifies only the milk vessel of the Ashwins and the hot milk which forms its content.

The *gharma* is accordingly often mentioned in such Vedic hymns as are dedicated to the Ashwins and invite them to their sacrifice. From this it follows that the Pravargya sacrifice was in the main well-known already in the age of the Rigveda.

We have the essential regarding the Pravargya sacrifice before us when, for example, it says in the Ashwin hymn *RV* VII,70,2:

> *átâpi gharmó mánusho duroné*

"The gharma was made hot (or glowing) in the dwelling of man". Or in the Ashwin hymn *RV* I,119,2: *svádâmi gharmám* ("I make the *gharma* tasty (sweet)"). Or also in the Ashwin hymn *RV* V,76,1:

> *arvâñcâ nûnám rathyehá yâtam*
> *pîpivâmsam açvinâ gharmám ácha*

"Come here now, you two chariot-driving Ashwins, to the swelling *gharma*!"

---

ihre ethnologischen Grundlagen, p.209; he points also to O. Jordan's 'Hymnus an den Mond', the "Death's head of the heavens". And there is no contradiction in the fact that the clay clods out of which the Ukhâ, the fire-pot for the sacred sacrificial fire, is formed is likewise called the "head of Makha" (cf. Hillebrandt, *op.cit.*, Vol.III, p.428n). For even the sacrificial fire represents the sun. The Ukhâ with the sacrificial fire in it can as well be considered as a symbol of the sun as the Gharma with its hot milk. These are variants of the same idea.

Similarly when Atri, in the hymn *RV* VII,73,6 says of himself that he is setting the immaculate *gharma* in undulating motion for the Ashwins, i.e. is cooking it (*gharmám arepesám bhuranyáti*). And there is no deviation from the known ritual when the gharma is designated as *mádhumant* or *mádhumattama*, i.e. filled with mead, sweetness, with sweet drink, for here by "mead" is understood, as it is often, certainly nothing but the sweet milk of the Pravargya. Thus it says in *RV* VIII,76,2:

> *píbatam gharmám mádhumantam açvinâ*
> *â barhíh sîdatam narâ*

> "Drink the *gharma* filled with sweetness (*mâdhu*), you Ashwins! sit down on the sacrificial straw, you two men!"

And in the Ashwin hymn *RV* I,180,4: *yuvâm ha gharmâm mâdhumantam – avrnítam*, "You two have chosen the *gharma* filled with sweetness."

Indeed, the hot milk of this Ashwin sacrifice is occasionally called precisely "sweet soma". Thus in the Ashwin hymn *RV* VIII,9,4 and 7:

> *4. ayám vâm gharmó açvinâ*
> *stómena pári shícyate*
> *ayám sóma mádhumân vâjinîvasû*
> *yéna vrtrám cíketathah*

> *7. â nûnám açvínor ríshih*
> *stómam ciketa vâmáyâ*
> *â sómam mádhumattamam*
> *gharmám siñcâd átharvani*

Even that hardly creates a difference. Like "mead", the appellation "soma" serves only for the glorification of the sweet milk drink.

The Atharvaveda (7,73) similarly contains a hymn which is obviously designed to accompany a Pravargya offering for the Ashwins. In it heated or glowing *gharma* (*tapto gharmah*) is often spoken of; similarly the Cow that provides the milk for this sacrifice.

But especially noteworthy seems a verse (7,73,3) in which this offering for the Ashwins, the *gharma*, is called *camasó devapánah*, "the beaker out of which the gods drink" – whereupon the poet continues:

tam u víçve amŕitáso jusháná gandharvásya prátyâsnâ rihanti

"All the immortals love to lick it with the mouth of the Gandharvas". The expression is not very clear here but nevertheless noteworthy and deviating from the normal form of the Ashwin hymns. Here not only the Ashwins but all the immortals drink, or lick, the contents of the *gharma* and they do that with the mouth of the Gandharva. That sounds almost mystical. Perhaps by Gandharva is meant Agni.[41] Perhaps also there appears before the poet's eye a scene of the heavenly world where the gods united enjoy the contents of the solar vessel, just as they, according to other clearer passages, drink the lunar vessel empty. The Gandharva protects both of these.

Of what substance the *gharma*, the sacrificial vessel in the Pravargya, is made is normally not indicated in the Rigveda hymns. The ritual reveals clearly that it was an earthen vessel and describes its preparation in an elaborate manner. So much the more striking is it that, precisely in those passages of the Rigveda where – according to the *termini technici* – the ritual Pravargya sacrifice is most definitely spoken of, the vessel used is referred to as a bronze vessel. That occurs in the Dánastuti, the gift fees, at the end of a Indra hymn, *RV* V,30,15:

cátuhsahasram gávyasya paçváh práty agrabhîshma
ruçámeshvagne
gharmáèç cit taptáh pravríje yá âsîd ayasmáyas tám v âdâma víprâh

"We have received four thousand cows, O Agni, in the Ruçamas, even the hot kettle, the bronze, that had to be offered, we the singers have obtained."

The hot *gharma* – *gharmáç cit taptáh* – would itself actually suffice to demonstrate to us what ceremony is being spoken of here. But the expression *pravríje yá âsît* proves that even more clearly, for *pravríje* is

---

[41] [See below pp.158,261,272].

indeed the infinitive of the verb to which the word Pravargya belongs. But the *gharma* contains here the epithet *ayasmáya*, i.e. made of *ayas*, i.e. indeed bronze, of metal – perhaps also of iron or copper, in any case metallic. The clay pot is quite firmly established throughout the ritual in the Pravargya and bears in addition a very antique character. But we shall have to conclude from the cited *RV* passage that, along with the clay pot, exceptionally, presumably in the sacrifices of especially rich and distinguished people, even a metal vessel could be used in this sacrifice, the subsequent gifting of which to the officiating priests naturally deserved special attention since it was a valuable gift.

The Vedic *áyas* (=latin *aes, aeris*)[42] is normally translated as metal or even iron. In any case the word means a metal. It is the only known name for a metal that can be traced back to the oldest Aryan period and it originally means in any case copper, the only metal that the still unseparated Aryans knew and used.[43] The word had later a varied fate and had to finally mean metal or even iron. Both have been accepted for the Veda (cf. the dictionaries of Böhtlingk-Roth and Graßmann). Zimmer, on the other hand, attempted to show that *áyas* in the Veda could mean only metal or copper.[44] In fact it seems to have been a red metal. Copper-ore, perhaps even copper, as in the earliest Aryan period.

Let us now remember that the milk vessel in the Pravargya sacrifice was meant to represent the sun, then it appears revealing that a shiny bronze or even copper kettle with hot milk was certainly much better suited to render an image or symbol of the sun than a corresponding earthen pot. Indeed, the comparison of the sun with a copper kettle is so apparent that it could enter the language of even a modern poet, in a poem which lies very far from all mythology: Fritz Reuter (*Ut mine Stromtid*, Vol.II, ch.19): "and the sun looks through the tree as round and red as a copper kettle".[45]

---

[42] Avestan *ayah*, Gothic *aiz*.

[43] Cf. O. Schrader, *Reallexicon der indogermanischen Altertumskunde*, p.540,541.

[44] Cf. H. Zimmer, *Altindisches Leben*, p.52.

[45] Cf. Fritz Reuter, *Sämtliche Werke*, popular edition in 7 volumes, Vol.VII, 5th edition, 1890, p.66.

This comparison apparently lies beneath a remarkable, for us important, saga which the Mahâbhârata narrates. There indeed it is narrated that Yudhishthira, after he, on the advice of Dhâumya, has practised ascesis and praised the sun in a hymn, receives as a gift from the sun-god Vivasvant, a copper cooking pot (*pithara*) which replenishes itself by itself according to one's wish.[46] Thus a sort of Indian wishing-table. All are fed from this pot. But this copper cooking pot is an image of the sun, or originally the sun itself. The miraculous things which are at the disposal of the solar and lunar gods indeed seem, as a rule, to be these heavenly lights themselves in some special conception that is especially varied in the case of the moon, on account of its changing appearance. Strikingly important here is, naturally, the circumstance that this copper cooking pot of the sun-god continually replenishes itself at will, enables all to eat, and indeed feeds and in this way helps Yudhishthira in case of all need and natural want during the years of banishment in the forest. Before we follow this important trail further which already points us energetically to the Grail, we must discuss another conception of the sun in the ritual and myth of the Veda, and that is: the sun conceived of as a porridge vessel.

Along with the milk-pot or milk-kettle of the Ashwins there appears, as a symbol or image of the sun in the ritual – and indeed in the popular ritual of the Atharvaveda – also a porridge, or a hot-pot with porridge, called *odana*, also with the apposition *odana vishtârin*, which latter word is unfortunately of obscure meaning.[47] A

---

[46] In the Vanaparva, the third book of the Mahâbhârata, the beginning; or III,3; cf., for example, verse 73: *grihnîshva pitharam tâmram mayâ dattam narâdhipa*, etc. the words of the munificent sun-god Vivasvant; and verses 83-85: the development of the feeding miracle through the cooking-pot of the god. At first the brāhmans receive the inexhaustibly produced food, finally Yudhishthira and Drâupadî eat. Cf. M. Winternitz, *Geschichte der indischen Literatur*, Vol.I, p.291; H. Jacobi, *Mahâbhârata* (Bonn, 1903) p.31.

[47] Apparently *vishtârin* means scattered with straw, brought forth on straw, which gives a good meaning. It is derived from vishtâra which word probably means straw (the *barhis*) in *RV* V,52,10, from *vi-star* "to scatter". The closely related *vishtara* means "bundle of reeds", and the like, used for sitting.

39

large section – *AV* 11,3 – is devoted to its offering. Quite rightly does Whitney remark on it in his translation of the *Atharvaveda*, Vol.II, p.625: "The rice-dish, hot and yellow and nourishing, is a symbol of the sun".

He refers thereby especially to v.50 of this section. That says: "*etad vâi bradhnasya vishtapam*[48] *yad odanah*", i.e. "this *odana* is the zenith of the red". Of this zenith of the red there is frequent mention in the Veda. We shall encounter it later too. Thereby is meant doubtlessly the zenith of the red sun or of the solar horse, or the sun in its highest position in the heavens. That is a place of the highest holiness, where the dead, who now participate in such a joy, feast in the company of gods and semi-gods and enjoy the highest bliss. In the well-known hymn *RV* IX,113, Soma is beseeched to bring his pious worshippers there:

10. yátra kâmâ nikâmâç ca
yátra bradhnásya vishtápam
svadhâ ca yátra tríptiç ca
tátra mâm amrítam kridhi

Roth translates that in its essence excellently in the Seventeen Hymns,[49] p.111:

Where wish and longing are stilled,
At the red zenith of the sun,
Where pleasure and satisfaction are at the same time,
O Soma, make me immortal!

In another Rigveda hymn (VIII,58,7) the singer expresses the hope of reaching this "red zenith" along with Indra and being able to drink mead with him there:

---

[48] *bradhná*, "red, flame red" appears as an epithet of the solar horse; *vishtápam*, like the closely related *vishtáp* means "the top, the highest region, peak, zenith".

[49] [*Siebenzig Lieder des Rigveda*, tr. K.Geldner and A. Kaegi, with contributions by R. von Roth, Tübingen, 1875.]

úd yád hradhnásya vishtápam
grihám índraç ca gánvahi
mádhvah pîtvâ sacevahi
tríh saptá sákhyuh padé

I translate:

When Indra and I go
To the red zenith, into the house,
Drinking wine, then we are united
Three times seven, at the friend's place.

And closely related is the idea when it says, in *AV* X,10,31, that the Sâdhyas and Vasus, the blessed or demi-gods, drink the milk of the Cow at the red zenith – *bradhnásya vishtápi* – and worship her moisture. Milk, mead, porridge – all these seem to be found up above at the sun, at its highest position, but is attainable only by the gods, demi-gods and the blessed.

But the ritual offering of the porridge-pot, of the *odana vishtârin* – of the porridge-pot onto the straw, as I would like to translate it – aids such heavenly blessedness. Thus does *AV* IV,34,3 say: "Those who cook the *odana vishtârin* never lack anything; he (such a person) sits with Yama, he attains the gods, he delights (intoxicates himself, feasts) in the company of the Soma-loving Gandharvas.[50]

In the previous verse it is said that such a sacrificer of the *odana vishtârin* enters the world of light, without bones, cleansed, refined, pure[51] – thus provided with a new transfigured body, just as we found it promised above to the sacrifice-bearers of the milk-pot for the Ashwins, the Pravargya. To the sacrificer of the *odana* however it is also promised (v.2) that the fire (of cremation) will not burn his manly member and that for such people there are many women in the

---

[50] *AV* IV,34,3:
vishtârínam ódanam yé pácanti nâinân ávartih sacate kadâcaná
âste yamá úpa yâti devânt sám gandharvâir madate somyébhih

[51] *AV* IV,34,2:
anasthâh pûtâh pávanena çuddhâh çúcayah çúcim ápi yanti lokám

41

heavenly world. In the verses following v.3 of the same hymn, such heavenly bliss is further depicted. Yama does not rob the sacrificer-bearers of the *odana vishtârin* of their manly seed. As a charioteer such a person hastens in the chariot, provided with wings he moves beyond heaven. There he find streams that swell with sweet moisture, lotus ponds, lakes of molten butter, rivers with mead (*madhu*) such as are filled with milk, sour milk and water, but also such as conduct brandy (*surâ*) instead of water. This and much else. Hence does the singer at the conclusion of the hymn, which obviously accompanies the offering of the porridge-pot, "This porridge I set before the brâhmans, the *vishtârin* which obtains the heavenly world, swelling the way it does it shall not dry up for me, an omniform milk-cow shall it be to me from which wishes are milked."[52]

The last words are especially significant. The porridge-pot on the sacrificial straw is supposed to become to the sacrificer a milk-cow that fulfils all possible wishes for him. Thus a miraculous thing like that copper kettle which, according to the Mahâbhârata, the sun-god gifts Yudhishthira. Only of a more comprehensive significance, since the kettle gives only every possible kind of food, but the wishing-cow fulfils its owners' wishes in general as any other cow gives milk from itself.

It is well-known that such a wishing-cow likewise plays a role in the Mahâbhârata. The famous conflict between Vasishtha and Viçvâmitra is about this cow. But we find it evidenced here already in the Veda. It stands as a wishing-animal next to the kettle of the sun-god rather like the naïve donkey Bricklebrit next to the wishing-table in Grimm's fairy-tale. The Atharvaveda mentions it more often,[53] whereas it does not appear in the Rigveda. That is perhaps explained by the fact that

---

[52] *AV* IV,34,8:

viçvárûpâ dhenúh kâmadúghâ me astu

[53] In *AV* IX,5,10, it is said of a goat, which is gifted along with 5 porridge-pots to a priest, that it is (for the donor) an omniform wishing-cow; according to v.25 such a person should receive 5 wishing-cows. In *AV* XI,1,28, the image of the wishing-cow appears again during a gifting of porridge. In *AV* XII,1,61, the earth is called a wishing-cow. In *AV* XVIII,4,33, certain funeral gifts for the dead are supposed to become wishing-cows that await him in the other world.

the Atharvaveda is so much more popular than the Rigveda and it is here doubtless a question of a popular, fairy-tale-like idea. Obviously a very old idea of this sort. Basically the wishing-cow is perhaps essentially the same as the wonderful copper kettle of the sun-god. Just another image of the sun thought of as a miraculous thing giving gifts. Indeed the sun is conceived of not only as a vessel but also as an animal, a bull, a horse, a bird – not to mention other images. And precisely when the wishing-cow is basically nothing but the sun is it more important for the singer who offers the pot signifying the sun to wish that it should be as a wishing-cow for him.

But that the porridge (*odana*) or the pot with porridge actually signifies the sun becomes so much clearer through the corresponding myth in the Rigveda. For the Rigveda mentions many times a heavenly *odana*, a heavenly porridge-pot, porridge or cooked porridge which Indra seizes, his battle comrade Vishnu carries away, and which is obviously nothing but the sun. This *odana* of the Rigveda cannot be a rice-dish as Whitney translates the word in the *AV* since the Indians of the Rigveda indeed generally did not yet know of rice.[54] It must have been a porridge of some other corn – perhaps barley or millet. We do not know exactly what. Rice however emerges first in the Atharvaveda, at a time when the Indians had already entered the Ganges valley.[55]

Mainly it is hymn *RV* VIII,66 which speaks of the heavenly porridge and its seizure by Indra. It is that exquisite hymn rich in original and ancient traits which narrates directly in the introduction how Indra, immediately after his birth, asks his mother: "Who are the powerful? Who are famous?" The strong woman[56] named to him

---

[54] Cf. [Heinrich] Zimmer, *Altindisches Leben* [: *Die Cultur der vedischen Arier nach den Samhitā dargestellt*, Berlin, 1879], p.239.

[55] [This dating of the Atharva Veda later than the Rigveda is obviously doubtful since the term "atharvan" is itself Indo-Iranian and the Atharva Veda is indeed the Veda that is associated with the highest Brahman priest, whereas the Rigveda, Yajurveda and Sāma Veda are associated only with the more practical Hotar, Adhvaryu and Udgātr priests respectively].

[56] [Śavasi, an epithet of Aditi, Indra's mother.]

Aurnavābha and Ahīśuva:[57] "These, my son, are the ones who must be overthrown". Then the slayer of Vrtra killed them both as spokes are hammered into naves; the slayer of demons had grown big (and strong). At one draught he, Indra, drank 30 vats – of the Soma drink.

And now the concise and terse narration moves to further adventures of Indra which it describes quickly in brief strokes. First of all comes the seizure of the "cooked porridge" (*pakvám odanám*) which is then also called a milk-cooked porridge up beyond in the airy region:

abhí gandharvám atrinad
abudhnéshu rájahsu â
índro brahmábhya id vridhé

nír âvidhyad giríbhya â
dhâráyat pakvám odanám
índro bundám svâtatam

"He pierced the Gandharvas into the groundless airy regions, Indra, for the prosperity of the worshippers. He shot from the mountains and seized the cooked porridge – (Indra) shot the well-aimed arrow".

The situation is mostly perfectly clear. The battle is conducted high above in the groundless airy region. The battle prize which Indra seizes and holds with a firm hand is the "cooked porridge". His opponent is the Gandharva who here protects the "cooked porridge" as he is otherwise considered a Soma-protector. But Indra hits him with his arrow shooting from the mountains – the cloud-capped mountains. He pierces him and obtains the battle prize for the use and joy of his pious worshippers.

The "cooked porridge" in the groundless airy region, which does not seem unworthy of a divine battle – what else can it be but the sun, thought of in a naïve image as a hot yellow porridge? The porridge in the heavens to which the sacrificial porridge in the ritual corresponds, which, on the other hand, finds its loftier counter-

---

[57] [Schroeder translates the names as "the spider's son" and "the cobra". Nothing definite is known of these demons.]

image in the heavenly Soma to which, in turn, the earthly soma drink corresponds. The image is naïve but not so bad after all.

The singer praises the victorious arrow of Indra which bestows blessings:

çatábradhna íshus táva
sahásraparna éka it
yám indra cakrishé yújam

téna stotríbhyo â bhara
nríbhyo nâribhyo áttave
sadyó jâtá ribhushthira

"Your arrow, which you, O Indra, have made your comrade, is provided with hundred (red) spikes, it alone with thousand feathers. Through this create food for the singers here, for men and women – immediately after your birth, you wonderfully strong one."

It would perhaps be better if the text offered a preterite (*â bharo*) instead of an imperative (*â bhara*). "Through this you created food for the singers here, for men and women". The slight change would commend itself so much more since the apposition sadyó jâtáh, "when you were born", fully points to the past. If one does not wish to emend, one must recognise in the text the typical, regularly repeated heroic deed of Indra which he must do even today and ever again, for the use and piety of the entire world. The interpretation is possible, but harder than if the text merely narrated.

The meaning of this verse too is essentially clear. Indra's arrow is praised. With this has he won victory, with this has he created food for his hymners, men and women – since he pierced the Gandharva and seized the cooked porridge. And so may he do ever again!

That by acquiring the "cooked porridge" Indra also creates food for men and women is perhaps to be noted – whether one relates it directly to the sun in its natural characteristic or whether one supposes that the poet here had that fabulous miraculous object in mind, the Indian wishing-table, the miraculous kettle, that is thought of as a porridge-pot. Certainly that cannot be ruled out. But we shall

soon enough encounter such a wonderful porridge-pot among our own people.

Of the last three verses of the hymn I wish to pick out only v.10, where the porridge is mentioned once again:

víçvét tâ vishnur âbharad
uritkramás tvéshitah
çatám mahishân kshîrapâkám
odanám
varâhám índra emushââm

"All these things did Vishnu bring, the one with the wide strides, goaded by thee (i.e. by Indra), brought hundred buffaloes, the milk-cooked porridge, Indra (brought) the pernicious boar."

According to this verse Vishnu, the battle comrade of Indra, seems to bring the "milk-cooked porridge", whereas Indra similarly gets the boar, a deed which corresponds to those of Hercules and has been mentioned elsewhere too but does not need to be discussed here.

In my opinion, a verse of a remarkable Indra hymn that belongs to the same book of the Rigveda (VIII,58) speaks of the same heroic deed of Indra; a hymn in which the folk-song-like tone of some verses already struck Hillebrandt.[58] I shall translate that verse in the following manner:

The strong one, he, Indra, despises
Them, all the foes.
The youth divided the porridge
Being cooked, far on the mountain.

Indra divides the porridge, i.e. he opens the solar vessel containing the porridge. The mountain is naturally the highest heaven. Up there is the solar porridge cooked.[59] The appellation "youth" agrees admirably

---

[58] Cf. Hillebrandt, *Vedische Mythologie*, Vol.I, p.144.

[59] The text of *RV* VIII,58,14:
átîd u çakrá ohata índro víçvâ áti dvíshah
bhinát kanîna odanám pacyámânam paró girá

with the fact that in *RV* VIII,66,6 Indra carries out the seizure of the porridge immediately after his birth. One may believe so much more in a connection of the two passages in that the two are found in the same book.

The "cooked porridge", which is nothing but the sun, seems to be mentioned in yet another passage of the Rigveda under the rather general appellation of *pacatam*, "the cooked", "the cooked food". It is that of *RV* I,61,7. It is a Indra hymn, and there is throughout only mention of Indra in it. But in v.7 again Vishnu comes in out of the blue – and here so disturbingly that Graßmann preferred to take the word in this passage as an epithet of Indra's and to translate it as "the efficient". Then there appears a good meaning but it cannot be denied that this translation has some doubts. And that so much more in that, in *RV* VIII,66,10, Vishnu, impelled by Indra, actually seems to bring the heavenly porridge which Indra himself previously won. I give here, for a better understanding of the connection, also the preceding verse:

RV I,61,6 *asmâ íd u tváshtâ takshad vájram*
svápastamam svaryàm ránâya
vritrásya cid vidád yéna márma
tujánn îçânas tujatâ kiyedhâh

7 asyéd u mâtúh sávaneshu sadyó
maháh pitúm papivân cârv ánnâ
mushâyád vishnúh pacatám sáhîyân
vídhyad varâhám tiró ádrim ástâ

I construe *parás* as an adverb and girâ as locative of *girí* "the mountain", like *agnâ* along with *agnâu*, and so on; I therefore do not derive it, as otherwise happens, from *gir*, "the song" (Ludwig: "the voice"). In this way the verse has an excellent meaning and linguistically everything is well-grounded. The verb *bhinát* can mean "he split". If Graßmann translates: "The youth refuses the porridge that is prepared without blood", this is indeed linguistically impossible. Somewhat better is Ludwig: "He cut the swollen cake still smaller, when he cooked, in the distance with the voice of thunder". Here too the conclusion is unsuccessful. For the mountain, cf. das *giríbhya â RV* VIII,66,6; also in VIII,45,5 the mountain is mentioned in Indra's first battles, only unfortunately in an unclear phrase (*girâv ápso ná yodhishat*).

"6. For him did Tvashtr make the pointedly effective heavenly thunderbolt for the battle, with which he discovered Vrtra's vulnerable place, striking with the strong penetrating versatile bolt, he the strong penetrating ruler. 7. As soon as the great one had consumed the repast, the beloved food, at the libations of his mother, the efficient (*vishnúh*) incomparably strong one robbed the cooked food (*pacatám*); he wounded the boar, shooting through the mountain."

As one sees, it is hardly possible to bring in Vishnu here since, before and after, the sentence speaks only of Indra. But taking *vishnúh* directly as an epithet of Indra also certainly remains doubtful. We may perhaps leave this question *in suspenso* here, especially since the passage is of secondary importance for us. That even here it is a seizure of the heavenly porridge, the cooked food that is being spoken of may be considered, after what was discussed earlier, as very probable. In all probability Indra performs here too the heroic act. He first heavily drinks Soma at his mother's, shoots through the mountain, wounds the boar – all features that remind us of the accompanying circumstances of the act in hymn *RV* VIII,66.

After the above discussion, it may be considered as proven, or at least as very probable, that the Vedic Indians considered the sun also in the image of a heavenly porridge-pot – of a cooked, hot, yellow porridge that, according to the myth, Indra seized, that was represented in the ritual by a porridge, that ensured to the sacrificer a future blessed existence with the most select pleasures in the heavenly world, that indeed played the role of the wishing-cow for him.

But this naive imagination of the sun as a heavenly porridge or porridge-pot is, I believe, quite suited to solving a riddle of Vedic mythology that was earlier quite obscure to me – and perhaps to others. I mean the so clearly expressed strange passage where the sun-god Pushan is said to be a porridge eater, a *karambhâd*. He is apparently toothless, and is mocked as a "porridge eater", as is clearly apparent from the warning of the singer against all such sacrilegious mockery (*RV* VI,56,1). How does one fall into such a strange thought? It is almost self-explanatory if one considers the idea of the sun as a hot porridge as natural. Then at least one of the gods must become a porridge-eater. And to such a god then naturally an offering of porridge or groats had to be brought.[60]

The wonderful food-dispensing kettle of the Indian sun-god – the porridge offering representing the sun which is supposed to become a wishing-cow for the sacrificer – the heavenly porridge in the Vedic myth – they remind us of many related sagas and fairy-tales of the European Aryans.

A Russian fairy-tale narrates of a peasant who climbs up to heaven on a giant cabbage-stalk and finds there a wonderful hand-mill that grinds for him wheat-cakes, butter and cheese-cakes and a pot with porridge.[61]

So we have here also a heavenly porridge-pot but it comes, along with other delights, only from the heavenly hand-mill. The sagas and fairy-tales of the wonderful mill are spread in countless variants throughout Europe. One of the best-known and most famous is the Sampo saga in the Finnish epic Kalevala. Its connection to the Grotti saga in the Edda has for long been undoubtedly correctly recognised. But, along with this, is ranged another manifold connection in the most diverse forms. I have already dealt with this subject in an earlier work,[62] and do not wish to discuss it here at length referring to it and to the studies of other researchers.[63] But it is certainly pertinent to

---

[60] Cf. Oldenberg, *Religion des Veda,* p.232n. - I find a solar sacrifice that recalls the porridge sacrifice, recorded in America among the Indians, in Taylor, *Anfänge der Kultur,* Vol.II, p.288: "The Pottawatomis sometimes used to climb up on their huts, kneel and offer a bowl full of maize to the shining disk".

[61] Cf. A. Schiefner, in the *Mélanges russes* of the St. Petersburg Academy, IV, p.206; L.V. Schroeder, *Germanische Elben und Götter beim Estenvolke,* p.43 (Sitzungsbericht der Wiener Akademie der Wissenschaften, philos.-histor. Klasse, Vol.153, Vienna, 1906).

[62] Cf. L.v. Schroeder, *Germanische Elben und Götter beim Estenvolke,* pp.41-63.

[63] Cf. Felix Liebrecht, *Zur Volkskunde* (Heilbronn, 1879), p.302,303; Laistner, *Nebelsagen,* pp.324ff; Asbjörnsen and Noe, *Norske Folkeeventyr,* 2nd edition, Christiania [Oslo], 1852, p.488, where the Norwegian fairy-tale of the wishing-mill is compared to the Sampo; Asbjörnen and Moe, *Norwegische Volksmärchen,* tr. Fr. Bresemann, Berlin, 1847, Vol.II, pp.182ff; Colshorn, *Märchen und Sagen,* p.173, No.61 and 25 and 32; Mannhardt, *Germanische Mythen,* p.399n; Harry Jansen, *Märchen und Sagen des estnischen Volkes,* 1st edition, Dorpat, 1881, pp.20ff.

us. For the wonderful mill that gives all possible good gifts is most closely related to the wonderful pot or kettle. That becomes clearer when one considers that the form of the "mill" in the most ancient period is indeed far removed from that form that the Grotti saga reports, where two giant maidens turn the mill-stones. The most ancient "mill" is indeed nothing but a vessel of wood, a hollow stone, a primitive mortar in which, with the help of a pestle, the corn is ground. Such a primitive grinding vessel is not far removed from the cooking vessel, pot or kettle; and the wonderful mill in its original form is therefore most closely connected with the wonderful pot or kettle not only through its miraculous character, but already through its form. Here as well as there it is a matter of wonderful, gift-giving vessels.

But a very characteristic trait of of these European mill sagas is the circumstance that the mill works, and can likewise be brought to a halt again, only with a certain phrase, a certain instruction. Otherwise it continues to grind without stop and thereby brings about serious catastrophes or also pleasant situations which can be, and were, realised in splendid narrative. Thus the sea became salty through the mill continuously grinding salt at the bottom of the sea, and so on.

In the Grimm collection we find a fairy-tale that likewise has this characteristic in it and most finely relates the European mill sagas to the heavenly porridge-pot of the Indians. It is so brief that I may present it here literally.

The Sweet Porridge[64]

There was once a poor, pious maiden that lived alone with her mother and she had nothing more to eat. So the child went into the woods and there she was met by an old woman who already knew her sorrow and gifted to her a small pot to which she had to say: "Little pot, cook" and it cooked good, sweet millet porridge and

---

[64] In the complete edition of the *Kinder- und Hausmärchen gesammelt durch die Brüder Grimm* [1812-1815], it is No.103.

when she said, "Little pot, stop", it stopped cooking. The maiden brought the pot home to her mother and now they were free of their poverty and hunger and ate sweet porridge as often as they wanted. Once when the maiden had gone out the mother said, "Little pot, cook", and it cooked and she ate to her fill; now she wants the little pot to stop but she does not know the magic phrase. And so it continues to cook and the porridge rises above the rim and still continues to cook, filling the kitchen and the entire house, and the second house and then the street, as if it wished to make the entire world full, and the danger is great and nobody knows how to solve it. Finally, when there is only one house left, the child comes home and just says, "Little pot, stop", and then it stops and ceases cooking; and anybody that wished to return to the city had to eat his way through.

The porridge-pot of this naïve and certainly very old fairy-tale has all the characteristics that we otherwise find in the wonderful mills. Not only the unlimited gift-giving but also the obedience to a certain order. And indeed it is a porridge-pot similar to the heavenly *odana* that Indra seizes in the groundless airy region, to which in turn the *odana* of the ritual corresponds that is said to become a wishing-cow to the sacrificer that satisfies all his wishes.

We have already seen that the Indian porridge-pot is, or signifies, the sun. But even the European wonder mill is the sun, as I have demonstrated in my above-mentioned work.[65] And that indeed agrees most accurately with the inference that we have just arrived at, according to which porridge-pot and wonder mills are originally not different but one and the same thing.

The representation of the sun as a heavenly mill has already been ascertained by Kuhn.[66] "In German folk-songs the morning sun appears as a mill when it grinds silver and gold on the mountain. On the representation of the sun as a mill is based the fact that the Milky Way, in which the sun is supposed to stand at noon, is called the Mill

---

[65] Cf. L.v. Schroeder, *op.cit.*, pp.61-63.

[66] Cf. A. Kuhn, *Herabkunft des Feuers und Göttertranks*, p.115; 2nd edition, p.102,103.

Way. That is why Kuhn and Schiefner have traced back the Grotti mill as well as the Sampo derived therefrom to the sun conceived of as a wonderful mill." The full proof of the correctness of this interpretation however has been brought forward only by the most recent Kalevala research, and indeed in a remarkable song from Ingermannland in which the liberation of the sun and moon from the power of the evil Louhi emerges quite clearly as just another version of the acquisition of the Sampo. The best expert on the subject, Kaarle Krohn, thereby reached the concise inference that "The song of the liberation of the sun and that of the stealing of the Sampo are, as O. Donner already rightly recognised, variations on the same theme, or rather they are variations on one and the same song."[67]

Therefrom arises further the conclusion that the wonderful mill Sampo is originally nothing but the sun, the sun imagined as a mill.[68]

And that agrees, as we have already seen, perfectly with our inferences arrived at above, and is well suited to support the latter further.

But, following the above, there arises as the original idea the representation of the sun as a heavenly vessel that can have diverse contents and gives wonderful gifts.

Such a representation could quite probably form the mythical foundation of the idea of the Grail.[69]

It is to be observed besides that that above-mentioned hymn from Ingermannland sings of the liberation of the sun and moon as a variant of the acquisition of the Sampo. Therefore the moon would have as much a claim to be the original image of the Sampo – or of

---

[67] Cf. Kaarle Krohn, *Zur Kalevalafrage, Finnisch-ugrische Forschungen*, Vol.I, pt.3 (1901), p.201.

[68] Cf. L.v. Schroeder, *op.cit.*, p.62,62.

[69] In Wolfram, as is well-known, the Grail appears not as as vessel but as a wonderful precious stone. It seems that even this idea is sometimes connected to the sun. The splendid necklace, Freya' jewel, *bringsamen*, is called "the beautiful sea-kidneys". It is doubtless the sun represented as a beautiful piece of amber. From there the passage to a precious stone would not be difficult at all. But I would like to consider it more probable that Wolfram formed his idea of the Grail as a precious stone from oriental sources – naturally indirectly, as L. Iselin presumes (cf. above p.26).

the Grail. And it cannot be denied that the moon through its waxing, waning, and regrowth could, much more than the sun, occasion the idea of a vessel that is emptied and replenishes itself ever anew. It is therefore not at all improbable that this idea first originated from the moon and was transferred only later to the sun. But this must have happened rather early, as emerges already from our previous investigations. We can only touch lightly upon the question here and will have occasion to return to it later.

We have encountered milk and porridge as the contents of the sun or the vessel representing the sun, according to the Vedic conception. But that, up above, there was also a heavenly intoxicating drink – mead, soma – to be found in the sun can be concluded from many passages of the Veda. In three passages of the Rigveda that Hillebrandt already cited it is clearly said that Indra drank Soma with Vishnu – i.e. with the sun-god.[70] And when in another passage it says that the gods enjoy themselves, or intoxicate themselves (*mâdáyante*) in the house of Vivasvant, another sun-god, Hillebrandt rightly concludes therefrom that the sun-god Vivasvant must be in possession of the Soma.[71] The question is difficult in many passages of the Veda since the appellation "mead" (*madhu*) that so often signifies soma is used, in a transferred sense, also of milk, as we have already seen.

In the Vishnu hymn *RV* I,154 it says at the end of v.4:

> *víshnoh padé mádhva útsah*
> i.e. "In Vishnu's highest step is the fount of the mead".

---

[70] Cf. Hillebrandt, *Vedische Mythologie*, Vol.I, p.480. It says in *RV* VIII,12,16:
yát sómam indra vishnavi yád vâ gha tritá âptyé
yád vâ marátsu mándase sám índubhih
And further, in *RV* VIII,3,8:
asyéd índro vâvridhe
vrishnyam çávo máde sutásya víshnavi
The pressed drink (*sutá*) can only be soma. Further in *RV* X,113,2, where the name *amçú* likewise clearly indicates soma.

[71] Cf. Hillebrandt, *op.cit.*, p.479. It is the passage *RV* X,12,7: *yásmin devâ vidáthe mâdáyante vivásvatah sádane dhâráyante*. That Indra obtains the Soma vat from Vivasvant (*RV* VIII,72,9) we shall discuss further below.

Vishnu is an ancient sun-god. His three steps are, in all probability, the rise, the high point and the setting of the sun. His highest step however is, by more or less general consensus, the sun in its highest position. Thus essentially the same that we already encountered earlier under the appellation "*bradhnasya vishtapam*", "of the red zenith". There the blessed feasted and enjoyed themselves in the company of the gods, and quite accordingly it says also previously in our verse *RV* I,154,5: "These his beloved places I would like to reach, where the pious men enjoy themselves (or intoxicate themselves, *mádanti*), there indeed are the host of friends of him who traverses the universe (Vishnu)"[72] – and then follow the words already cited.

That the blessed do not drink milk there but enjoy mead, i.e. Soma, an actual intoxicating drink, may perhaps be considered probable *a priori*. It becomes still clearer through the previously cited verse *RV* VIII,58,8 in which the singer expresses the hope of reaching Indra at the bradhnasya vishtapam and of drinking mead with him there. This mead must in any case be an intoxicating drink, in all probability Soma, Indra's drink. Indra is unthinkable as a milk-drinker.

All the three steps of Vishnu are, moreover, filled with mead, and imperishable. That is expressed by the verse that immediately precedes the above-cited one.[73] The verse immediately following it however shows clearly that Vishnu's highest step is actually the sun. *RV* I,154,6 says – and the entire hymn closes with these words:

átrâha tád urugâyásya vríshnah
paramám padám áva bhâti bhûri

"For there shines the great, the highest footstep of the wide-striding strong One."

That can certainly only be the sun – the sun in its highest position. And the place of the blessed is thought to be there, for which the

---

[72] *RV* I,154,5:
   tád asya priyám abhí pâtho açyâm náro yátra devayávo mádanti
   urukramásya sá hí pûrnâ bandhúr itthâ víshnoh padé paramé mádhva útsah
[73] *RV* I,154,4: *yásya trî pûrnâ mádhunâ padâny ákshîyamânâ.*

singer longs quite in accordance with other passages that have already been observed.

The same conclusion arises from hymn *RV* I,22 whose last part is similarly addressed to Vishnu. There we hear of the three steps of Vishnu and then it says:

tád víshnoh paramám padám
sádâ paçyanti sûráyah
divîva cákshur âtatam

"The sacrificers look forever at this highest step of Vishnu spread like an eye in the heavens".

The eye in the heavens can indeed be only the sun. And the following last verse of the hymn makes it still clearer. It says (v.21) in Graßmann's translation:

And this step of Vishnu, which
Is the highest, is lit constantly by
The priests, attentively, commendably.

The priests light the sacrificial fire and therewith presumably also the solar fire, which is identified hieratically-mystically with the former. When it says that the priests light the step of Vishnu the latter can certainly be understood as nothing but the sun.

This conception of the Veda of the font of the mead in the step of Vishnu, the sun-god - or, up above in the sun itself, becomes especially noteworthy through a pair of little songs of the Latvians that demonstrate a related conception.

The Latvian verses sound highly enigmatic:

A lark brews beer
In the footstep of the horse.[74]

---

[74] The concluding lines of the four-line poem are:
   I hurried to drink the mash,
   Got it in the back with the cooking spoon.
This original conclusion seems to point to the unapproachability of the beer brewed

What they signify was first made clear to me only by a parallel verse in which, instead of the lark, the god Uhsing is named:

> Uhsing brews beer,
> In the footstep of the horse.

Uhsing is the sun-god, the god of the sun rising anew in the spring, as Pastor R. Anning has shown in a fine monograph.[75] and as can be confirmed further. From this it emerges with fair probability that the horse, whose step is being spoken of here, may be the solar horse. His footstep in which Uhsing brews beer corresponds to the footstep of the sun-god Vishnu in the Indian songs and may signify the very same thing. But when, instead of Uhsing, it says "the lark" or "a lark", we remember that among the Aryans the sun is not seldom conceived of as a bird. And that is understood so much better in that the verse is obviously meant as a riddle or enigmatic question. The solution is: The sun-god brews beer up there in the footstep of his horse, of the sun. Brewing does not accord badly with the sun-god. And when the Latvian thinks he sees in the sun brown beer that the sun-god brews, that is certainly no worse an idea than that of the Vedic poets who glimpse milk, porridge or soma-mead in the sun. However the comparison makes it certainly probable that such an analogy existed already in the most ancient period. It is primitive enough for that.

Among the Latvians there is found also the conception of the sun as a vessel – especially as a pot, a golden pot, which is sometimes related to "little Johann", the naïve personification of Johannis day, sometimes to the sun's daughter. Thus, for example, it says in a Latvian sun-song:

> Little Johann shattered the pot,
> Sitting on a stone,

---

by the lark – or Uhsing. Clearly, the bold tippling singer must run away and gets it in his back with the cooking spoon. That he must retreat I assume from the fact that he receives a blow in his back.

[75] Cf. Robert Auning, "Wer ist Uhsing?", in the Magazine of the Latvian Literary Society, Vol.16, pt.2 (Mittau, 1881), pp.1-42; see especially p.20,27.

The son of god bound it together
With silver staves.[76]

The song says openly that little Johann shatters the pot because on Johannes day the ascent of the sun comes to a stop and its decline begins.

Another of these songs says:

Dive, Perkun, to the source,
Up to the bottom
Yesterday evening the sun's daughter drowned
While washing the golden pot.[77]

When the sun sinks in the evening into the sea, one imagines that the young sun-goddess, the daughter of the sun, washes the golden solar vessel there. Frequent reference is made to her drowning or the danger of her drowning at sunset.

The image of a silver pot, and indeed precisely in connection with the feast of Johannis, I find also in a communication from Tyrol. Indeed this seems even more vivid insofar as the wonderful pot also reveals an enticing content:

"In the Tyrolean Loser valley one sees on Johannis eve on Mt. Pechhorn a giant silver pot, out of which liquid gold issued like beer from the foaming jug. But no lucky child came to obtain the pot and the gold".[78]

This is a regular miraculous vessel and Johannis makes one think of the sun. But since it is a silver pot that shines at night, the moon can also perhaps be meant.

That the conception of the sun as a heavenly vessel was alive among the Germans and Russians is demonstrated already by some

---

[76] Cf. Mannhardt, "Lettische Sonnenmythen" in *Zeitschrift für Ethnologie*, Vol.VII; according to him it is song no.57.

[77] Cf. Mannhardt, *op.cit.*, Song no.39; no.40 is a variant.

[78] Cf. Feuilleton, *Wiener Fremdenblatt*, 23 June 1904, "Sonnwendzauber", p.14, signed "M.K."

of the popular confirmations communicated by Mannhardt.[79] Thus a German rain song shows us the sun conceived of as a bowl:

Sun, sun, come again,
With thy golden feather,
With thy golden bowl,
Shine on us forever.

And a popular Russian riddle says: "A bowl full of oil is enough for the entire world." The answer is: the sun.

The aptness of these images – the sun as a golden bowl, a bowl full of yellow oil – is self-apparent.

Among the Greeks, as is well-known, the sun is thought of sometimes as a beaker. Thus it appears as δέπας in Stesichoros and also in Peisandros of Kameiros.[80] According to the saga, Hercules travels over the Ocean in a solar beaker. Here the idea of the solar beaker seems to coincide with that of the solar boat. Thereby an Babylonian or Assyrian influence was considered. The Assyrian monuments from Nineveh reveal beaker-shaped vehicles such as served for upstream ship voyages on the Tigris.[81] Perhaps that is coincidental. But the saga may have also developed quite organically from the doubtless ancient Aryan ideas of the sun as a vessel and of the solar boat. Whether these ideas, that is, of the boat, originally perhaps of the moon – where they have a better derivation – may be transferred to the sun we may leave undecided here.

That the ancient Germans and Scandinavians of the Edda were accustomed to consider the sun as a vessel out of which mead was drunk or could be drunk, can perhaps be rendered to a certain degree probable in an indirect way. The Völuspa says (in Gering's translation):

I know Odin's eye hidden
In the water source of Mimir, the world-famous,

---

[79] Cf. Mannhardt, "Lettische Sonnenmythen", p.101.

[80] Cf. Mannhardt, *op.cit.*, p.102,103.

[81] Cf. [Ludwig] Preller, *Griechische Mythologie*, 3rd edition, Vol.I, p.355.

Mimir drinks mead daily in the morning,
Through Walvater's[82] pledge – can you understand the rest?[83]

There can be no doubt that the eye of Odin, the god of the heavens, is the sun. He has only one eye, the other he had to once give to the water-god or water-spirit Mimir as a pledge in order to acquire wisdom from the latter. This second, pledged eye he never gets back. Thus does the myth narate – what does it mean thereby?

I think that it understands by Walvater's pledge, the second eye which the water-god Mimir has received and never returns, nothing but the sun reflected in the waters, or the mirror-image of the sun in the water. Uhland was already of this view and Mühlenhoff followed him in it; likewise Wilhelm Müller and recently E. Meinck.[84] The vapid mockery with which E. Siecke sought to make this view ridiculous and thereby dismiss it completely misses its mark.[85]

---

[82] [An epithet of Odin as the father of the heroes killed in the battlefield.]

[83] Cf. Hugo Gering, *Die Edda, translated and explained*, Leipzig and Vienna, Bibliograph. Inst., p.8; also note 8 on p.7.

[84] Cf. [Karl] Müllenhof, *Deutsche Altertumskunde*, Vol.V, p.102; Wilhelm Müller, *Geschichte und System der altdeutschen Religion*, p.184; Ernst Meinck, "Über die Verehrung der Sonne bei den Germanen", in *Bayreuther Blätter*, 32 (1909), p.115. However we shall leave two possibilities open here. The pledge of Walvater should be either the mirror-image of the sun in the water or the pledging of the eye should be manifested in the apparent setting of the sun in the world-sea every evening. E. Mogk, *Germanische Mythologie*, 2nd edition, p.76,77 (305,306); H. Gering, *op.cit.*, p.8n represent only the latter hypothesis. I can consider only the first hypothesis as probable. But in Mogk's and Gering's hypothesis the sun is, moreover, more directly thought of as a vessel from which Mimir drinks mead. According to v.27, even the World-Tree is watered by Walvater's pledge. According to this too, therefore, Odhin's eye is clearly thought of as a vessel, bowl and so on.

[85] Cf. Ernst Siecke, *Mythologische Briefe*, Berlin, 1901, p.36. He says the same: "I think everybody, whether he has pawned or pledge something, perhaps his watch as a student, just once or not, will admit that the essential thing in the pawning or pledging of something consists in no longer having it for a while, that one gives it away, to be sure with the hope of getting it back. On the other hand, if one holds an object before the mirror in such a way that one sees its reflection in it while one has it itself in one's hand, this action can never be called a pawning". That sufficiently justifies my judgement above.

There is something of the great, originally grown, picturesque poetry of the primordial age, of the age of the birth of myth, in this thought. Up above shines the sun, the eye of the god of the heavens. He has only one, since the other one is glimpsed only deep down in the waters, as deep down as the first is high above. He had to once pledge it to a wise water-god or a water-spirit in order to buy wisdom from him. But now he will not get it back.

And Mimir, the clever water-spirit, drinks mead daily in the morning out of this pledge, the eye of the god of the heavens, out of the second sun, which he has in his power. Since the one eye must be basically the same as the other, it can be concluded with great probability that, along with the image of the eye, that of a vessel also - out of which mead is or can be drunk – for the sun was not unknown to the ancient Germans.[86] The connection or mixing of the two images does not have anything objectionable at all about it – as little as when, in the above-cited hymn *RV* I,22, the sun is described as the footstep of Vishnu, the eye of heaven and the sacrificial fire in close sequence – or when Goethe indeed says that the golden tree of life is green.[87] This is of course poetry, not logic.

It is perhaps possible, even if not entirely necessary, that the conception of the sun as a vessel which is drunk out of continuously was originally transferred to it from the moon, as the lunar mythology postulates. It is clear that the ever waxing and again waning moon could, much more than the sun, inspire the image of a vessel that is filled and again emptied. For the rest, however, the image of a vessel

---

[86] The lunar mythology sees in Odhin's pledged eye the moon (cf. E. Siecke, *Hermes der Mondgott*, p.16 and p.72n5 *Mytholog. Bib.* II, Pt.3). If we admit the possibility of this interpretation, this too would form only a further support of our view that will be presented later that the moon, not only among the Indians, but also among the Germans (that is, already in the earliest period) was seen as a vessel for heavenly drink. For our specific investigation the difference is not essential since, according to it, both the sun and the moon were held as a wonderful heavenly vessel. And I admit that the watering of the World-Tree by Walvater's pledge is perhaps better suited for the moon than for the reflection of the sun in the water.

[87] I remark that in relation to E. Meinck, *op.cit.*, p.115n, which shows a mixture of two quite different interpretations since in the same strophe the sun is first interpreted as an eye and then as a bowl.

in manifold forms is, according to our explanations above, certainly attested and was certainly current already in the earliest Aryan times. Even if less than the moon, the sun is indeed also apt to be compared to a round vessel. Indeed the imagination does not shy away from comparing it also to a pot or a beaker, as we have already seen. Likewise, as we saw, the wonderful characteristic of giving food or other gifts was attributed to this vessel in India as well as in Europe. There is no doubt that this too goes back to the earliest times; there is no doubt that many related representations in the sagas and fairy-tales of later times go back to the representation of the solar vessel dispensing food and other gifts – and that leads us directly to the Grail saga.

It was especially and chiefly the food-dispensing power of the Grail which allowed earlier researchers to suppose a connection between this wonderful vessel and certain magical vessels of the Celtic saga, the wishing-table of the German fairy-tale, and so forth. They were, in my view, completely right; by itself that wonderful characteristic of the Grail was not sufficient to ascertain the connection completely convincingly. There were similar wonderful objects also among other peoples – and could not a similar wonderful characteristic have been attributed later to the holy vessel of the Christian legend quite independently of those sagas and fairy-tales?

Birch-Hirschfeld, who – hardly rightly – wishes to place Robert de Boron at the head of the Grail poem, energetically stresses that in him the Grail is simply a "vessel of grace" that gives to the diners a purely spiritual, incomparable pleasure, not a vessel that, endowed with wonderful powers, gives food and drink, youth, health and strength (*op.cit.*, p.215), as emerges in Wolfram and others. Heinzel confirms the negation for Robert de Boron, though with a noteworthy conclusion. He says: "That the Grail gives actual food is said nowhere and was also not what was meant by the poet, who therein departed from the older significance which perhaps seemed to him too crude."[88] According to this then, the food-dispensing power of the Grail was an older idea which Robert, in his attempt to raise the Grail to the

---

[88] Cf. Heinzel, *Über die französischen Gralromane*, p.102.

highest possible spiritual sphere, had avoided or discarded. And that seems completely credible – just as Wagner intentionally removed from his Grail vessel the naïve, childish fairy-tale like ideas that are found in Wolfram and that were well-known to him.[89]

It is striking how Gottfried Baist judges this feature in Wolfram's poem. He is convinced that Wolfram knew no other source than Crestien and that all deviations from Crestien in him derive from his own design. The food-dispensing power of the Grail does not emerge clearly anywhere,[90] so Wolfram must have added them. On this Baist says: "That the Grail becomes a wonderful stone rests on a misunderstanding; Wolfram did not know the French word. Or the meaning of the food-dispensing power of the Grail".[91] So this characteristic of the Grail is supposed to have entered his Parzival through a mere misunderstanding! How is that thinkable when the same characteristic of the Grail however emerges quite clearly in other French poems? Poems that are certainly not dependent on Wolfram.

In the second interpolator in Pseudo-Gautier,[92] the Grail appears as a golden vessel which at the court of the Grail king dispenses food swaying in the air. Joseph of Arimathea once had it made and collected the blood of Christ in it. Already Joseph and his people were nourished in a wonderful way by the Grail. The Grail goes round and gives everyone whatever he wants. Heinzel affirms expressly that the author of the interpolation departs from Crestien through the swaying Grail that serves at table and dispenses actual food, along with which there is no lance and no procession.[93]

Even the Grand St. Graal narrates that the Grail gave to anyone the food that he wanted. "As a miraculous effect of the Grail is considered

---

[89] H. St. Chamberlain, Richard Wagner, 4th edition (1907), p.442.

[90] A relic of this idea can perhaps be recognised in the fact that in Crestien the Grail is carried past at every course of the meal. Cf. E. Wechssler, op.cit., p.168.

[91] Cf. Gottfried Baist, Parzival und der Gral, p.13 of the offprint, p.37 of the official edition.

[92] [See p. 13 above]

[93] Cf. Heinzel, Über die französischen Gralromane, p.36,37; cf. also p.46,47.

the satisfaction of the owner and of his community with actual food – which everybody wants for himself". However, that is granted only to the virtuous. The Grail also multiplies existing food. It also produces supernatural satisfaction without actual food. But the food-dispensing characteristic emerges clearly.[94]

Likewise in the *Quête*. Here too the Grail gives everyone the food that he wishes.[95]

In Manessier, the Grail feeds the royal company. According to him too, Joseph of Arimathea was sustained in prison by the Grail, which he saw daily twice or thrice.[96] And in the Pseudo-Crestien Introduction, the Grail serves automatically.[97]

It is therefore clear that not only Wolfram but an entire series of French Grail poems are aware of the food-dispensing power of the Grail in a very naïve form. And we can leave undecided whether Crestien and Robert de Boron did not yet know this feature of the saga or legend – which I would much rather believe – or intentionally avoided or spiritualised it. In any case it is clear. And the obvious explanation is certainly that this feature entered the Christian legend through some of those European sagas and fairy-tales of wonderful, food-dispensing vessels and similar wonderful objects. It cannot be contested that other possibilities are also thinkable. It will be a question of whether, along with this characteristic and completely fabulous feature, others appear in the course of our investigation which allow our explanation to be recognised as the most probable.

THE MOON

It is an everlasting service of Alfred Hillebrandt that he provided the evidence that soma in the Rigveda does not signify merely the intoxicating drink in the sacrifice but at the same time, in its widest scope, also the moon, which is thought of as a heavenly intoxicating

[94] Cf. Heinzel, *op.cit.*, p.48,130,132.

[95] Cf. Heinzel, *op.cit.*, p.48,160.

[96] Cf. Heinzel, *op.cit.*, p.60.

[97] Cf. Heinzel, *op.cit.*, p.78.

drink, as the intoxicating drink of the gods and the blessed – or as a vessel with such wonderful intoxicating drink that ever anew replenishes itself and empties itself. Hillebrandt brought forward this evidence in the first comprehensive volume of his *Vedic Mythology* so fundamentally and convincingly and further defended it so successfully, especially against Oldenberg, that I can spare myself a thorough explanation of this view, through which both the hymns of the Rigveda and a great part of the ritual have been revealed in a quite new light.[98] What one hardly thought of earlier can be at present considered as firmly established: the most outstandingly important central point of the ancient Indian ritual is formed by a mystical cult of the moon, the heavenly Soma, that corresponds, and is indeed equated, to the earthly soma in the same way that the sun as the sacrificial fire of the gods corresponds to the sacrificial fire of men. We have also seen the modest milk-pot of the Ashwins and the equally modest porridge-pot, the *odana vishtârin*, identified with the sun in the ritual. But the soma-sacrifice is the highest and most important sacrifice of the Indian ritual; incomparably more significant is therefore the identification of the highly celebrated soma drink with the moon, both of which are actually lauded in an exalted manner in a hardly dissoluble unity as one and the same highly important and powerful potency. The soma that the priests press is supposed to enliven the gods, strengthen Indra for the battle against the demons; indeed Indra also drinks the Soma up above in heaven, in his father's house, with his mother, or elsewhere; up there he conquers the Soma from Vrtra and other envious demons, up there there are many

---

[98] Cf. A. Hillebrandt, *Vedische Mythologie*, Vol.I, Breslau, 1891; Vol.II, pp.209ff. "Once again soma" - Hillebrandt's view has received in the meanwhile also a powerful confirmation through comparative ethnology. Paul Ehrenreich states in his recently published book, *Die allgemeine Mythologie und ihre ethnologischen Grundlagen* (Leipzig, 1910), p.144: "States of intoxication are, like dreams and visions, an effect of the moon, which, as the vegetational god, rules plantal life and the bowl of which contains the revitalising magical drink. Such divine drinks and foods as nectar, ambrosia, honey, soma, wine, pulque [a central Mexican alcoholic beverage] are therefore mythologically most closely related to the moon and its forms, a feature that likewise belongs to those things that are universally and regularly recurring."

struggles for the Soma, revelling in the Soma, on the part of gods and the blessed. What happens in the sacrifice corresponds in a secret way to the processes in the heavenly dome, as Preuss has shown us also in the sacrificial feasts of the Pueblo Indians.[99] And it has an influence on those regions. When the priests light the sacrificial fire, they let the sun light up there; when they let the soma drops run, then they cause the rain to fall. When they enjoy the different soma beakers, the milk-pot of the Ashwins, the porridge-pot, they drink and eat, in the primitive sacrament, the moon and sun, as such a sacramental consumption of their own god among primitive peoples has indeed already been sufficiently proved a long while ago.

In spite of all the mystical approximation of the earthly with the heavenly Soma, men however remain conscious that the actual enjoyment of the heavenly Soma is refused to them, that this remains a privilege of the gods. That is occasionally clearly expressed. So in a hymn that does not belong to the actual Soma hymns but perhaps to the most important interesting pieces of the Rigveda. I mean the great wedding hymn, *RV* X,85, in which the wedding of the young sun, Sûryâ, the daughter of the sun-god Savitar, to the Moon is celebrated. The hymn was, and is up to the present day, recited at the weddings of Indians, and the heavenly wedding, which thereby appears as the prototype of the earthly, casts its transfiguring shimmer on the wedding celebrations of men. That such was the age-old custom of the Aryans can be inferred from the Latvian solar hymns that are similarly sung at weddings and celebrate the heavenly wedding of the daughter of the sun or sun-maiden, Saules Meita.[100] In all probability, such hymns were sung originally at the spring- and solar festivals of the Aryans, while the wedding of the celebrated heavenly beings who, as the greatest vegetational powers, rule the flourishing of the earthly world was represented in cultic-dramatic manner. The King

---

[99] [Konrad Theodor Preuss (1869-1938) was a German anthropologist who studied native American culture in Mexico and South America. His major work was entitled *Die geistige Kultur der Naturvölker* (1915)].

[100] [Saules Meita is the daughter of the sun-goddess Saule in Latvian and Lithuanian mythology.]

of May and Queen of May, appearing in festive costumes, united in an arbour, are the relics of this play, whereas the May betrothals of young people significantly elaborate the old generative ritual.

Now at the beginning of the great Rigveda hymn, the heavenly bridegroom Soma, the Moon, is celebrated in noteworthy verses.

Already in the first verse it is clearly said that Soma is up there in heaven, is situated in heaven (*diví sómo ádhi çritáh*):

> The earth stands firm through truth,
> The heaven stands through the sun,
> The Âdityas through the sacred law,
> Soma stands there in the heavens.

We hear further of Soma's power and that it is to be found among the stars:

> Through Soma are the Âdtyas strong,
> The earth is great through Soma,
> There in the middle of the astral womb,
> There is Soma seated.[101]

Here there can be no doubt about what is being spoken of. It can only be the moon, the heavenly Soma:

> And now follow the most significant verses:
> One who drinks thinks it is Soma,
>
> And when one pounds the soma plant;
> The Soma that the priest knows,
> Is never enjoyed by a man.[102]

The Soma that the priests know – so it says actually in the text – clearly stands here in opposition to the soma that is obtained and

---

[101] *átho nákshatrânâm eshâm upásthe sóma âhitah.*

[102] v.3:

> *sómam manyate papivân yát sampimshánty óshadhim*
> *sómam yám brahmâno vidár ná tásyâçnâti káç caná*

drunk through the pressing of the soma-plant; it is the heavenly Soma that the wisdom of the priests knows, in contrast to the earthly. That is enjoyed by nobody – says the verse – i.e. by no mortal, as long as he lives on earth, for the fifth verse says clearly enough that the gods drink it. Perhaps one thinks of it, perhaps one has it in mind when one drinks the soma in the sacrifice – in reality, however, only the gods and the blessed enjoy it. The circumstance described above is thereby indeed sufficiently confirmed.

Even the following verse, even more remarkable on account of other expressions, strengthens the unattainability of the heavenly Soma for mortals:

> Concealed by a series of covers,
> Watched over by Brihat singers, O Soma,
> You stand there listening to the stones,
> No earthly person enjoys you.[103]

The heavenly Soma listens to the sound of the pressing stones (*grâvan*) with which the priests press the earthly soma down below; it itself however is enjoyed by no earthly being (*pârthivah*).

Highly noteworthy and singular are the first words of this verse: "Concealed by a series of covers", *âchâdvidhânâir gupitáh* however cannot, in my opinion, be translated any other way: *âchâd* cannot mean anything but "the cover, covering, envelope" and *vidhâna* means "the series". It is used especially in an interweaving, for example, in the famous Varuna hymn RV VII,87, where it says (v.5): "Three heavens repose in him (Varuna), three earths below, forming a series of six" (*shádvidhânâh*). Hillebrandt leaves *âchad* untranslated since the word has not yet found an adequate explanation.[104] The same appears also with the meaning "cover" in *VS* XV,4,5. It is also not only according to its etymology derived from *chad* with the preposition

---

[103] The text runs:
âchâdvidhânâir gupitó bârhatâih soma rakshitáh
grâvnâm íc chrinván tishthasi ná te açnâti pârthivah

[104] Cf. Hillebrandt, *Vedische Mythologie*, Vol.I, p.302. He thinks it is a corruption of *ât shadvidhânâih*, but does not explain it further and places a question mark there.

â,[105] but we have along with it the forms immediately related to it, *âchâdaka*, "covering, concealing", *âchâdana*, "to covered, concealed", *âchâdin*, "covering, concealing", *âchâda*, "garment, robe" as the cloaking, the covering, the cover. Thus Roth too translates in PW[106] *âchadvidhana* as "protective device, means of covering", whereby only the second part of the composite did not gain acceptance. Similarly Graßmann in his dictionary, "Protective device for covering, defence". In the translation he says simply "provided with protection". Ludwig combines it, hardly successfully, with the following and says: "Protected, O Soma, with covering devices of Brihatî-strophes". If we translate it precisely according to the established meaning of *âchad* and *vidhâna*, it doubtless means: "Concealed in a series of covers". And that gives a completely good, blameless sense, even if the idea emerging here appears only in this passage of the Veda. Now if – which is in my opinion probable – the clouds may have been thought of as covers or envelopes of the heavenly Soma, or if the imagination played thereby in a different way, objection cannot indeed be made against the sense that the wonderful heavenly Soma vessel that no mortal can approach, that is guarded by elfin guards, the Gandharvas, was concealed in protective covers. And in the most remarkable manner this idea corresponds to those of the wonderful Grail vessel, of which it is often reported that it is normally covered with some cover or lid, or is "uncovered" at the moment of the celebration.[107]

The following words have caused difficulties for translators and exegetes: *bârhatâih soma rakshitâh*, "protected, O Soma, by the Bârhatas". What does it mean? The word *"bârhata"* is well attested. It means either 1. standing in relation to the Bríhat Sâman; or 2. standing

---

[105] The root *chad* with *â* means nothing but "cover, cloak, envelop"

[106] [the Petersburger Wörterbuch]

[107] Cf. R. Heinzel, *Über die französischen Gralromane* (Vienna, 1892), p.4,8,82,90. In Crestien's *Perceval* 4479 the cauldron is carried around fully uncovered *tot descouvert* (p.4,8). In the Quête a velvet cover is mentioned (p.8). In the so-called Demanda, a Portuguese romance about the Round Table and the Holy Grail, Gawan complains that the Grail was *cuberto* (p.8). In Manessier 45234 the Grail appears *en apert* (uncovered, opened). In Robert de Boron, it appears at first covered, then uncovered (p.82,90).

in relation to the Brihatî metre, representing this, derived from it (cf. PW, *s.v.*[108]). It is thus in no way right when Graßmann says simply: "Protected, Soma, by sayings", or Hillebrandt: "Protected by (series) of Brihats" – quite apart from the fact that these two do not supply any satisfactory meaning. Let us stick to the well-attested first significance of the word: "standing in relation to the Brihat Sâman". The Brihat Sâman and the Rathamthara Sâman are the oldest and most famous sacrificial melodies. They were, as Hillebrandt has shown, sung at the solstices.[109] The Rathamthara, the hymn moving the chariot, stood in a special relation to the sun. It was supposed to bring the sun, the sun-chariot or the sun-wheel forward. But the Brihat is already valued in the Rigveda "as an especially beloved melody for the rainy season or its start".[110] If the Rathamthara is supposed to bring the sun forward, the Brihat is clearly supposed to produce rain. That is a clear correspondence and these two belong completely together and are wont to supplement each other. We may, I believe, translate the word *bârhata* without hesitating as Brihat singer; for "belonging to the Brihat Sâman" could certainly be understood in this sense: "expert in the Brihat Sâman, taking part in or dedicated to the Brihat, knowing or singing the Brihat". And then we receive the best thinkable sense for our passage. If we remember that the heavenly Soma, the moon, like the earthly soma sacrifice, stands in the closest relationship to the rain, is supposed to give or produce it, then it appears completely appropriate that the heavenly Soma was surrounded by Brihat singers, i.e. by singers of rain-hymns, and was guarded by them. But it is well-known that the Gandharvas are wont to serve as protectors of the heavenly Soma, and it would be, in my view, a completely reasonable conception if we wish to think of these heavenly singers and musicians, the protectors of the Soma, especially as singers of the Brihat hymn. But we may leave it undecided who is meant here by the Brihat singers – that such are being spoken of here I consider as hardly doubtful.

---

[108] ["under the word']

[109] Cf. A. Hillebrandt, *Die Sonnwendfeste in Alt-Indien*, p.23 (cf. the entire section pp.22-27).

[110] Cf. Hillebrandt, *op.cit.*, p.25.

And now further the following, not less important verse of our hymn:

> When they, O god, drink thee up,
> You immediately swell again!
> The guardian of the Soma is the Wind-god[111]
> The month is the image of the Year.[112]

Above all, the first two lines of this verse are of significance for us. They give expression with great clarity to the idea that the heavenly Soma, the Moon, is thought of as a vessel that is drunk fully and then swells again in order to be drunk up again. In this way month after month, the whole year through. An idea completely well-grounded in the situation, a clear and fine thought of the primitive-mystical imagination that is so illuminating that we already had to mention several times the possibility that from this the idea of a drinking vessel could first have been transferred even to the sun. Who drinks the heavenly Soma cannot be doubtful. To men it is forbidden, it could be only the gods, and in addition perhaps also the blessed dead. Perhaps that was originally directly expressed in the verse. At least it is very advisable to substitute the apparently unnecessary vocative *deva* "O god" with the nominative plural *deváh*. Then the verse would run:

> When the gods drink thee up,
> You immediately swell again.

But one may think of this conjecture as one wishes. It is not completely necessary. It cannot be doubtful to anybody that it is the gods who drink the heavenly Soma.

Therewith the glorification of Soma in our hymn is completed and there follows the glorification of his bride, Sûryâ, the wedding-chariot, the bridal journey, etc.

---

[111] [Vāyu; cf. the identification of the Gandharvas as wind-gods below p.272]

[112] *RV* X,85,5:

> *yát tvâ deva prapíbanti táta âpyâyase púnah*
> *váyúh sómasya rakshitâ sámânâm masa âkritih.*
> [The Year is, in the Vedas, a synonym for the universe.]

The moon is normally simply called Soma in the Veda; and also as the "drop" (*indu, drapsa*), the "wave" (*ûrmi*), the "flood" (*samudra*) and the like. Relatively rarely is the vessel spoken of in which this heavenly intoxicating drink is.[113] But such a thing is indeed naturally to be presupposed already. When one sees it shining up there in a firm enclosure, when the hymn discussed above sings how it is drunk up and replenished, that is difficult to think of without the idea of a vessel which contains the heavenly drink. Hillebrandt therefore claims, certainly rightly, for the Veda the idea that the moon is "a container full of Soma".[114] When it says in *AV* X,2,31 that there stands a golden, heavenly vat, covered in light, in the impregnable fortress with nine gates, the moon is in all probability meant, as a heavenly Soma vat (*koça*).[115] Similarly we have to perhaps refer to the moon when, in RV VIII,61(72),8, it is narrated that Indra brought the Soma vat (*koça*) from the sun-god Vivasvant.[116] During the conjunction the moon is with the sun, which can and is conceived of mythologically as a violation or possession of the moon by the sun-god. The hero Indra gets the moon vessel back from the house of the sun-god. Whether those Vedic passages in which it is narrated that Indra or the gods in general drink Soma with the sun-god are similarly to be referred to the conjunction I would like to leave undecided. It is conceivable but I do not consider it to be very probable, and think rather that the sun, independently of the moon, also is considered as a place where heavenly Soma is to be found and is enjoyed. However this idea recedes greatly before those of the moon as the heavenly Soma.

---

[113] Cf. Hillebrandt, *Vedische Mythologie*, Vol.I, pp.319ff.; p.329.

[114] Cf. Hillebrandt, *op.cit.*, Vol.I, p.314,329,330.

[115] Cf. Hillebrandt, *op.cit.*, Vol.I, p.330. The verse in *AV* X,2,31 runs:
   *ashtâcakrâ návadvârâ devânâm pûr ayodhyâ
   tásyâm hiranyáyah kóçah svargó jyótishâvritah.*
If Eggeling is right in construing the word *kuçî* in *Çat. Br.* III,6,2,9 as the same as *koçî*, and if there actually two golden bowls are being spoken of in which the Soma is contained, then I would like to maintain that this relates to the sun and the moon.

[116] *RV* VIII,61,8 *á daçábhir vivásvata indrah kóçam acucyavít*; cf. Hillebrandt, *op.cit.*, p.329;p.479.

In a hymn of the Atharvaveda (IX,4) something is said obscurely for the first time that an old man rich in seed carries a barrel or a vessel with good things – perhaps filled with good drink.[117] Immediately after however it says quite clearly that Tvashtar carries a bowl or a beaker (*kalaça*) filled with soma.[118] He is therefore perhaps that old man. The divine artificer Tvashtar, Indra's father, in whose house Indra drinks the beloved Soma for the first time, is however also celebrated as the creator of a splendid bowl which is certainly nothing but the heavenly Soma vessel. That can be inferred clearly from the well-known myth that the clever Ribhus had been able to produce out of the wonderful bowl, or divine beaker, of Tvashtar four of them, whereupon Tvashtar seeks to hide himself in shame and envy.[119] Therewith in all probability are meant the lunar phases that emerge from one moon. In this way does not only Hillebrandt, but also Macdonell and other researchers interpret it.[120] And it is obvious that a more satisfactory explanation for this wonderful story cannot be found. But it agrees completely with the undoubtedly correct idea that the moon was thought of as a wonderful heavenly vessel filled with the drink of the gods, Soma.

This interpretation is confirmed in the most decisive manner by many passages of the Veda. Above all by the fact that the wonderful vessel of Tvashtar, out of which the Ribhus make four, is called "the beaker out of which the gods drink" – *camasó devapânah*. Thus, in the Ribhu hymn IV,35, their beaker trick is mentioned many times and in v.5 it says of that: "with artifice you have formed the beaker out of which the gods drink".[121]

Also in the hymn *RV* I,161 the beaker feat of the Ribhus is reported.

---

[117] *AV* IX,4,3 *vásoh kábandham.*

[118] *AV* IX,4,6 *sómena púrnâm kaláçam bibharshi tváshtâ rûpânâm janitâ paçûnâm.*

[119] Cf. A. Kaegi, *Der Rigveda*, p.54; Macdonell, *Vedic Mythology*, p.133 etc.

[120] Cf. Hillebrandt, *op.cit.*, p.515; Macdonell, *op.cit.*, p.118; that Siecke and the other lunar mythologists understand the matter similarly is easy to understand; they are also certainly right. Cf. Paul Ehrenreich, *Die allgemeine Mythologie und ihre ethnologischen Grundlagen*, Leipzig, 1910, p.165. In the footnote he says with regard to the certainly unfounded doubt of Oldenberg: "There is in all mythology hardly anything more certain than that".

[121] *RV* IV,35,5: *çácyâkarta camasám devapânam.*

Then it says:

> But Tvashtar, when he saw four beakers formed,
> Hid himself, slipping into a bevy of women.

He sees in it a mockery of his splendid work, the beaker out of which the gods drink; that is why he even wishes to kill them:

> As Tvashtar spoke: "Let us kill these men,
> Who have insolently desecrated the drinking cup of the gods
> in mockery
> Drinking, they gave themselves new forms,
> Then a maiden saved them so disguised."[122]

Even here the wonderful beaker of Tvashtar is called camasó devapânah – the beaker out of which the gods drink. It can only be about the moon, the heavenly drinking vessel of the gods.

Somewhat different is the appellation of the beaker in the Ribhu hymn *RV* I,110. There it says in v.3: "That beaker there, the drinking vessel of the Asuras, which was one, you have made fourfold".[123]

Practically there is no difference, naturally.

It says of the four beakers of the Ribhus that they shine like the day or, actually, like the "days". *RV* IV,33,6: "When Tvashtar saw the beakers shining like the day, he became envious".[124]

We saw above that, in the *RV*, Tvashtar carried a beaker filled with soma. According to *RV* X,53,9 he carries several of these vessels, or he carries "salutary vessels out of which the gods drink". The Ribhus are not thought of here and he is called the "cleverest of artificers". In any case he does not stand in hostile opposition to the many vessels. The wonderful power or magical power (the *mâyâ*) of Tvashtar is also

---

[122] *RV* I,161,5: *hánâmâinân íti tváshtâ yád âbravîc camasám yé devapânam ánindishuh.* I have given here Graßmann's translation.

[123] *RV* I,110,3: *tyám cic camasám ásurasya bhákshanam ékam sántam akrinutá cáturvayam*; asura, the lord, lord of the gods, seems here to indicate the previously mentioned Savitar.

[124] *RV* IV,33,6: *vibhrâjamânâmç camasân áhevâvenat tváshtâ catáro dadriçvân.*

thereby highlighted with praise.[125]

This is one of those interesting dialogue hymns which treat of the regaining of Agni, of the new beginning of the sacrificial period. If Tvashtar, the wonderfully powerful artificer of the gods, brings salutary vessels from which the gods drink, it can only be soma vessels. Through Agni's return the holy fire is gifted to the sacrifice. Tvashtar, the creator of the heavenly beaker, brings the salutary vessels as well from which the gods are supposed to drink. The one stands next to the other and complements the other, like sun and moon, fire and intoxicating drink of the gods.

For us one of the most important appellations of the Soma-vessel from which Indra drinks, whose blessing he grants even to men, is the word *carú*. It appears in the *RV* only rather seldom but is of special importance for the comparison on account of the corresponding words in the related languages that make it certain to us that precisely this word already belonged to the earliest period and in all probability played a significant role in the myth.

In the Indra hymn of Viçvâmitra and Jamadagni - *RV* X,167 - the *carú*, pot or bowl, appears clearly as a vessel in which one brings Indra the soma drink. The hymn begins:

> For you, Indra, is the mead poured here
> You are lord of the pressed drink and the beaker,
> You produce wealth for us, gift us a heroic army,
> You produce warmth, and have won the heavenly light,
> We call Çakra to the pressed drink, etc.

Then in the fourth verse it says: "With enthusiasm I have partaken of the drink in the *carú*",[126] etc. The connection permits no doubt at all about the meaning of the word. It is a vessel out of which Indra is said to drink the soma.

A soma-vessel is perhaps a *carú* also in the Soma hymn *RV* IX,52.

---

[125] *RV* X,53,9: *tváshtâ mâyâ ved apásâm apástamo bíbhrat pâtrâ devapânâni çámtamâ.*

[126] *RV* X,167,4: *prásûto bhakshám akaram carâv ápi*; in the previous v.3, as in v.1, the Soma vessels are called "beakers" *kaláça*.

Here the word appears in a very remarkable verse which nevertheless poses some difficulties in interpretation, so my translation can only be a tentative one.

As in many Soma hymns here too one speaks interchangeably of the earthly and heavenly soma. The third verse, of which it is a question here, can be translated rather in the following manner: "Him who is like a *carú*, shake him! O drop, shake the gift! With strokes, you striker, shake him!"[127]

The "drop" that is addressed is Soma itself, the god of the moon and of the sacrificial drink. The verb "*îūkhaya*" means "sway". It is used of the swaying of the solar ship in the sea of air, of the swaying of Bhujyu in the sea, of the swaying of the just born Indra. Typical is also the idea of the sun as a swing (*preūkha* from *pra-îūkha*) which moves up above. In the ritual, a swing is built that represents the sun and is pushed in the feast. In the popular spring festival Dolayâtrâ, an image of the sun-god Krishna is similarly pushed.[128] Swinging is a primordial fertility rite that is practised among various primitive peoples. As the comparison of Latvian and Slavic customs with the Indian teaches, it was practised even in the earliest Aryan times in the solar feasts, as I have elaborately explained and demonstrated in the second volume of my *Ancient Aryan Religion* which hopefully will soon be in print.[129] The Latvians sing even today continuously during the solar festival their songs with the refrain "swing, swing!"(*lîgo, lîgo!*).[130] One swung oneself or – as in India – a swing that represented the sun, or an image of the same, and carried an image of the sun-

[127] *RV* IX,52,3:
    *carár ná yás tám înkhayéndo ná dânam înkhaya *
    vadhâír vadhasnav înkhaya
    The one that is like a *carú*, bowl, pot or cauldron, that would be indeed the moon vessel.

[128] Cf. Hillebrandt, *Sonnwendfeste in Alt-Indien*, p.38n, following Wilson, *Religious festivals* (Works II, p.225).

[129] [The second volume of Schroeder's *Arische Religion: Naturverehrung und Lebensfeste*, was published in Leipzig, 1914-1916].

[130] Cf. my essay "Lihgo, Refrain der lettischen Sonnwendlieder" in *Mitteilungen der Anthropologischen Gesellschaft in Wien*, Vol.XXXII (Vol.II of the third series).

god, in order to receive the fertilising efficiency of the sun. I would now like to suppose something analogous in our verse about the moon. The moon-god Indu is requested to swing the moon-vessel, to set it with powerful strokes, or pushes, in a swinging motion so that it may release its gifts.[131]

In the Indra hymn *RV* I,7,6, *carú* means quite clearly the heavenly vessel which the god Indra is supposed to open up and tap for the benefit of men. That is the well-known heroic act of Indra through which he produces for the world the fertilising water, the rain. It is already mentioned in verse 3, in another typical expression along with the other great deed of Indra's, the formation of the sun: "Indra let the sun rise to the heavens to attain a distant perspective; he cleft the rock for the cows" (i.e. for the sake of the fructifying waters contained therein). And then it says in verse 6: "You strong one, bestowing all, you who are irresistible, open for us that *carú*, for us."[132] That *carú* means a vessel, a bowl, pot or cauldron, is quite certain. That here it is a question of a heavenly vessel emerges from the context. The question can only be what sort of heavenly vessel is meant here. Graßmann understands by it, corresponding to an earlier conception, the clouds.[133] He has the authority of the *Nâighantuka* behind him where, at 1,10, the word carú is listed among the appellations for cloud (*meghanâmâni*). But we find listed there also *odana, camasa, varâha*, etc. Recent research rightly emphasises that the moon is the

---

[131] Graßmann translates: "Shake him who is like a cauldron, O Indra, shake gifts down, with blows, sticks, shake him"; however, *înkhaya* means "shackle" and Graßmann's explanation, "the one that is like a cauldron is the enemy filled with goods whose possessions should be shaken out for the pious people" I consider as being most improbable. In the following verse where enemies are actually being spoken of, the verb *înkhaya* does not appear any more as one could assume following Graßmann's translation.

[132] *RV* I,7,6:
   sá no vrishann amúm carúm sátrâdâvann ápâ vridhi
   asamábhyam ápratishkutah

[133] Graßmann translates: "Open that cauldron for us, the cloud, you who gift everything, O strong one, the untameable". But the cloud is only an explanatory addition of Graßmann's. Ludwig translates: "You, strong as a bull, uncover that pot for us, you who provide for ever, without eluding us here".

heavenly Soma-vessel. But thereby the older view is not so completely dismissed as may at first glance appear. There can be no doubt that the soma-sacrifice forms a rain-sacrifice. No doubt also that the view firmly established among so many peoples that the moon is related to rain and produces rain lies at the basis here. But there can have been little doubt among any people on earth that the rain comes from the clouds. Here a secret relationship must have been thought of between the moon and the rain – a primitive natural philosophy that has still not been sufficiently explained to us. That is why so much in the myths of Indra's acquisition of the Soma and production of rain is still unclear to us – quite apart from the fact that his liberation of the waters may refer partly in any case to the liberation of the rivers and other waters from the winter ice, as Hillebrandt has made probable.[134]

When, in our song, Indra opens the heavenly pot – *carú*, which clearly corresponds to his earthly soma-vessel in the first cited passage, it is indeed illuminating that the moon is meant thereby just as the *camasó devapânah*, the wonderful beaker of Tvashtar, from which the gods drink, can only be the moon – that the Ribhu saga shows us without a doubt. They are only different appellations of the same heavenly thing.

Carú means also otherwise pot or bowl in several sacrifices, in the Rigveda as well as in the Atharaveda.[135] Later it designates in the ritual one of the customary sacrificial foods, a sort of corn-mess cooked in milk, butter, water, etc.[136] Originally it must have meant the pot in which this mess was contained. For the original meaning of carú which emerges clearly in all passages of the Rigveda is "pot" or "bowl", in any case a "vessel" - and indeed such as was used in the sacrifice. In

---

[134] Cf. *Vedische Mythologie*, Vol.III, pp.162-254.

[135] So in the horse-sacrifice in *RV* I,162,13; in the donkey-sacrifice of the Vrishâkapi in *RV* X,86,18; in the goat-sacrifice in *AV* IX,8,6; in the rice-sacrifice in *AV* XI,1,16; XI,3,18f; in the offerings to the dead in XVIII,4,16. In the *RV*, the word *carú* appears altogether only 6 times. Apart from the already cited passages, only in *RV* VII,104,2. Here it appears in a comparison: *carúr agnivân iva*, like a pot on the fire. A cooking-pot is clearly meant – nothing else can be gathered from the passage.

[136] Cf. *Peterburger Wörterbuch, s.v. caru; Zeitschrift der deutschen morgenländischen Gesellschaft*, Vol.IX, p.63f.

the soma-sacrifice, but also in other sacrifices.

Now the word *carú*, as the comparison demonstrates, corresponds to the old Nordic hverr, the cauldron that Thôrr obtains from Hymir according to the "Hymesqvidha".[137] Likewise to the old Anglo-Saxon old High German *hwer*, "cauldron". But also to the Irish *coire*, the Cimmerian *pair*, the Cornish *pêr*, "cauldron". And by extension so do the Russian *čára*, Polish *czara*, "drinking bowl".[138]

That opens up further perspectives.

First the old Nordic *hverr* in the Hymesqvidha and further also in the Lokasenna. That is no ordinary vessel but a wonderful mythical one which the gods use for their feasting. They wish to celebrate similarly with Ägir, but the latter explains that he needs for it the vessel, then he would indeed gladly brew the beer for the gods. So, a vessel in which to brew beer for the gods. Thôrr should make it. He goes out with Týr to get the vessel from the giant Hymir who has it in his possession. He has indeed nine such vessels – a significant number. However, when the beam on which they stand breaks, eight of these vessels tumble down and break. Only one remains intact. Before Thôrr gets this, he rows out with Hymir to catch fish. The giant catches two whales, but Thôrr fishes the frightful Midgard serpent and hits it on the head with his hammer. But it sinks back into the sea. Finally Thôrr carries the vessel on his head and bears it away while the cup-handles ring against his heels. Hymir and the other giants follow him but are struck by him with his hammer Mjolnir:

Thôrr went to the Thing[139] of the gods, the mighty,
And had the vessel that Hymir owned,
Now the Aesir can thoroughly carouse
Until winter in Ägir's hall.

[137] ['Hymiskviða', or the poem of Hymir, is part of the *Poetic Edda*].

[138] Cf. [Christian] Uhlenbeck, [Kurzgefasstes] *Etymologisches Wörterbuch der Altindischen Sprache, s.v. carús,* with a cauldron, pot, sacrificial porridge. – In the Celtic forms a further development through a j-suffix is to be supposed whereby the i then entered the root syllable.

[139] [assembly]

This feasting is then further described for us in the prose introduction to the Lokasenna with noteworthy characteristics: "Instead of fire, bright gold served for illumination, the beer flowed automatically; it was a grand haven of peace".[140]

The bright gold that provides illumination makes us think of the sun or the moon. The beer that flows automatically points in the same direction since the great heavenly lights present themselves moving freely, but it finds in the Grail saga also its clear correspondence. For the Grail serves at the table as an attendant, it serves automatically; it floats through the air, a golden vessel that provides food.[141]

When it says: "It was a great haven of peace", the idea arises of a celebratory festive meal that was sanctified by a decree of peace. Analogous to a cultically sanctified festive celebration of men on earth. We remember the idea of the Indians: As the men here below light their sacrificial fire and drink soma, the gods above have their sacrificial fire in the sun and drink from the vessel of the moon the heavenly Soma that flows out continuously. The Eddic passage can be interpreted in a similar way: the gold of the sun gives illumination, the moon provides the beer that flows automatically.

Earlier, Hymir's vessel, from which the gods drink beer, was interpreted differently. Uhland saw in it the sea, which during winter is in the power of the ice giants, from which only the thunderstorms of spring free it. Others, like Gering too, agree with him in this.[142] I cannot. The idea of the sea as a brewing vessel that must be got from afar and whose content the gods then drink seems to me nothing less than probable and convincing. As little can I agree with researchers who wish to recognise that brewing vessel in the ever-present, all covering heavenly vault.[143] On the other hand, the moon can without doubt be very well thought of – as the Indians show – as a wonderful

---

[140] Cf. H. Gering's translation of the *Edda*, p.29.

[141] Cf. H. Gering's translation of the *Edda*, p.30.

[142] Cf. R. Heinzel, *Über die französischen Gralromane, Denkschriften der kaiserlichen Akademie der Wissenschaften zu Wien,* philosoph.-histor. Klasse, Vol.XL (Vienna, 1892), p.26,28,36.37,53,78,160.

[143] Gering, *op.cit.*, p.24n3.

vessel with heavenly drink that is drunk by the gods, while it remains unattainable to men, who can only tell fairy-tales about it.

The bowl can likewise point to the sun, which was viewed by the Aryans in any case also as a wonderful vessel, but we have already seen that the moon possesses a greater right to be considered as a vessel for intoxicating drink. Its waxing and waning speaks for it just as the Indian analogy does and therefore exhibits the basis of comparison that best agrees with this supposition in general ethnology and that shows us especially the moon, returning in an almost routine manner, in the closest relation to the intoxicating drink.[144]

And, as among the Indians, so also among the ancient Germans the sun may have, during the divine festivals, played another important role. To the soma feasts of the Indians corresponded, I believe, the spring and summer feasts of the Germans during which the fire blazed and mead or beer was drunk in abundance. The Norwegians called the solstitial fire *brising*, as Jakob Grimm already observed. But the precious neck jewellery of the sky-goddess Freya was called *Brisingamen* – the "beautiful necklace" which we already spoke about and which was certainly nothing but the sun. But from the correspondence between *brising* and *brisingamen* I think I may conclude that the sun up there and the solstitial fire were felt and thought of as something related and corresponding to each other, just as the heavenly beer of the divine feasts corresponded to the beer and mead of the human feasts. Thus a similar view as in India. And, as in India the sun and divine drink are stolen and won again by Indra, Loki too steals the *Brisingamen* but must return it; and Thôrr retrieves the beer cauldron from Hymir after a strenuous battle, as Indra brings back the Soma vat from Vivasvant, or strikes Vrtra to take the Soma from it, thereby solar fire and divine drink, sunshine and rain, are acquired again for the world, for the gods and for men. And, like men down here, the gods up there celebrate their joyful feast. In this way was it considered in India, in this way, I believe, also originally among

---

[144] Recently K. Schirmeisen, *Die arischen Göttergestalten* (Brünn, 1909) also refers Hymir's cauldron to the heavenly vault (op.cit., p.248). In addition he offers many pertinent remarks on this saga cycle, cf., for example, p.183,185, 247,248.

the ancient Germans. As down below the fires (*brising*) blazed, and beer and mead were drunk, up there shone the solar gold, the solar fire (*brisingamen*), and the beer in the vessel taken from Hymir - the lunar vessel, in our estimation - served the host of gods automatically during their feast.

The manifold sagas, already discussed many times, of the acquisition of the divine drink among the Indians, Germans, Greeks, etc., we cannot go into more closely here. There we find a number of parallel forms in which, as a rule, a divine or semi-divine hero obtains that drink. One of the oldest forms of this sort may be the narration about Odin, how he obtains the stimulating drink in the vessel Odherir. The especially antique character of this saga lies in the description of the origin of this drink, from which it emerges clearly that even the ancient Germans once knew about an intoxicating drink that was obtained through chewing and spitting out a certain substance. This primitive acquisition of an intoxicating drink, which many primitive peoples still practise (*kava-kava*,[145] and so on), is – as I have shown – also known to the Rigveda and is preserved there especially in a girls' pubescence ritual.[146] It was doubtless ancient Aryan and older than the preparation of any mead or beer.

With the Celtic vessel names – *coire, pair, pêr* – corresponding to the ancient Indian *caru*, the Nordic *hverr*, we move very close to the Grail saga. The Celts possessed a great number of sagas that told of a wonderful vessel, magical cauldron, magical beaker, and so on, and fabulous or epic heroes, Peronnik, Peredur, Perceval, and others, obtained these vessels after all sorts of adventures. Whether it is permitted to relate the name of the magical beaker – *pêr* – somehow with the first part of the name of the Grail seeker I wish to leave decided. That is a matter for Celtologists to decide. But nothing is more obvious than to relate the saga of Parsifal and other Grail

---

[145] Cf. Paul Ehrenreich, *Die allgemeine Mythologie und ihre ethnologischen Grundlagen*, Leipzig, 1910, p.144; above p.41n. [Kava is a plant with sedative properties that is used both in religious rituals as well as socially in the Pacific Ocean cultures.]

[146] Cf. my essay on "Das Apâlâlied", *Wiener Zeitschrift für die Kunde des Morgenlandes*, Vol.XXII, pp.223-244.

seekers to the sagas of those magical vessels and their acquisition, to view them as a Christian transformation of an older heathen material or even to presume a merging of Christian legends with heathen sagas. So much the more obvious is it in that the Grail saga was current essentially on Celtic ground and even otherwise intertwined with Celtic sagas. Indeed the matter was considered rather generally in this way also earlier. So also by the so careful and critical Heinzel, who in 1872 stated about it: "As regards the Grail, the bowl has clearly taken the place of the heathen symbol in the legend of Joseph of Arimathea".[147] Nutt and E. Wechssler consider it in this way even today.[148] However, on the other hand, the large majority of researchers have, since Birch-Hirschfeld's attack,[149] completely given up the old view of some connection between the heathen and Christian symbol.

So also R. Heinzel in his later years. In his work, *On the French Grail romances*, he spoke against Nutt's views (p.97). When Bran the Blessed, a demonic giant, receives the cauldron of revivification, this cauldron of Bran's however has, in Heinzel's opinion, "as good as no similarity with the Grail bowl". The same is true – as he says further – of most of the Celtic magical cauldrons and vessels "that have been cited from Villemarqué to Nutt". Bran's cauldron is similar, rather, to Medea's cauldron, in which old people become young; "the cauldron of the Ulton cycle (Nutt 185) has just the characteristic that each of the guests received the portion belonging to him, Ceridwen's cauldron (Nutt 210) is a vessel of intoxication like the Nordic Odhrerir, the vessel of the Fionn saga contains a magical balsam for wounds (Nutt 187)", etc. "Now, closer to the Grail stand the cauldron of Diwrnah that leaves nobody unsatisfied, the basket of Gwyddneus, which,

---

[147] Cf. R. Heinzel, "Ein französischer Roman des 13. Jahrhunderts", *Kleine Schriften*, ed. M.H. Jellinek and C.v.Kraus, Heidelberg, 1907 (originally published in the *Österreichische Wochenschrift für Wissenschaft und Kunst*, 1872).

[148] [Alfred] Nutt, *Studies on the legend of the Holy Grail*, 1888; E. Wechssler, *Die Sage vom heiligen Gral in ihrer Entwicklung bis auf R. Wagners Parsifal*, Halle a.S., 1898, p.9.

[149] Cf. *Adolf Birch-Hirschfeld, Die Sage vom Gral, ihre Entwicklung und dichterische Ausbildung in Frankreich und Deutschland im 12. und 13. Jahrhundert. Eine literarhistorische Untersuchung*, Leipzig, 1877.

when one places in it food for one, feeds hundred and that with the food that each wants, and the pan with dishes of Rhegnydd Ysgolhaig which also possesses the last-mentioned magical characteristic".[150]

The admission in the last sentence is in itself not insignificant. However we may not, on the basis of the wider foundation that the treatment of the question has obtained through our observation above, strictly deny other Celtic magical vessels a relationship with the Grail vessel in the way Heinzel does. Or, in other words, we cannot completely dissociate these from those vessels in which such a relationship is essentially granted even by Heinzel.

If the cauldron of Ceridwen is a cauldron of intoxication and is comparable to the Nordic Odherir, then it is definitely to be emphasised – what was already indicated above – that Odherir with its intoxicating drink is as closely related to the heavenly Soma vessel of the Indians as the cauldron which Thôrr gets from Hymir for the feast of the gods, whose activity with the automatically served beer reveals the characteristic of a relationship with the Grail that has already been noticed earlier.[151] The variants of the narration of the heavenly Soma, its acquisition, its characteristics, etc. are very numerous in the Veda, so that they cannot at all be discussed in brief. The heavenly Soma vessel, whose contents are inexhaustible since it swells ever anew for the drinking gods, is basically not at all different from the heavenly Soma vessel from which Indra and other gods too quaff the intoxicating drink – or, at most, differ from one another only as variants of the same basic idea. One can never mistake Hymir's cauldron for the Odherir but one can yet recognise that both go back to the same basic idea: the idea of the wonderful heavenly drinking vessel of the gods, in the case of which we must think first of the moon, whereas occasionally even the sun comes into consideration.

Bran's cauldron has, in Heinzel's judgement, as good as no similarity with the Grail bowl, since it is a revivifying cauldron. It can rather be

---

[150] Cf. R. Heinzel, *Über die französischen Gralromane, Denkschriften der kaiserlichen Akademie der Wissenschaften zu Wien, philosoph.-histor. Klasse*, Bd.LX (Vienna, 1892), p.97.

[151] Cf. Heinzel, *op.cit.*, p.97.

compared to Medea's cauldron in which old people are brewed young again. These cauldrons of rejuvenation and revivification agree almost entirely with the rejuvenating mills that, according to the saga, like the fountains of youth, ground men and made them younger.[152] In its oldest form the mill is indeed, as we have already seen, only a vessel, a mortar, not essentially different from a pot or a cauldron. But the rejuvenating mill is generally not to be separated from the miraculous mill that gives all possible good things in inexhaustible abundance, at first indeed material things, drink and food, salt, gold, etc., but then also peace and happiness of all sorts. We were able to trace back this idea to the sun, without wishing to keep the moon at a distance for that reason. Bran's revivifying is after all impossible to separate from the wonder mills and the food-dispensing vessels. They belong close together and go fully back to the basic idea of the wonderful heavenly vessel that gives all possible good things - one may find this now in the sun or the moon or also sometimes in both, which I consider to be right.

That the revivifying cauldron and the food-dispensing vessel go inseparably together is also demonstrated very clearly by the Brythonic fairy-tale of Peronnik the Fool – a genuine popular fairy-tale which however is most closely associated with the Grail saga. Not in such a way that it could have arisen from the Christian one about the Passion vessel – that is, by its character, excluded – but perhaps in this way that it contains an abundance of fairy-tale characteristics that found their way into that Christian saga.[153]

Peronnik sets out to obtain the golden bowl and the diamond lance (*le bassin d'or et la lance de diamant*) from the giant Rogéar in Kerglas castle who has hidden these in his fortress. The bowl's characteristics

---

[152] Cf. Felix Liebrecht, *Zur Volkskunde*, Heilbronn, 1879, p.303.

[153] Cf. Emile Souvestre, *Le Foyer Breton, Traditions populaires,* (W. Coquebert), Paris; the Peronnik l'idiot fairy-tale is there too, pp.192-211, along with the notes to pp.212-216. I have with me a manuscript translation of the same by Dr. Victor Junk, from which the sentences cited in the text are extracted. This fairy-tale is of outstanding significance for the history of the Grail saga, especially for the recognition of their popular, pre-Christian roots. Dr. Junk will presumably devote to it an appropriate treatment in the near future, so I restrict myself here to short notes on it communicated directly to me.

however are described in the following manner: "Apart from the fact that the bowl is capable of producing in a moment all the food and wealth that one wishes, it is also enough to drink from it to be cured of all ills, and the dead themselves regain life when they touch it with their lips".

This power of the bowl of reviving even the dead is maintained even at the conclusion of the fairy-tale to Peronnik's great advantage. It is a characteristic of the same bowl, along with the food-dispensing and illness-curing power. The bowl thus unites the power of the Grail and that of the revivifying cauldron. But if it can at the same time cure all illnesses, it follows therefrom that the vessel of the Fionn saga which contains a magical balsam for wounds can as little be separated as something quite different and far removed – as Heinzel wishes to do.

The different magical cauldrons and other magical vessels of the Celtic saga go together and are to be judged uniformly as variants of the same basic idea – of the wonderful heavenly vessel. A cultic quality can hardly be detected in them, which cannot be surprising any longer since the concerned narrations from the age of an Aryan-heathen cult are too far removed and bear purely fairy-tale, or saga-like characteristics. Their agreement with the corresponding Indian and Germanic vessels however are striking and consists certainly not merely in an analogous but in a genealogical relationship. If, at least in one appellation that appears here significantly – *caru, hverr, pêr* – there is also a linguistic agreement, that certainly serves to strengthen such a supposition. In the case of the Indian vessels however, the connection with the cult of the sun and moon is clear and even in that of the German some traces point clearly to it. Thus we shall have to suppose not only mythical but also cultic roots that go back to the earliest Aryan times also in the background of the manifold Celtic narratives of magical vessels and their acquisition.

It may be asked now if the Grail saga strengthens the supposition of this connection through certain characteristic traits – where possible such as have up to now remained unexplained – and thereby also in its way points to the heathen prehistory of the Aryans – apart

from the already oft-mentioned food-dispensing power of the Grail. Something of the sort has already been touched upon occasionally in the preceding discussion – thus the covers of the heavenly Soma, in *RV* X,85,4; the beer in the Edda that serves the assembled guests automatically like the Grail. Our futher investigation will uncover more of such characteristics. Here, in brief, only one more thing that is perhaps related to the automatic service. In many of the Grail poems, the Grail floats through the air. Thus, in Psuedo-Gautier, the Grail is a golden vessel that, swaying in the air, dispenses food.[154] And even in the *Quête*, the Grail needs no bearer since it floats freely in the air.[155] If it spreads around it light and radiance,[156] its origin from the radiant great bodies, the sun and moon, freely floating in the heavens, appears perhaps a little clearer even though not too much weight should be placed on the last characteristic. But I consider the free floating of the Grail to be very significant.

---

[154] Cf. R. Heinzel, *Über die französischen Gralromane*, p.36f,53,160.

[155] *Ibid.*

[156] Cf. Heinzel, *op.cit.*, p.82,102,109. In Crestien the Grail is a bowl whose radiance dims the candles; cf. Baist, *op.cit.*, p.10 of the offprint, p.34 of the official edition.

III. RAIN PRODUCTION. THE STORM WEAPON

The soma sacrifice was a rain magic. The flowing drops of the celebrated intoxicating drink, compared to the running raindrops and sympathetically equated with them, are supposed to let the rain fall from the heavens.[157] It is a great drinking feast of the gods and men, or of the priests representing men. But as the most often and most highly celebrated god of this sacrifice, surpassing by far all others, appears Indra, the mighty hero, the storm-god, armed with the thunderbolt, who accomplishes the double heroic deed: reacquisition of the sun and the liberation of the waters from the demonic power. He frees – in the spring thunderstorm – the earthly rivers from icy bands, he frees the heavenly waters of the clouds and lets them fall on the thirsting earth. His conquest of the heavenly Soma produces not only the beloved intoxicating drink for himself but also especially the fructifying moisture that is needed by the men of the earthly world.

In the solstitial sacrifice Mahâvrata, a great soma festival, along with the magic with the drops of the intoxicating drink, other rain magic is practised. Drums or kettle-drums are struck. They are supposed to imitate the thunder and thereby attract the storm. Women transform the fire with filled water-pots and finally pour the

---

[157] Cf. Oldenberg, *Die Religion des Veda*, p.459.

contents of the pot into the fire. And this too is undoubtedly a rain magic.[158]

The last ceremony is comparable to the remarkable custom of European Aryans of rolling a burning wheel into the river. The wheel represents the sun. The sun is bathed. The fire of the sun and the moisture of the rain, whose union determines all fertility, are brought together. Essentially it is the same when in a festive way those water-pots are poured out into the fire symbolising the sun.

The spring and summer festivals of the European Aryans which are most closely related to the Soma festivals reveal other usages of water and rain magic. Apart from baths and spraying, especially the throwing into water of certain persons who represent the vegetation spirit. But we will have to presume that here too – as in India – the festive intoxicating drink and the myth of the acquisition of the heavenly beer cauldron were originally related to storm and rain.

It is Thôrr, the storm-god, who obtains the beer cauldron of the gods from Hymir, just as it is Indra, the storm-god, who obtains the Soma or the Soma vat from Vṛtra, Vala, Vivasvant, etc. The parallel is clear enough. But the Edda offers us another, it seems to me, not less instructive parallel. I mean the narration of the Thyrmsqvidha, as Thôrr gets back the hammer stolen from him from the control of the giant Thyrmr. The thunder-hammer, the storm-instrument. This splendid poem, to which nothing corresponds in the Veda, makes amends to us for the fact that the Edda is not so rich as the Veda in variants of the narration of the acquisition of the heavenly intoxicating drink. Hymir's cauldron corresponds to the Soma vat, Thôr's Mjolnir to the Vajra, the thunderbolt of Indra, with which he obtains the heavenly Soma. But that the Thyrmsqvidha is to be considered as a parallel poem of the Hymesqvidha, related most closely to it in its mythical core, that emerges, I think with unquestionable clarity

---

[158] Cf. Hillebrandt, *Sonnwendfeste in Alt-Indien*, p.29,39,40. Compare to the custom last cited also the Estonian custom notified by Wiedemann: "During severe aridity beer was carried three times around his (i.e. the thunder-god's) sacrificial fire and then poured into the flames with the request that the thunder-god may finally rain", [Ferdinand] Wiedemann, *Aus dem inneren und äusseren Leben der Esten*, p.427.

from that noteworthy Estonian fairy-tale that I have already earlier discussed *in extenso* in these meeting reports,[159] and represents a very remarkable fusion of Thyrmsqvidha and Hymesqvidha, or much rather a completely independent mythic poem originating certainly from Scandinavia, in which elements of both those Eddic poems seem to have grown together quite organically, with the great advantage, at the same time, that the natural process that it deals with is quite clearly expressed. Here there is no mention of either a cauldron or a hammer, but of the thunder instrument that appears as a musical instrument, a bagpipe or a horn, in any case a wind-instrument – and yet Jakob Grimm already in his time recognised with astonishment in this fairy-tale Thyrmsqvidha and Hymesqvidha at the same time. And that cannot at all be underestimated.

I shall outline the contents only in brief.

The earth has for a long time been waiting in vain for rain. The devil has stolen the thunder-instrument from the thunder-god. The thunder enters in the form of a boy into the service, as a page, of the fisherman Lijon who lives by a lake, in whose water the devil hides from the thunder. The devil organises for his son his wedding feast, steals for that fish from the fisherman, is caught, and now invites the two to the wedding in order to conciliate them. There the thunder succeeds in getting back his instrument through cunning. No sooner does he play on it than the devil and his house-servants fall dead to the ground. Now the thunder plays freely on his instrument. Heavy rain falls down and vivifies the earth after seven months of long drought.

The instrument plays the role of the thunder hammer. The fisherman and the fish remind us clearly of the Hymesqvidha, the wedding feast of the Thyrmsqvidha. According to the version of the fairy-tale reported by Wiedemann (*op.cit.*, p.427), the thunder has a page, the son of the rattler, as a helper in the acquisition of his instrument, as Thôrr has Týr in the Hymesqvidha. But everything

---

[159] Cf. my essay, *Germanische Elben und Götter beim Estenvolke, Sitzungsberichte der kaiserlichen Akademie der Wissenschaften in Wien*, philosoph.-histor. Klasse, Vol.153 (1906), pp.80-82.

happens in order that the long missed rain of the earth is finally obtained again.

Everything becomes clear if we consider the Hymseqvidha and Thrymsqvidha as parallel poems. The thunder hammer places Thôrr once again in a position to arouse thunder and produce rain. But the acquisition of Hymir's cauldron must likewise have had an analogous effect, exactly like the acquisition of the heavenly Soma vat by Indra.

Like the sun and moon, the thunderbolt of Indra too appears in the ancient Indian ritual and especially in the soma sacrifice. The staff of the dîkshita, the consecrated, in the soma sacrifice, who has the character and the duty to drive away the demons, is identified with the thunderbolt of Indra and called such. A similar role is played also, in another context, by the Sphya, a wooden chip, which is tossed and is supposed to destroy the demons.[160] Here therefore Indra's weapon functions along with the Pravargya pot, which is identified with the sun, and the most important ingredient of the sacrifice, the Soma, which is identical to the moon. Indra's weapon next to the two heavenly vessels whose acquisition it aids.

I believe that these three mythical things should be recognised again next to one another in the well-known fairy-tale of the wishing-table. The donkey Bricklebrit would be the sun, the wishing-mill the wishing-object in a theriomorphic version, as it is well-known to us in India as a wishing-cow and has already been mentioned by me above. The wishing-table would be the moon, the lunar vessel, the inexhaustible, ever renewing itself, the wonderful object dispensing heavenly food. The cudgel in the sack, however, would naturally be the thunder-hammer that helps its owner to obtain those two wonderful objects. The fairy-tale points back to a myth in which the thunder-god gets back the sun and moon with his hammer. And the circumstance that the wonderful objects are at the beginning divided among three brothers as owners is naturally not an obstacle. They all come finally into one hand, for the welfare of an entire family. The cudgel in the sack has proved itself victoriously.

---

[160] Cf. Oldenberg, *Religion des Veda*, p.493.

But we must also think of the diamond lance of the Peronnik fairy-tale that the hero obtains along with the golden bowl from the giant Rogéar in the castle Kerglas and with which he then kills thousands of enemies. Of this lance it is said: "It kills and strikes down everything that it touches" (*elle tue et brise tout ce qu'elle touche*). Thus not a bleeding lance but a powerful, irresistible weapon like the thunderbolt of Indra.[161] It is also called the merciless lance (*la lance sans merci*). It shines like a flame. No man dares to attack the giant when he carries this lance.

If the thunderbolt has been transformed here into a lance, one may consider that as a contemporary change, no more striking than its transformation into a cudgel in the popular fairy-tale. Above all one may also think of the fact that Indra does not only, and not always, carry the thunderbolt as a weapon. In the Rigveda, he also shoots occasionally with bow and arrow – as the Estonian thunder-god shoots *pikse-nôled* (thunder arrows), lightnings (Wiedemann, *op.cit.*, p.427). And then in the Mahâbhâratha Indra appears also armed with a spear or lance (*çakti*). This spear never fails its target, and when it is hurled, it returns by itself into the god's hand.[162] It is clearly the old thunder weapon transformed into a spear.

But if we remember that the Peronnik fairy-tale is not to be separated at all from the Grail saga, that the bleeding lance of the Grail mountain corresponds to the diamond, merciless lance of the fairy-tale, then we cannot evade the further conclusions. When the lance

---

[161] I would like to recognise a variant of this weapon in the same fairy-tale in the iron ball that, once it has reached its goal, returns by itself into the hand of the slinger – that boomerang effect, thus, which we occasionally find mentioned in the case of Indra's and Thôr's weapon too. Here a black man has this iron ball who, however, is also overcome by Peronnik. And even the manner in which this happens is significant. The black man is put to sleep by Peronnik as Indra puts Dhuni and Cumuri to sleep and Hercules the giant Alcyoneus. A most antique feature which has survived along with many equally ancient features in the Peronnik fairy-tale.

[162] *Mahâbhârata*, Vanaparvan, ed. of Pratap Chandra Roy, Calcutta, III, 309,24. Indra says the same of his spear (*çakti*): *amoghâ hanti çataçah çatrûn mama karacyutâ, punaç ca pânim abhyeti mama dâityân vinighnatah.* In this manner does Thôr's hammer too return after the throw into the god's hand. Cf. W. Mannhardt, *Germanische Mythen*, p.111,141.

appears in the Grail procession along with two wonderful or sacred vessels, that can correspond to the ancient Aryan cultic custom, just as, in the Indian soma sacrifice, the cultic symbols of the lunar vessel, the solar vessel and the thunderbolt are all three represented. And as the three are preserved together as desired objects in the fairy-tale of the wishing-table. But the Grail vessel can appear alone or along with the lance – as in the Peronnik fairy-tale bowl and lance, that constitutes no contradiction. It is not necessary that they all appear together, but when it is the case, then we have the greatest objects of wonder of a very ancient cult, the symbols of the greatest wonders of the heavens – sun, moon and thunder-weapon – next to one another.

Even the so-called lance of Longinus in the Grail saga can be a Christian transformation of an ancient heathen motif.

On closer observation, the investigation above throws a new light on many points of the Grail saga and allows, I think, something that was up to now hard to understand to be better understood.

So it is perhaps one of the most striking and least explained features in the mediaeval Grail poems that the Lord of the Grail Mountain to which the Grail seekers must advance is called the Fisher or the Rich Fisher and is occupied in fishing. Now I think I may point out that the giant Hymir, from whom Thôrr and Týr get the bowl, appears and works as a fisherman. He lives in the east of the Eliwagar, the "stormy waves", invites Thôrr after the first meal to accompany him on a hunt and this consists in fishing. He angles whales though it is for Thôrr poor game. Hymir might also perhaps be called a Rich Fisher even though Thôrr then makes him poor. He has nine bowls, of which one suffices to remedy the need of the gods. For that he has the chalice, the precious jewel, that Thôrr throws on his skull so that it shatters. And at least one of the two cauldron seekers stands in the closest blood relationship to him – but the less of the two, Týr. And yet it looks as if they hardly know each other, in any case are very distant, otherwise the mother would not have needed to hide Týr under one of the cauldrons. There hovers a certain obscurity over the relationship as over that between the Grail seeker and the Lord of the Grail Mountain, the Rich Fisher.

We have encountered the Fisher also in the related Estonian fairy-tale, though the relationship here too is somewhat displaced. The Fisher is here the helper of the thunder-god. The Hymesqvidha however should offer the more original version. A mythical background, similar to this, could bring the remarkable characteristic into the Grail saga which then, after the Christianisation of the material in many ways, was interpreted as biblical or Christian with reference to the fishing and fishing of men of the apostles, the Christian fish symbol, and things of the sort. But this feature did not become really understandable through all these interpretations, as it remained unexplained even to me. Naturally, a mythical background of the sort of the Hymesqvidha also does not explain the matter completely, but precisely such strongly adherent, obscure, irrational characteristics point not seldom to the highest antiquity. They belong to the content of the oldest myth.

A very remarkable feature still unexplained in many of the mediaeval Grail romances is that the land around the Grail Mountain is described at times as desolate, deserted, waterless, dry, apparently on account of some transgression, a murder of a brother of the Grail Lord, an insulting of the fairies of the fountain. Only the redeeming act of the successful Grail seeker, the discovery of the Grail Mountain or the right question brings about, in a miraculous manner, a transformation of these sad circumstances. The misery of the drought is over and everything good as before.

The majority of the Grail romances have the motif of the serious illness of the Fisher King which is remedied by the magically powerful question of the Grail seeker. Thus in Crestien, Manessier, the *Perceval of Rochat*[163] and Didot,[164] the *Grand St. Graal*, the *Quête*, *Perlesvaus* and

---

[163] Alfred Rochat published in 1855, in his dissertation *Ueber einen bisher unbekannten Perceval li Gallois: eine literarhistorische Abhandlung* (Zurich), selections from a Berne MS containing part of a continuation of Chrétien by Gautier de Doulens.

[164] [The Didot-Perceval is a 12th century manuscript that was owned by the publishers Firmin-Didot that may be a rendering of the *Perceval* and *Mort Artu* branches of an original poetic tetralogy by Robert de Boron (which began with *Joseph d'Arimathie* and the mostly lost *Merlin*) into prose and includes transcriptions

Peredur – except that in Manessier and *Peredur* the ailing Fisher King is not healed by the question but by revenge. Instead of the motif of the ailing Fisher King, there is, in an entire series of other Grail romances, a completely different one, namely "the premise that the land of the Fisher King was made in a magical way desolate and arid through a baleful stroke, that is, through the murder of Goon, the brother of the Fisher King". Thus in Pseudo-Gautier, the second interpolator of Pseudo-Gautier, Gautier and Gerbert. This evil is remedied here by the question of the Grail seeker, as also the illness of the Fisher King. Even in the Pseudo-Crestien Introduction, we have the infertility of the land, but it has arisen here through a crime against the fairies of the fountain and is remedied by Gawan's finding of the Grail Mountain.[165]

Even the *Grand St. Graal* and the *Quête*, in which the illness of the Fisher King stands in the foreground, refer to the infertility of the land as a consequence of a murderous act that was committed against a member of the Grail house. But this deed lies here far in the past, long before the time of the Grail heroes. It is not brought into relation with either with the magical question or with the avenging of the deed or remedied by these, much rather it seems to have been forgotten thereafter. It emerges only as a narration from ancient times, according to which the old Fisher King Lambor was victorious against his opponent Bruillan, who had to flee but then returned and clove the Fisher King as well as his horse asunder. Thereby the land became infertile or laid waste by plague. "But, in Ch.XII of the *Quête*, where Galaad gets the Grail, it is not indicated in any words that thereby the condition of the land became better".[166] It has receded entirely to the background.

That looks as if an older, obliterated, suppressed, half-forgotten motif that has been pushed back by a more recent one, the illness of the Fisher King, survives only as an old history of an ancestor, whereas it has retained its full significance in other Grail romances where, however, there is no mention of an illness of the Fisher King.

---

of several sections of Chrétien's *Perceval* and that of his continuator Wauchier].

[165] Cf. R. Heinzel, *Über die französischen Gralromane*, p.18; also p.28,31,52,61,68f,71,72,77,79.

[166] Cf. Heinzel, *op.cit.*, p.18,68.

The motif survives clearly also in the *Conte du Graal* (Crestien). "Even in the latter there is reference to a lord of a castle who is in possession of, even if not magical characteristics, still magical objects, whose castle is very hard to find, whose land has as a result of a crime lost its fertility which it can in a magical way regain through the question of a visitor".[167]

That is clearly only a variant of the Grail Castle story and, I think, one that preserves older features, and thus survives alongside the more recent and more viable ones. However, Heinzel sees the matter differently, though I do not wish to blame him completely for it. The main reason on account of which I must consider the motif of the drought and infertility of the land as very old was not yet known to him. He considers the narration in Pseudo-Crestien's Introduction as a contamination. Pseudo-Crestien "traces back the infertility of the land and the rapture of the Grail Castle, whose lord is a magician, to the crime of King Mangon against the fairies of the fountain - if the Grail Castle is found, the fertility will return".[168] According to Heinzel that is a contamination of a fairy-tale such as the *Conte du Graal* reports with the narrative of the Grail Castle and the sick Fisher King, whom he identified with the lord of the magical castle.[169] I think that Pseudo-Crestien, even if he were not a great poet, preserved precisely in his narration an older, popular tradition.

In Pseudo-Gautier, Gawan, the Grail-seeker asks the king about the bleeding lance, receives information too, but then falls asleep and thereby misses further questions and further instruction. He thereby attains not everything but still something essential. When he rides out again he finds the land that lay waste on account of the mentioned murderous deed well-watered and full of green woods and meadows. The recovered fertility is the result of the question about the lance.[170]

Heinzel found it "striking that, in Pseudo-Gautier and, according to him, in Pseudo-Crestien, the return of the water in the dried

---

[167] Cf. Heinzel, *op.cit.*, p.71.

[168] Cf. Heinzel, *op.cit.*, p.70.

[169] Cf. Heinzel, *op.cit.*, p.71.

[170] Cf. Heinzel, *op.cit.*, p.28.

up rivers is highlighted as an essential symptom of the improved situation".[171] I think that we have here the most striking point of the old saga before us.

The land lies waste and infertile, dry and desiccated. If meadows and woods should become green again, the fructifying water must be obtained again, the rain must fall, the rivers must swell. That is effected with a magical stroke by the finding of the Grail Castle or the magic question through which the Grail-seeker becomes the lord and owner of the Grail. This wonderful process, which seemed up to now obscure and incomprehensible, and therefore was gladly pushed aside – not only by the researchers of the present time, but much earlier already by the most outstanding poets of the Middle Ages who represented the Grail saga in poetic form – this wonderful process becomes understandable only through the connection with the myth and cult of the earliest Aryan times, becomes perfectly clear and understandable only through the connection in which we have sought to bring it above.

When Indra obtains the heavenly Soma, the wonderful, inexhaustible self-replenishing vessel, after heroic adventures, he lets the rain, the heavenly mead, fall on the earth, he lets the waters swell, the imprisoned rivers stream once again. When Thôrr – in a parallel poem – gets back his hammer, he can once again produce rain, even if the poem does not describe this expressly. Indeed, apart from the obvious clarity of the matter, what is the striking of the giant with Mjolnir also but a thunderstorm? And when the Estonian thunder in a doubtlessly related narrative obtains once again his thunder instrument and plays on it, not only the devil and his fellows fall to the ground, but also heavy rain falls down and saturates the thirsting earth. That the acquisition of Hymir's cauldron by Thôrr must have originally had the same result, even if the Edda does not mention a word or know about it, that follows, it seems to me, necessarily from the unquestionable connection of this myth with the myths and fairy-tales mentioned above – with Thyrmsqvidha and the Estonian fairy-tale of the *müristaja mäng* on the one hand, and with the myths of Indra's acquisition of the Soma on the other.

---

[171] Cf. Heinzel, *op.cit.*, p.71,72.

If we consider the Grail vessel as a Christian transformation of that wonderful heavenly vessel – of the lunar (or also solar) vessel – which conceals the intoxicating drink of the gods and gives rain to the earth, then this remarkable feature of the saga of the infertility and the later irrigation of the land can be understood immediately. It very probably survived in sagas and fairy-tales of the Middle Ages that were not yet influenced by Christianity. The great poet Crestien - perhaps following older schemes – set in place of this motif the purely humanly touching one of the ailing Fisher King which could also be deepened and utilised in a moral way. It was followed by others. Others again, but perhaps no great poets, although familiar with the sagas and fairy-tales of the people, adhered to the old motif and left the new one aside, whereas yet others did not give it up at least and let it survive in further episodic narratives. Understood in this way, nothing seems to me to interrupt the development.

This feature of the saga however leads us to another no less important and remarkable feature, whose connection with it, at first not at all to be expected, emerged only through the ancient Indian material.

We know Parzival as the foolish, the pure, boyish youth, inexperienced in worldly ways, without falsehood from Wolfram, see him ethically elevated as a "pure fool" in Wagner's Parsifal. His character as a fool is, according to Heinzel, the typical characteristic in the personality of Parzival. But Heinzel thinks that this fool by nature stands quite far from the legend of the Grail,[172] wherein I cannot agree with him. Heinzel in his time formulated the type somewhat differently in saying: "A youth, brought up not as a knight, becomes a mirror of knighthood and an ornament of the Round Table. If we ignore the Grail, this is the formula that the romance of Parzival and that of Fergus[173] could be reduced to".[174]

Certainly this interpretation has its justification for the knightly romances but it is not sufficient for the understanding of the character,

---

[172] Cf. Heinzel, *op.cit.*, p.22.

[173] [The *Roman de Fergus* is a 13th century French Arthurian romance about Fergus, Lord of Galloway.]

[174] Cf. Heinzel, "Ein französischer Roman des 13. Jahr.", in *Kleine Schriften*, p.73; see also p.84,85.

not deep, and too temporally conditioned. It is more correct, as Heinzel later does, to speak of the foolish nature which is indeed also known and preferred in the fairy-tale. I recall here above all Peronnik l'idiot. But this foolish nature consists of two chief factors: 1. inexperience, unfamiliarity with the world and its ways, with the entire wonder of the world, 2. purity of heart, especially also in sexual relations.

Purity, chastity, even virginity, forms an important trait in the character of the Grail hero, though this is not naturally not expressed equally strongly in all poems.[175] Alain and Galaad are virginally chaste, as the *Grand St. Graal* indicates. In the *Quête* and in the *Demanda*[176] Galaad is even compared to Christ; a manuscript compares the virginity of Galaad with that of Mary.[177] The *Quête* places the greatest weight on chastity. Of its three Grail heroes, Bohort has sinned only once, Galaad and Perceval never. In the *Conte du Graal*, on the other hand, Perceval shows himself to be truly manly.[178] Wolfram's Parzival is also no longer as virgin as when he comes to the Grail castle. He has indeed already lived together in matrimony with Konwiramur. Nevertheless, he is of a morally pure nature. According to the disposition of the author there are, here, naturally nuances.[179]

We encounter an image of the "pure fool" in ancient India, as I have presented in greater detail in my book *Mystery and Mime in the Rigveda*, pp.292-303. It is the story of Rishyaçringa which is narrated in the Mahâbhârata and also in the Jâtaka[180] and Kanjur,[181] and was originally also perhaps dramatised, and indeed, I believe, as an artistic

---

[175] Cf. Heinzel, *Über die französischen Gralromane*, p.53,131,132,142,162,172.

[176] [The *Demanda del Santo Grial* is a Spanish translation dating from 1515 of the French *Quête*.]

[177] Cf. Heinzel, *op.cit.*, p.131,132,142.

[178] Cf. Heinzel, *op.cit.*, p.162; also the note there.

[179] This feature is not lacking even in the popular Peronnik l'idiot. He is a *pauvre innocent* and, before he reaches Castle Kerglas, undergoes a hard test of chastity.

[180] [The Jātakas are popular stories of the former lives of the Buddha that were composed in India around the 4th century B.C.]

[181] [The Kanjur ("translated words [of the Buddha]") along with the Tanjur ("translated treatises") constitute the canonical literature of Tibetan Buddhism.]

version of the ancient generative rite performed at the solstitial sacrifice.

The form of the narrative that, from a comparison of the different versions, emerges as the oldest is, in my view, the following:

The youth Rishyaçringa lives entirely sequestered from the world with his father, an ascetic, in the woods, in a hermitage. He has never seen the world, never looked upon a woman, indeed he does not have any idea that there is a difference between the sexes. In the country however there has for a long time already been a drought and lack of rain so that everything threatens to perish. Then the king learns that this want can be remedied if one succeeded in bringing the fully chaste Rishyaçringa into a love-union.[182] The beautiful daughter of the king succeeds in reaching this goal, and while a happy pair is formed of the two, the heavens unlock their sluices and revive the thirsting land. The spell in broken – through the ancient theurgical-cultic magic of the generative act. But this magic is only effective if it is practised by a brahmaçârin, a member of the brāhmanical caste who has been sexually abstinent at least for a while. Rishyaçringa naturally represents the ideal of such a person, the absolutely pure fool. Hence the extraordinary success.

What the Indian "pure fool" effects here through the generative act is thus clearly the rainfall, is the removal of the drought and infertility of the land through the production of water – the same thing therefore that Indra effects through the acquisition of the Soma, Thôrr and the Estonian thunder-god through the reacquisition of their thunder instrument – the same thing that the chaste Grail seeker, in a series of Grail narratives, effects through the discovery of the Grail castle or the magic question. As a narrative it is to be

---

[182] The reason of the great aridity and lack of rain is given differently in different versions. In the *Mahâbhârata* it is a fault of the purohita or the illness of a brâhman, in the *Jâtaka* it is Indra's fear of the all-too strong penitence of Isisingo, in the Kanjur the wrath of the rishi. These motivations may be of entirely later origin and inconsequential. Indeed it requires no motivation. The essential is the rite of rain-creation that was practised at a specific time during specific festivals. If a drama or a narration was created from the rite, then however the missing rain had indeed to be given a motivation somehow.

compared to these narratives, as a rite to such rites as the pressing of the soma, the striking of the thunder drum, and so on – a rain magic, a fertility magic.

To be sure, it is something essentially different if the pure folly of the Indian forms only to a certain degree the foundation of a great success of the generative act, whereas, in the case of the chaste Grail-seeker, this appears as a lasting moral characteristic whose loftiness and purity qualifies him for the sacred office. Common to both however is the thought that the practice of chastity provides extraordinary power. Even the most primitive peoples practise fasts and abstinence and attribute a value to them. The greatest gap between the Rishyaçringa and the Grail-seeker corresponds fully to the enormous gap between the most ancient Indian and the mature Christian culture. And if there is a historical and cultural historical connection between the festivals of primitive peoples and ours, such is not unthinkable here too, even if we are however not in a position to be able to demonstrate the connecting threads.

If the chaste person operates here through the generative act, there through the magic question, then even the latter deserves a closer investigation. But this is difficult and riddles still lie hidden here. But that in the magic question something specifically Christian is to be recognised is not very probable and, to my knowledge, has also not been maintained by anybody. Much more probable may it be that precisely in this point is hidden ancient heathen belief or superstition, ancient heathen magic or cult practice. This thought has also clearly directed those who have used the term "magic question" – i.e. a question employing magical effects – for the Grail question.[183]

---

[183] Cf. R. Heinzel, *Über die französischen Gralromane*, p.14: "The questions are of a magical character since the healing can be effected only through them – whether they may be called fabulous is not clear to me since I have at my disposal no clear parallel in the traditional literature. More certainly traditional is the motif of the forborne question". And further below: "But one can doubt whether the magical character was always peculiar to the questions of the Grail hero. Indeed they have a double meaning, first magical healing – in some versions also the fertilisation of the deserted land – and legitimisation of the Grail hero as the successor of the Grail king". I think the last circumstance does not seriously speak against the inherently

My material for the judgement of this subject is still completely insufficient, yet I believe I should make at least some observations on it. And I hope that in this direction some further enlightenment may soon be obtained.

It seems that, in the ancient Aryan cult, riddling questions or, more correctly, riddle-like questions about the secrets of the world, the natural powers, the gods and their character, the sacrifice, etc. played a certain role. This character is borne by the remarkable, obscure dialogue hymns of *RV* X,27 and 28, where Indra and the singer hold an exchange of speeches which was apparently performed in a somewhat dramatic way, i.e. with assigned roles. There is no further action therein. To this belongs also the well-known Dîrghatamas hymn *RV* I,164, the great riddle hymn that begins with cosmogonic questions and then moves to the change of the seasons and the diurnal periods, to the sun and moon, fire, lightning, wind, to the heavenly and earthly sacrifice, the metres, the sacred speech, the relationship between gods and men, and so on, throughout in a mystical riddling form that still poses so many riddles to us as well.[184] Already there appears in this hymn the idea of philosophical unity (v.46) and so many of the questions and disputations in the Upanishads seem to me precisely a continuation of these ancient cultic riddling questions and riddling conversations. Even there questions are asked about secrets of the sacrifice, the sacrificial fire, many individual rites, and even there one speaks of the sun and moon, wind, aether, etc., until everything culminates in the most perfect possible answer to the great question of that time, the question about the Âtman-Brahman, the "world-soul" which is at the same time "the sacred" (*brahman*). From cultic questions one steps ever higher to philosophical questions.[185]

That the riddling questions and riddling conversations of the Rigveda played a role in the most ancient cult or indeed in the

---

magical character of the question.

[184] Cf., now, regarding this song, especially Paul Deussen, *Allgemeine Geschichte der Philosophie*, I, i, pp.105-119.

[185] Cf. especially in the *Brhadâranyaka* [Upanishad] the famous disputation at the court of King Janaka of Videha.

course of the sacrificial festivals I should like to conclude from the circumstance that these are found in the Rigveda. But that it is here a question of a most ancient type seems to me to be attested, above all, by the circumstance that we have preserved in the Edda something quite similar of interrogatory conversations. I perhaps need to recall only "Vafthruthnismâl" and "Alwissmâl". What Odhin speaks oraculously in the "Grimnismâl" before King Agnar seems like a series of answers to similar questions concerning the world and the gods. Unfortunately we know next to nothing about the recital and use of the Edda songs, but one must perhaps consider it as probable that these go back to a type that originally played a role during the cultic festivals of the ancient Germans. The relationship of the Vedic and the Eddic songs however makes it perhaps further probable that the type of song in the form of a speech that is in question here – like other such types – may have already been a most ancient Aryan one.

The secret question with a significant answer, posed and given on a festive occasion, perhaps appeared in itself as something powerful and potent – like the song that praised the deeds of the gods, sang their fate or the course of the world, or like many important cultic practices of a material character.

The so-called "magic question" of the Grail seeker can, in my opinion, quite probably be considered as such a potent question. The questions: "Whom does one serve with the Grail?" - "Where is it being taken?" - "Why does the lance bleed?",[186] these are questions about the secret character or the motivation of the festive solemnity that the naïve world-alienated Grail seeker sees with astonishment developing during his visit to the Grail castle. It can be compared especially well to those Vedic questions which are related to objects of the cult, the fire, the soma (= the moon), and so on.

I do not want to dare to maintain that with these fleeting observations the difficult problem has already been clarified sufficiently; but perhaps they are suited to initiating its solution.[187]

---

[186] These are the essential principal questions. Cf. Heinzel, *Über die französischen Gralromane*, p.12,13.

[187] One finds much that is informative in Georg Hüsing, *Die iranische Überlieferung*

und das arische System, Leipzig, 1909, (*Mythologische Bibliothek*, Vol.II, pt.2);
cf. also Wolfgang Schultz, *Rätsel aus der hellenischen Kulturkreise*, Leipzig, 1909
(*Mythologische Bibliothek*, Vol.III, pt.1).

IV. LAND OF SOULS, LAND OF THE SWAN
ELVES, SOMA-PROTECTORS
AND GRAIL-PROTECTORS

A very noteworthy feature of the Grail poems that has not at all been sufficiently explained consists in the fact that the resting place of the Grail is characterised as a sort of land of souls or kingdom of the dead. In the prose romance of *Perceval li Gallois*,[188] the Grail castle, as Birch-Hirschfeld points out,[189] bears three names: Eden, Castle of joys, Castle of souls. This, especially the last name, points to a land of the blessed dead, a heavenly land or elysium. Heinzel says in his discussion of Crestien's poem: "The miraculous castle is a sort of land of the dead".[190] He too points out that in *Perlesvaus* – the same work of which Birch-Hirschfeld speaks under a different title – the Grail castle is called "Castle of souls", "Castle of joys", "Eden". Martin wished to conclude directly from an analogous trait of the Arthur saga that Arthur was a Grail – or Fisher-King. Lohengrin comes to Brabant from his subterranean court, as, in Wolfram, from the Grail castle. Heinzel is of another opinion. He

---

[188] [i.e. *Perlesvaus*, cf. p.14 above]

[189] Cf. Birch-Hirschfeld, *Die Sage vom Gral*, p.132.

[190] Cf. Heinzel, *Über die französischen Gralromane*, p.23,175. The "wonderful castle" is doubtless a variant of the Grail castle.

remarks: "The land of the dead is indeed appropriately attributed to Lohengrin as his homeland and, since he was a hero, especially that of King Arthur". But when, in Wolfram, he comes from the Grail castle, Heinzel considers this as a later fabulous transformation.[191]

The question whether Lohengrin belonged by nature to the Grail castle or – as many think – was only later and secondarily brought into a connection with it we shall return to later. For now let us establish only the remarkable fact that the Grail castle sometimes appears as a land of the blessed dead – a land of souls, Eden

This feature, which cannot in any way be traced to the Christian legend, is explained immediately in a surprising manner in light of our investigation above. If we recognise in the heavenly Soma vessel the prototype of the Grail vessel, then this feature agrees very well with it, for we recall at once that the kingdom of the heavenly Soma in the Vedic hymns emerges clearly as the kingdom of the blessed dead, where they enjoy indescribably high pleasures. We remember the fine Rigveda hymn IX,113 in which (v.7-11) Soma is entreated to lead the pious worshipper into this kingdom of blessedness where Yama, the son of Vivasvant,[192] is king, and to make him immortal there. In the translation of the "Seventy Hymns"[193] these fine verses go thus:

Where there is light that is never extinguished,
And where the heavenly light shines,
There, into immortality, -
The eternal, Soma, bring me!

Where Vâivasvata is king,
 And where the heart of heaven is
Where those eternal waters are -
O Soma, make me immortal!

Where one moves at will,
 In the third height of the heavenly kingdom,

[191] Cf. Heinzel, *op.cit.*, p.67.

[192] Cf. p.118 below.

[193] [See above p. 40n.]

Where all spaces are brilliant, -
O Soma, make me immortal!

Where wish and desire are stilled,
At the zenith of the red sun,
Where pleasure and satisfaction are at the same time, -
O Soma, make me immortal!

Where pleasure and joy and gaiety,
And bliss abide, where the wishing
Of the wisher finds fulfilment, -
O Soma, make me immortal!

If the "the red zenith" here is interpreted as "the zenith of the red sun", i.e., its highest position, we have already explained above that we agree with that. Hillebrandt thinks the "red" in this context is the moon.[194] We saw above the blessed enjoying themselves also in Vishnu's highest step, which we can only refer to the sun. However, besides, the blessed dead, the manes, the fathers, are in fact, especially in the later period, brought into much closer connection with the moon than with the sun.[195] In the doctrine of the transmigration of souls developed later we encounter the idea that the souls of good men, who however are not yet freed for ever from the transmigration of souls, enjoy a period of blessedness in the moon or in the region of the moon and finally return to earth with the falling rain. That the close relationship of the moon with the dead souls is a most ancient Aryan one can hardly be doubted.[196] That is indeed why the gods of

---

[194] Cf. Hillebrandt, *Vedische Mythologie*, Vol.I, p.396 note1.

[195] The sun and moon as the dwelling place of souls, especially of chieftains and the brave, thus of the outstanding dead – these are ideas that are found often also among primitive peoples; cf. Taylor, *Anfänge der Kultur*, Vol.II, p.69,70.

[196] Plutarch mentions the ancient doctrine that Elysium is in the moon; see Taylor, *op.cit.*, II, p.70. The idea that the starry heavens as a whole is the "land of souls", the land of the mythical ancestors, to which the souls of the dead return, is an idea that is spread over almost the whole world. Cf. Paul Ehrenreich, *Die allgemeine Mythologie und ihre ethnologischen Grundlagen*, Leipzig, 1910, p.132.

souls, the leaders of souls, stand so often in the closest relationship with the moon for which reason the lunar mythologists call them simply lunar gods.

For the Rigveda, the close relationship of the Gandharvas to the heavenly Soma is, in the same context, especially important. They are its militant guards and protectors, a view that persists from the earliest to the most recent times. But the Gandharvas are, as has been long established, nothing but a certain, and in their way, very old form of the host of dead souls. They live in blessed companionship with the beautiful, nymph-like, swan-elfin Apsaras, correspond to the Greek satyrs, sileni,[197] and centaurs, Germanic elves, etc.[198] The awareness of their spiritual character must however have been alive in India already in the time of the developed doctrine of the transmigration of souls, already in the time of Buddhism too. Only in this way can be explained the remarkable theory of conception that is developed in the Assalâyanasutta[199] and which was in his time so badly misjudged and misinterpreted by Pischel that he sought to use it as a support of his completely untenable view that the Gandharva was originally nothing but the embryo and to explain its nature from it.

This passage has been very finely translated by Hillebrandt, who rightly opposed Pischel:[200]

"We know, O Lord, how conception comes about. Father and mother live together and unite. The mother becomes utunî (menstruating) and the Gandharva comes in as well. In this way through the union of the three does conception come about". Do

---

[197] [The sileni were drunken followers of Dionysus, god of wine.]

[198] Cf. E. Windisch, *Buddhas Geburt und die Lehre von der Seelenwanderung* (Leipzig, 1908), p.12f,27f,67f,72f, especially the entire Ch.II of this profound work; further, my book *Griechischen Götter und Heroen*, I, pp.69ff; *Mysterium und Mimus*, pp.57ff *et passim*.

[199] [The Pali "Assalayana Sutta" (Skt. Ashwalayana Sūtra) is part of the *Majjhima Niyaka* collection that forms part of the canonical literature of Theravada Buddhism.]

[200] Cf. Hillebrandt, *Vedische Mythologie*, I, p.327n. The Pali original is given in the text.

you know if this Gandharva is a Kshatriya or Brāhman, or Vâisya, or Çûdra? "We do not know, O Lord, if, etc."

The Gandharva can obviously not be the embryo here, which comes about only through the union of the productive factors, and is not itself one of these factors. But it cannot also be merely "the spirit of fertility with its blessing", as Hillebrandt interprets it, although the Gandharvas actually operate in this character. Here the Gandharva is quite clearly one of the three factors through which the embryo, the new human being, arises. According to the doctrine of transmigration of souls, there belongs to it however, apart from the father's and mother's seed, a separate soul that enters into the new body. That is the Gandharva. Only under this precondition does the question have a meaning whether this Gandharva is a Kshatriya, Brāhman, Vâisya or Çûdra. Applied to the spirit of fertility it would be meaningless; on the other hand, it is important and significant if it is a matter of a separate soul that enters into a new maternal womb.

Besides, the spiritual character of the Gandharvas has also, even otherwise, been clarified, even if not in a sober scientific form but in a mythological form. The Gandharvas and the heavenly Soma belong inseparably close together. That is so well-known that it requires no further proof here.

But especially important for our investigation is the constant, firm connection of the Gandharvas with the Apsaras, whose character as swan-elves emerges in an unquestionably clear manner especially in the story of Purûravas and Urvaçî. I have dealt with this story already many times in a thorough manner and pointed already almost a quarter of a century ago to the undoubtedly close relationship between the Lohengrin saga and the saga of Eros and Psyche.[201] We do not have here to do with mere analogies – we may speak of relationship, because these and many other sagas, of the type of the Melusina fairy-tale,[202] of

[201] Cf. my book, *Griechischen Götter und Heroen* (1887), I, pp.52ff; *Mysterium und Mimus*, pp.232ff,257ff.

[202] [Melusina is a water-spirit or mermaid who is featured in several mediaeval folk tales.]

rough Else,[203] and so on, all go back to a very ancient basic form of the swan-elf saga. The swan-elfin being unites with the human under a certain condition: it cannot be known in its elfin, superhuman character by the human lover. That is, one cannot investigate or ask questions about its "name" and "species". The regularly appearing violation of the condition then produces necessarily the tragic departure, which was only later occasionally changed through false sentimentality.

Normally the swan-elfin being is a woman corresponding to the female sex of the Apsaras and swan-virgins. But sometimes it is also a man, whether it is now that the swan-elfin nature in a certain case was transferred to a manly being of the same circle, or that these manly inhabitants of the land of souls were by nature estimated and capable of acting as heroes of such an adventure since they too indeed, like their female partners, bear the half-theriomorphic, half-human nature and form, or a corresponding character capable of transformation, in themselves – wherein, however, the non-human, theriomorphic or superhuman nature always appears as the real nature that must remain hidden from the purely human partner.

The most outstanding figure of this sort is Lohengrin, the swan-knight, the knight with the swan, whose nature indeed clearly goes back to a superhuman, swan-elfin being of the cited type, but in the poetry of the Middle Ages has acquired a highly poetic form, fully cloaked and as it were transfigured in a cloud of spiritual knighthood. Its knighthood however is, in its core, similarly very ancient, for, as a professional militant protector of the Holy Grail vessel, he corresponds unmistakably clearly to the Gandharva who, in India, is the professional militant protector of the heavenly Soma.

Thus this connection of Lohengrin with the Grail is in its core and essence most ancient, for it corresponds precisely to that which appears quite clearly in the most ancient Indian tradition, where the Gandharvas, inseparably connected to the swan-elfin

---

[203] [Rough Else is a character in the 13th century epic *Wolfdietrich*. She has at first the repulsive features of a fish and Wolfdietrich refuses her request to marry her, until she reveals her real beautiful self under her piscine form.]

Apsaras, belong most closely together with the heavenly Soma as its militant protectors. It was one of the great mistakes of modern Grail research that it thought it had to represent the connection of the Lohengrin saga with the Grail saga as a secondary, not original one that arose only later without there being any compelling proof thereof. The Rigveda offers the most striking proof for the fact that this hypercritical, negative, disintegrating and fragmenting tendency was a completely mistaken one.

Heinzel allied himself, as we have already seen, to the same in that he too considers the connection of Lohengrin to the Grail castle as a secondary one. Birch-Hirschfeld has, to my knowledge, assumed the same. He represents the view that it was Wolfram von Eschenbach who invented the the knightly brotherhood of the Grail protectors as well as the connection of the Grail saga with the those of the swan-knight, that this connection thus originates from him, and was not created from an ancient source.[204] What led him to, and determined him in, this view he expresses clearly in these words: "There is as little trace of this knightly brotherhood of Wolfram in Crestien as in the other Grail poems".[205] So they must have originated from Wolfram and been invented by him.

That is already not right since the connection of the swan-knight with the Grail saga is indeed found already in the French Grail poetry too. So in Gerbert, where the swan-knight appears as Perceval's offspring.[206] To be sure, the swan-knight here does not have the name Lohengrin that Wolfram gives him, but that is completely incidental. The close connection of the swan-knight with the Grail is the essential thing. It is unthinkable that Wolfram took this connection from Gerbert, whom he did not know at all. The only probability is that both created this from an older source.

And Wolfram indeed mentions, with great certainty, as a chief source of his Parzival – along with Crestien – the book of the

---

[204] Cf. Birch-Hirschfeld, *Die Sage vom Gral*, p.281,282.

[205] Cf. Birch-Hirschfeld, *op.cit.*, p.281.

[206] Cf. R. Heinzel, *Über die französischen Gralromane*, p.78; E. Wechssler, *Die Sage vom heiligen Gral*, p.174.

Provencal Kyot or Guiot, of whom unfortunately no trace has otherwise survived. He could therefore very well have created this connection of the swan-knight Lohengrin, or Loherangrin, with the Grail saga and the entire knightly brotherhood of the Grail from this source. But it belongs to the negative alleged results of the modern Grail research that this Provencal Kyot and his book are supposed never to have existed, that this is nothing but a deliberate invention of Wolfram, a deliberate deception of his readers. Because indeed this Kyot is otherwise not to be found and proven. Gottfried Baist, in this negative direction, considers the question as something to be completely dismissed and hardly discussed any more.[207] But I think that he is in the wrong there. I think that this fraud with the invented source hardly agrees with Wolfram's character, and it is also not easy to perceive to what purpose it should have compelled him. If he wished to lend to his own inventions the authority of older tradition, he could indeed have appealed in a general way to older traditions, he did not need to name by name so definitely a man of his age as his source and indeed cite his source. He speaks of him as of a famous poet known by all: *Kyôt der meister wol bekant* (cf. Wolframs *Parzival*, 453,11). If such a person did not exist at all, that could indeed only discredit his work and his love of the truth. In those days he was easier to check than today. If he names a source that is important to him by name it is hard to see why he should not be believed.

And now when important features of his poem are revealed in their core to be most antique – as the connection being discussed of the swan-knight and the entire host of knightly protectors with the Grail saga[208] – then, in all probability, he created them out of an

---

[207] Cf. Gottfried Baist, *Parzival und der Gral*, p.15 of the offprint, p.39 of the official programme: "He (Wolfram) did not know any other Grail poet than Crestien; what he provides beyond him is his own and fully bears the stamp of his character".

[208] That Wolfram did not invent this knightly brotherhood emerges already from the fact that the Templars are found in the French prose romance *Perlesvaus*, which cannot possibly depend on Wolfram. In the *Perlesvaus* the hero P. rules over two kingdoms: 1. the Grail kingdom, 2. a monastic community on a desolate island; the latter is "endowed with features that recall spiritual knightly orders and especially the Templars". Cf. Heinzel, *Über die französischen Gralromane*, p.176.

older source, which in its turn was based on some apparently popular tradition. And since the known source – Crestien – does not come into consideration, one must think of the source unfortunately unknown to us – Kyot or Guiot. Likewise indeed did we see already earlier that another characteristic feature in Wolfram's Parzival – the idea of the Grail as a precious stone – may very well go back to this source, or indirectly to the heathen Flegetanis used by Kyot. It is very plausible that this Moor, as Iselin has made probable, conveyed the original eastern idea and thus indirectly influenced our Wolfram.

In short – we have no ground at all to mistrust Wolfram's so definite citations of a source; rather these agree most finely with the facts or research results obtained by us on a quite different path.[209]

I cannot undertake to go deeper into the complicated field of the mediaeval Grail poetry and the research occupied with it. Here I am not an expert. In this direction the present investigation should be continued by my dear former pupil, colleague and friend, Dr. Victor Junk, with whom I can perfectly agree on the main point of view. My task here can only be to discover and ascertain the major connections between the mediaeval Grail poetry and the corresponding ancient Aryan myths, sagas and fairy-tales.

The role of the Gandharvas as the militant protectors of the heavenly Soma has been dealt with so often and so thoroughly that I do not need to say much more on it for this reason. Of course, in the great wedding hymn, Vāyu too is, as we have seen, called "the guardian of the Soma";[210] and even Agni is called Somagopāh, "Soma protector",[211] but the actual professional guardians of the Soma, who are often referred to in this character, are the Gandharvas. In the Rigveda this Gandharva appears in singular form, later a number of them are mentioned. They are *somarakshâh* or *somarakshayah*, Soma guardians.[212]

---

[209] Our investigation confirms completely what E. Wechssler arrived at, *op.cit.*, 176, that Wolfram's statements on his models are shown to be fully true in themselves. See also above p.27n.

[210] Cf. *RV* X,85,5 *vâyáh sómasya rakshitâ*; Hillebrandt, *Vedische Mythologie*, I, pp.352ff,436.

[211] Cf. *RV* X,45,5;12; Hillebrandt, *op.cit.*, I, p.275,330,333ff.

[212] Cf. Hillebrandt, *op.cit.*, I, p.79,289,437,443ff.

In the *Mâitrâyanî Samhitâ* III,8,10 (p.109,10) *somarakshayah*, Soma guardians, are named as such by name: Suvân, Nabhrâd, Anghâri, Bambhâri. In addition there are, in the *Mâitr.* S. I,2,5, finally also Astar (i.e. the archer), Ahasta and Kriçânu. The *Tâitt. Samhitâ* enumerates at the corresponding passage (I,2,7): Svâna, Bhrâja, Añghâri, Bambhâri, Hasta, Suhasta and Kriçânu. At the ceremony of the purchase of the soma which we should imagine as being dramatically represented, they function as sellers of soma.[213] Among the names cited, the one standing in the final place is the most important insofar as we find him already in the Rigveda, in a fine hymn that describes the stealing of the Soma by the falcon (*RV* IV,27).

The divine falcon or eagle steals the Soma from the heavens. Kriçânu, the archer, draws the string and shoots at it with his bow. But only one feather flies off from the falcon. Now Indra drinks the Soma. Clearly the falcon has stolen the Soma for him.

Kriçânu is not expressly called a Gandharva, but he is doubtless one.[214] The name and form are old. Kriçânu belongs together with the Keresáni of the Avesta, who likewise is related to the Haoma (=Soma).[215]

The Gandharva – not Kriçânu, but "the Gandharva" – appears in a sharper difference to Indra in the hymn discussed by us earlier of the acquisition of the heavenly porridge by Indra. There Indra shoots with his arrow and pierces the Gandharva in the groundless airy region. The connection leaves it hardly doubtful that the Gandharva is thought of here as the guardian of the heavenly porridge. But that was, as we have seen, the sun. Thus the Gandharva appears as the militant guardian and protector of the solar porridge as well as of the Moon-Soma, of the two heavenly vessels with their desirable content. Though the relationship with the Soma is by far the one that stands out more strongly.

But the Gandharva, it is well-known, stands in other ways as well in a rather close relationship with the sun. According to *RV* I,163,2, he seizes the bridle of the solar horse. But he stands closer to the Soma.

---

[213] Cf. Hillebrandt, *op.cit.*, I, pp.79-82.

[214] Cf. Hillebrandt, *op.cit.*, I, p.448.

[215] Cf. Hillebrandt, *op.cit.*, I, p.449.

The Gandharvas have placed the juice in the Soma. The Gandharva extols the drink of immortality.[216] Above all, he protects the site of the Soma.[217] In the hymn *RV* X,123, which doubtlessly glorifies the moon in a mystical way, the Gandharva stands erect on the back of the heavens, bearing shimmering weapons, clothed in a light garment. He clearly bears the weapons since he stands as the militant protector beside the Moon-Soma.[218]

But constant and important remains precisely the double relationship of the Gandharva to the sun and moon, to both heavenly vessels, whose content enlivens the gods and the blessed. And if we turn once again to the Grail saga, we recall immediately that, in Crestien, along with the Grail and the lance, a dish is also carried in the procession.[219] The militant Gandharva lives in the heavenly kingdom of light, the dwelling place of the blessed dead, where sun and moon shine and are watched by him, where Indra hurls his thunderbolt to obtain both; from whence the Apsara Urvaçî, the swan maiden, descends to earth, to make mortals happy until the violation of the condition destroys the union for ever. Lohengrin, the swan-knight, the militant protector of the Grail, comes from the Grail castle, the castle of souls, from Eden, where, along with the Grail, a lance and a dish are also preserved, in order to enter into union with an earthly woman, the tragic course of which, in spite of the enormous heightening and deepening of the poetic motifs, is still undoubtedly clearly and unmistakably related in its core to the Urvaçî fairy-tale.

Highly noteworthy no doubt is Burdach's reference to the Byzantine mass, where, along with a chalice and a plate, a knife representing the lance of Longinus appears. And it can hardly be doubtful that the image of the mass hovered before many mediaeval poets for the Grail ceremony. But all the fairy-tale like wonderful objects and all the rich relationships that bind the Grail saga with the Aryan myths, sagas and fairy-tales, from the Rigveda and the Edda up to the fairy-tales of

---

[216] Cf. *RV* IX,113,3; *RV* X,139,4-6.

[217] Cf. *RV* IX,83,4.

[218] Cf. *Mysterium und Mimus*, p.59,60; *RV* X,123,7.

[219] Cf. Birch-Hirschfeld, *op.cit.*, p.278.

Peronnik l'idiot and the wishing-table, are not thereby cast aside. The only satisfactory explanation of this remarkable double-relationship perhaps lies, in my view, in the fact that the Christian legends of the evening-meal vessel, of the bowl of Joseph of Arimathea, the lance of Longinus, and the image of the mass of the poetic fancy in the Grail saga are so closely connected to traditional Aryan sagas and fairy-tales that they grew together into a new wonderful unity that cannot and may not be claimed exclusively by either one side or the other.

V. SUMMARY AND CONCLUSION

We have recognised the roots of the Grail poetry – insofar as not Christian but ancient Aryan sagas come into consideration – in the most ancient representation of the sun and moon as wonderful heavenly vessels. Vessels with a precious, desirable content, dispensing rich gifts. They shine in the distant land of light, up there on the heavenly mountain, inaccessible to men, accessible only to gods, demi-gods and the blessed.

The lunar vessel whose content – the heavenly intoxicating drink – drunk by the gods, swells up ever anew; the copper cauldron of the sun-god Vivasvant that inexhaustibly dispenses food to Yudhishthira and his people according to their wishes; the porridge-pot of the ritual that represents the sun symbolically and that should become a wishing-cow for the pious sacrificer that fulfils all his desires; the inexhaustible porridge-pot of the German children's fairy-tale; the endlessly manifold stories of wonderful wishing-mills in Europe that are basically, or were originally, nothing else but wonderful gift-dispensing vessels, originally nothing else but, once again, the sun and moon represented in such a way; the wishing-table alongside the donkey Britlebrit in the German fairy-tale; the various magical vessels of the Celtic saga that dispense sometimes food and drink, sometimes also other gifts and powers that are related to one another just as closely as they cannot, on the other hand, be separated from the wishing-mills of different European peoples;

especially also the wonderful golden bowl that Peronnik, the fool in the Brythonic fairy-tale, obtains from the giant Rogéar, and that similarly dispenses food and drink, and as well makes dead people live and the sick healthy – they are all only variations of one and the same basic idea that proliferated with greater power and abundance among the imaginative Aryan peoples. The idea of the Holy Grail as a golden or other precious vessel that inexhaustibly dispenses food and drink in a miraculous way is classifiable here so naturally that perhaps nothing appears more natural than the assumption that the Christian poetry of the Middle Ages transferred onto the fabulous Passion relic of Joseph of Arimathea a number of fairy-tale like features that were from time immemorial so common to the Aryan people, and especially also to the Celtic, in whose area the Grail saga developed, and that were connected with so many saga – and fairy-tale – like vessels. Especially the food-dispensing power of the Grail is explained thus in the most natural manner. When Heinzel expresses the opinion that the identification of the vessel in which Joseph of Arimathea collected the blood of Christ with the bowl of the supper of Christ was an important step in the development of the saga, and that the food-dispensing power of the Grail is probably connected to it,[220] he should not therein be totally contradicted. Certainly the food-dispensing power would suit the last supper bowl better than the blood vessel. However, the food-dispensing power is not yet explained thereby in any way, at least in that naïve form in which it appears to us in Wolfram and some French poets – *spîse warm, spîse kalt*, etc. – whereas this can be immediately explained quite easily by the transfer of a familiar saga – and fairy-tale motif.

In this context, what Eduard Wechssler observes remains very remarkable: "In spite of its markedly religious character, the legend of the Church and the clergy is not acknowledged. No author of a religious position narrates to us of the Grail. Nowhere do we find even the name of the Grail mentioned in the very many works of churchmen that have been handed down except in the chronicler Helinand. And yet the wonderful myth of the sixfold symbol of faith

---

[220] Cf. R. Heinzel, *Über die französischen Gralromane*, p.46.

cannot have remained unknown to them. They have thus intentionally passed over the legend in silence".[221]

That is important. Clearly numerous narrations and fables were made of the Grail, and that in circles that did not stand far from the Church. It was not spiritual but secular poets who enveloped the Grail with their imagination, ornamented it with their poetic discoveries, clothed it with wonderful splendour and raised it to unapproachable heights. The Church clearly shied away from entering into a closer relationship with these plays of poetic fancy. Without being hostile, it spurned it and let the secular poem freely prevail. That was certainly right and fortunate for both sides. However this attitude of the Church to the Grail saga certainly indicates that we should not overestimate the Christian legendary element in it as regards its significance, and have full freedom to assume purely secular, purely poetical or also popular, saga-like and fairy-tale-like influences. If the Church had accepted and controlled the legend, many different things would have happened. It did not do that. And so every poet, big or small, had the fullest freedom to fabulate.

Along with the food-dispensing power of the Grail we find, in many of the mediaeval Grail poems, still other features which are completely suited to further support the assumption of a connection of the same with that sphere of ancient Aryan sagas which, in the final analysis, goes back to the representation of the sun and moon as heavenly vessels.

We have seen that, in some of these poems, the golden Grail vessel is not carried, but floats freely in the air spreading a bright light around it and serves the diners automatically. We were reminded thereby of the feast of the gods in the Edda where the beer in the vessel obtained from Hymir pours out by itself while bright gold provides the illumination to it. We had to admit that a more perfect and suitable prototype for a golden vessel that floats freely through the air shining cannot be thought of than the brightly shining lunar or solar vessel freely floating in the heavenly space, both of which

---

[221] Cf. E.Wechssler, *Die Sage vom heiligen Gral*, Halle, 1898, p.24. Cf. also what the author remarks on this, pp.24-27.

according to the most ancient Aryan idea offer their precious content to the gods and the blessed.

We were daring enough to connect the series of covers with which the heavenly Soma is, according to a passage of the Rigveda, covered with the various envelops or covers with which the Grail appears covered until it is uncovered at the festive hour. That this is a bold and naturally hypothetical assumption, since missing links between the Rigveda and the Grail poetry seem to be lacking here, we are fully aware. But that may not prevent us from listing even this point in the series of remarkable concordances.

A most important point of concordance that illuminates a feature of the Grail poetry that remained quite obscure up to now was that the acquisition of the heavenly Soma by Indra signifies at the same time the production of rain, liberation of the water streams for the earth and human world, that the soma sacrifice therefore represents a rain magic and that the Soma-Moon is a dispenser of rain – and that those Grail sagas agree with it in a remarkable way that describe the land around the Grail castle as withered, deserted and infertile until the discovery of the Grail castle by the Grail hero, or the magic question through which he becomes lord of the Grail, changes everything at one stroke, makes the meadows and woods turn green and the waters flow again. The great spring magic of the storm-god continues to live on therein in a saga-like form. And this correspondence was substantially supported by the proof that in the ancient German myth the reacquisition of the thunder-hammer by Thôrr is represented as a parallel story to his acquisition of the beer cauldron from Hymir for the feast of the gods, that the two appear inseparably melded together in the Estonian fairy-tale of the thunder-drum and here the production of rain emerges unquestionably clearly as the final aim of the whole.

The production of rain however is, according to the ancient Indian saga, the work of the pure fool – and thus it is a further remarkable feature of the correspondence that even the Grail hero, the seeker and discoverer of the Grail castle is represented clearly in this character: Parzival, the foolish, who so clearly corresponds to Peronnik l'idiot.

We wished also to illuminate a little the riddling obscure feature of the rich Fisher as the Grail lord by recalling Hymir, the whale fisher, who has the cauldron in his possession that the gods desire, and in addition other similar bowls and the precious chalice, and similarly the fisherman Lijon of the corresponding Estonian fairy-tale, in which admittedly a shift had taken place.

Of greater importance is the circumstance that the heavenly kingdom of light in which the solar vessel and and the Moon-Soma shine is clearly thought of in ancient India as the dwelling place of souls, of the blessed dead and that the latter appear as enjoying together the content of that heavenly vessel, that especially an important phenomenal form of the host of souls, the Gandharvas, emerge as weapon-bearing knightly protectors of the Moon-Soma and perhaps also of the solar porridge, whereas the female partners closely related to them, the Apsaras, are the Indian swan-maidens from whose midst Urvaçî detaches herself to undergo her typically swan-elfin amorous adventure with a mortal. In Scandinavia,the Valkyries correspond to the Apsaras, since these are also maidens and experience similar adventures;[222] and the Valkyries are directly related to the heavenly intoxicating drink of Valhalla since they serve it to the Einherjar,[223] another form of the male host of souls. There is no doubt that, already in the most ancient Aryan period, blessed hosts of the dead were thought of in the kingdom of light of the heavens, of the sun and moon, and among them swan-elves and militantly geared men. Above all the clear image of these ideas in the Veda solves for us a great riddle of the Grail saga. We understand why the Grail castle is called an Eden, castle of joys, castle of souls; we understand the connection of the swan-knight with the Grail for the swan-knight is an unquestionably ancient swan-elf that undergoes the typical swan-elfin adventure, and he is at the same time the knightly protector of

---

[222] Cf. L.v. Schroeder, *Griechische Götter und Heroen, eine Untersuchung ihres ursprünglichen Wesens mit Hilfe der vergleichenden Mythologie*, I, p.93.

[223] [The Einherjar ("lone fighters") are the warriors slain in battle who are brought to Valhalla by the Valkyrie. There they feast on an animal called Saerimnir, which may be a boar, and on mead milked from the goat Heiðrún.]

the Grail, he combines in his person in a certain way the nature of the Gandharvas and Apsaras, or certain specific traits of them – or summarily translated into German, the nature of the Einherjar and the swan-elfin Valkyries. We understand all this as soon as we assume the influence of an ancient Aryan saga world surviving silently in the people on the development of the Grail saga. And this assumption agrees with all our results.

Even the other-worldliness of the Grail, the unapproachability of its abode, the quest for the Grail by the Grail heroes through all sorts of adventures and the blessedness appearing immediately after the final victory cannot be satisfactorily explained at all by the Christian legend of the precious Passion relic; but perhaps directly by the numerous most ancient sagas and myths of the quest for and acquisition of the wonderful or heavenly vessel guarded and protected somewhere in a hidden place.

If in the Grail poetry mostly just a wonderful vessel emerges, sometimes however also two vessels appear next to each other, of which indeed one always far surpasses the other; if, thirdly, not seldom even a weapon, the lance, appears – then this relationship agrees excellently with the ancient Aryan saga and ancient Aryan cult, where sometimes sun and moon appear next to each other, as a rule however the narration is only of one of the two heavenly vessels, whereas as a third the weapon of the thunder-god – thunderbolt, hammer, arrow, even lance (in the Mahâbhârata) – comes in as well, as a rule, as the powerful instrument for obtaining the treasure that is sought, sometimes however also itself the object of the quest and acquisition. In the Peronnik fairy-tale, the golden bowl and the diamond lance, *la lance sans merci*, next to each other; in the German fairy-tale, next to the wishing-table and Bricklebrit the cudgel-in-the-sack that gets them both back.

That moreover the Grail procession was, in the case of some poets, perhaps influenced by the image of the processesion during the mass, especially of the Byzantine mass, we do not wish to deny. That is quite possible, perhaps probable. But our task here cannot be to determine the manner and the degree of this influence. They must be left to those who place a special weight precisely on this point.

We cannot also undertake to determine the scope of the actual Christian legend within the Grail poetry in a more definite manner. It must suffice us to establish in any case that a rich current of ancient myths, sagas and fairy-tales has combined with this legend. The legend was seized by the current and borne further by the free inventive appetite of secular poets. But precisely through the fact that the sublime Passion relic was spun round with the native wealth of sagas could a poem arise that satisfied all the poetic needs of the popular soul and at the same time developed into an incomparable symbol of Christian mediaeval feeling and faith.[224]

---

[224] Only after the printing of the present essay did I learn of the extremely valuable and comprehensive work of Jessie L. Weston, *The legend of Sir Perceval, Studies upon its origin, development and position in the Arthurian cycle*, London, 1906-1909 (Vol. XVII and XIX of the Grimm Library). It agrees quite often with my explanations above and comes to the same result insofar as it wishes similarly to trace the Grail saga back very definitely to the ancient nature cult. For more detail on that see my essay, "Der arische Naturkult als Grundlage der Sage vom heiligen Gral" in the Bayreuther Blätter of 1911.

BIBLIOGRAPHY

I. L. V. SCHROEDER: SELECT BIBLIOGRAPHY

Books:

Ueber die Mâitrâyanî Samhitâ, ihr Alter, ihr Verhältnis zu der verwandten çâkhâ's, ihre sprachliche und historische Bedeutung, Dorpat, 1879.
Pythagoras und die Inder. Eine Untersuchung über Herkunft und Abstammung der pythagorischen Lehren, Leipzig, 1884.
Indiens Literatur und Cultur in historischer Entwicklung. Ein Cyklus von fünfzig Vorlesungen, Leizig, 1887.
Griechische Götter und Heroen, Eine Untersuchung ihres ursprünglichen Wesens mit Hilfe der vergleichenden Mythologie, Berlin, 1887.
Die Hochszeitsgebräuche der Esten und einiger anderer finnisch-ugrischer Volkerschaften in Vergleichung mit denen der indogermanischen Völker, Berlin, 1888.
Buddhismus und Christenthum. Was sie gemein haben und was sie unterscheidet, Reval, 1893.
Germanische Elben und Götter beim Estenvolke, p.43 (Sitzungsbericht der Wiener Akademie der Wissenschaften, philos.-histor. Klasse, Vol.153, Vienna, 1906.
Mysterium und Mimus im Rigveda, Leipzig, 1908.

Aus meinem Leben: Wesen und Ursprung der Religion, ihre Wurzeln und deren Entfaltung, Riga, 1909.
Die Wurzeln der Sage vom heiligen Gral, Vienna, 1910.
Die Vollendung des arischen Mysteriums in Bayreuth, Munich, 1911.
Richard Wagner als Nationaler Dramatiker, Bayreuth,1913
Reden und Aufsätze vornehmlich über Indiens Literatur und Kultur, Leipzig, 1913.
Herakles und Indra. Eine mythenvergleichende Untersuchung. Pt. 1-2, Vienna, 1914.
Arische Religion. Vol.I: Einleitung. Der altarische Himmelsgott. Das höchste gute Wesen
 Vol.2: Naturverehrung und Lebensfeste, Leipzig, 1914-1916.
Houston Stewart Chamberlain. Ein Abriß seines Lebens, auf Grund eigener Mitteilungen, München, 1918.

Articles:

"Lihgo, Refrain der lettischen Sonnwendlieder", *Mitteilungen der Anthropo- logischen Gesellschaft in Wien,* Vol.32 (Vol.2 of the third series) (1902), pp.1-11.
"Das Apâlâlied", *Wiener Zeitschrift für die Kunde des Morgenlandes,* Vol.22 (1906), pp.223-244.
"Der arische Naturkult als Grundlage der Sage vom heiligen Gral", *Bayreuther Blätter* 34 (1911), pp.182-197.
"Der reine Tor in Indien (mit einem Nachtrag über arische Einflüße in der Bibel), *Bayreuther Blätter,* (1917), pp.277-289;290-295.

II. RELATED AUTHORS

P. Asbjörnen and J. Moe, *Norwegische Volksmärchen*, tr. Fr. Bresemann, Berlin, 1847.

P. Asbjörnsen and J. Moe, *Norske Folkeeventyr*, 2nd edition, Christiania [Oslo], 1852.

Robert Auning, "Wer ist Uhsing?", *Magazin der Lettisch-litterarischen Gesellschaft*, Vol.16, pt.2, Mittau, 1881, pp.1-42.

Gottfried Baist, *Parzival und der Gral*, Freiburg im Breisgau, 1909.

Adolf Birch-Hirschfeld, *Die Sage vom Gral, ihre Entwicklung und dichterische Ausbildung in Frankreich und Deutschland im 12. u. 13. Jahrhundert. Eine literarhistorische Untersuchung*, Leipzig, 1877.

H. Brunnhofer, *Arische Urzeit*, Bern, 1910.

Konrad Burdach, *Deutsche Literaturzeitung*, 1903, No.46; 1904, No.50.

H. St. Chamberlain, *Richard Wagner*, 4th edition, 1907.

C. and T. Colshorn, *Märchen und Sagen aus Hannover*, Hannover, 1854.

Paul Deussen, *Allgemeine Geschichte der Philosophie mit besonderer Berücksichtigung der Religionen*, Leipzig, 1894-1917.

P. Ehenreich, *Die allgemeine Mythologie, und ihre ethnologischen Grundlagen*, Leipzig, 1910.

K.M. Ganguli (tr.), *The Mahabharata of Krishna-Dwaipayana Vyasa*, translated into English Prose, Calcutta: P.C. Roy, 1883-1896.

R. Garbe, *Die Pravargya-Zeremonie nach dem Âpastamba-Çrâutasûtra, mit einer Einleitung über die Bedeutung desselben, Zeitschrift der deutschen Morgenländischen Gesellschaft*, Bd.34, pp.319-370.

K.Geldner and A. Kaegi (tr.), *Siebenzig Lieder des Rigveda*, with contributions by R. von Roth, Tübingen, 1875.

Hugo Gering, *Die Edda. Die Lieder der sogennanten älteren Edda*, Leipzig and Vienna, 1892.

W. Golther, *Parzival und der Gral in deutscher Sage des Mittelalters und der Neuzeit*, Munich, 1909.

W. Golther, "Lohengrin", *Romanische Forschungen* V (1890), pp.103-136.

Jakob and Wilhelm Grimm, *Kinder- und Hausmärchen gesammelt durch die Brüder Grimm*, 2 vols., Berlin, 1812.

Richard Heinzel, *Die französischen Gralromane, Denkschriften der kaiserlichen Akademie der Wissenschaten in Wien*, philosoph-histor. Klasse, Bd.40, Wien, 1892.

Richard Heinzel, *Kleine Schriften*, ed. M.H. Jellinek and C.v. Kraus, Heidelberg, 1907.

A. Hillebrandt, *Vedische Mythologie*, 3 vols., Breslau, 1891-1902.

A. Hillebrandt, "*Die Sonnwendfeste in Alt-Indien*", *Romanische Forschungen* V (1890), pp.299-340.

Georg Hüsing, *Die iranische Überlieferung und das arische System*, (Mythologische Bibliothek, Vol.II, pt.2), Leipzig, 1909.

Ludwig Emil Iselin, *Der morgenländische Ursprung der Grallegende, aus orientalischen Quellen erschlossen*, Halle a.S., 1909.

H. Jacobi, *Mahâbhârata*, Bonn, 1903.

Harry Jansen, *Märchen und Sagen des estnischen Volkes*, Dorpat, 1881.

'M.K.', Feuilleton, *Wiener Fremdenblatt*, 23 June 1904, "Sonnwendzauber", p.14.

A. Kaegi, *Der Rigveda. Die älteste Literatur der Inder*, Leipzig, 1881.

Kaarle Krohn, *Zur Kalevalafrage, Finnisch-ugrische Forschungen*, Bd.I, Heft 3 (1901), pp.185-210.

A. Kuhn, *Herabkunft des Feuers und Göttertranks. Ein Beitrag zur vergleichenden Mythologie der Indogermanen*, Berlin, 1859.

L. Laistner, *Nebelsagen*, Stuttgart, 1879.

Felix Liebrecht, *Zur Volkskunde*, Heilbronn, 1879.

A.A. Macdonell, Vedic Mythology, *Grundriss der Indo-Arischen Philologie und Altertumskunde* (ed. G. Bühler), Vol.III, Pt.Ia., Strassburg: K.J. Trübner, 1897.

J.W. Mannhardt, *Germanische Mythen. Forschungen*, Berlin, 1858.

J.W. Mannhardt, "Lettische Sonnenmythen" in *Zeitschrift für Ethnologie*, Vol.VII (1875).

Ernst Meinck, "Über die Verehrung der Sonne bei den Germanen", *Bayreuther Blätter*, 32, 4-6 (1909), pp.107-121.

E. Mogk, *Germanische Mythologie*, Leipzig, 1910.

K.V. Müllenhof, *Deutsche Altertumskunde*, 5 vols., Berlin, 1870-1908.

Wilhelm Müller, *Geschichte und System der altdeutschen Religion*, Göttingen, 1844.

A.T. Nutt, *Studies on the legend of the Holy Grail, with especial reference to the hypothesis of its Celtic origin*, London, 1888.

H. Oldenberg, *Die Religion des Veda*, Berlin, 1894.

L. Preller, *Römische Mythologie*, 3rd ed., 2 vols., Berlin, 1881-1883.

O. v. *Reinsberg-Düringsfeld, Das festliche Jahr in Sitten, Gebräuchen und Festen der germanischen Völker*, 2. ed., Leipzig, 1898.

Fritz Reuter, *Sämtliche Werke*, popular edition in 7 volumes, 5th edition, 1890.

F.A. v. Schiefner, *Mélanges russes*, tome IV, St. Petersburg Imperial Academy of Sciences.

K. Schirmeisen, *Die arischen Göttergestalten*, Brünn, 1909.

O. Schrader, *Reallexicon der indogermanischen Altertumskunde. Grundzüge einer Kultur- und Völkergeschichte Alteuropas*, Strassburg, 1901.

Wolfgang Schultz, *Rätsel aus der hellenischen Kulturkreise*, (Mythologische Bibliothek, Vol.III, pt.1), Leipzig, 1909.

Ernst Siecke, *Mythologische Briefe*, Berlin, 1901.

Ernst Siecke, *Hermes der Mondgott: tStudien zur Aufhellung der Gestalt dieses Gottes* (*Mythologische Bibliothek*, Vol. II, Pt.3), Leipzig, 1908.

Emile Souvestre, *Le Foyer Breton. Traditions populaires*, Paris, 1844.

E.B. Taylor, *Die Anfänge der Cultur*, 2 vols., Leipzig, 1873.

C.C. Uhlenbeck, *Kurzgefasstes etymologisches Wörterbuch der altindischen Sprache*, Amsterdam, 1898.

Eduard Wechssler, *Die Sage vom heiligen Gral und ihre Entwicklung bis auf Wagners Parsifal*, Halle a.S., 1898.

Jessie L. Weston, *The legend of Sir Perceval, Studies upon its origin, development and position in the Arthurian cycle*, (Vol.XVII and XIX of the Grimm Library), London, 1906-1909.

F.J. Wiedemann, *Aus dem inneren und äusseren Leben der Ehsten*, St. Petersburg, 1876.

H.H. Wilson, «The Religious festivals of the Hindus», JRAS 9 (1847), pp.70-74; also in *Works*, ed. R. Rost, London, 1862, Vol. II, pp.151-246.

E. Windisch, *Buddhas Geburt und die Lehre von der Seelenwanderung*, Leipzig, 1908.

M. Winternitz, *Geschichte der indischen Literatur*, 3 vols., Leipzig, 1905-1922.

H. Zimmer, *Altindisches Leben. Die Cultur der vedischen Arier nach dem Samhitā dargestellt*, Berlin, 1879.

THE INDO-EUROPEAN
ORIGINS OF THE GRAIL

ALEXANDER JACOB

I. THE INDO-EUROPEANS

II. THE SOLAR COSMOLOGY OF THE INDO-EUROPEANS

III. THE SOLAR RITUALS OF THE INDO-EUROPEANS

IV. THE GRAIL

I. THE INDO-EUROPEANS

To properly understand the several mysterious objects and actions associated with the stone in *Parzival*, and the head and the platter in the Breton and Celtic romances, it would be beneficial to follow Schroeder's example and go back several centuries to the early history of the ancient Indo-Europeans and to decipher the cosmological religion that characterised them.

The comprehension of the ancient religions of the Indo-Europeans has been hitherto hampered by the isolation in which the documents of Egypt, Mesopotamia, and their Āryan neighbours have most often been studied. Examining the documents of these apparently distinct regions of the ancient Near East together presents a much more coherent and comprehensive picture of the cosmological scheme which underlies the religions of the area. The recent comparative linguistic and mythological studies of scholars such as Giovan Semerano[225] and M.L. West[226] have happily shown that the origins of Indo-European religion are intimately linked to the civilisations of the ancient Near East and that the erstwhile tendency to distinguish, on the basis of the linguistic difference between agglutinative and

---

[225] See Giovanni Semerano, *Le Origini della Cultura Europea: Rivelazioni della linguistica storica*, Firenze: Leo Olschki, 1 984-94. The etymological dictionary provided in this work gives Akkadian and Sumerian origins for many of the ancient Greek, Latin and German words.

[226] See M.L. West, *The East Face of Helicon*, Oxford: Clarendon Press, 1997.

135

inflected languages, the Egyptian civilisation from the Sumerian and both from the so-called 'Indo-European' cultures of the Indo-Iranians and the Hittites and Greeks has ignored the possibility that they may have all been derived from a common racial and linguistic source.[227]

The similarities in the cosmological orientation of the religions of the three most ancient civilisations, Sumerian, Egyptian and Indian, certainly give credence to this possibility. And the references in the Sumerian epic of *Enmerkar and the Lord of Aratta*, 1 41-6, to a time when all the peoples of the region "in unison/To Enlil[228] in one tongue [gave praise],"[229] as well as in *Genesis* 11:1 to the sons of Noah [Shem, the Semite; Japheth, the Aryan and Ham the Hamite] speaking the same tongue originally reinforce such a hypothesis. Charvat has also recently noted the emergence of the first "universal religion of Mesopotamia" already in the Chalcolithic cultures of Tel el Halaf and Ubaid.[230] The possibility that the three most ancient civilisations may be derived from a common source is strengthened by the several similarities of religious terminology that are to be found in their

---

[227] Indeed, it will be necessary henceforth to rename the current linguistic term "Proto-Indo-European" as "Proto-Aryan", since "Proto-Indo-European" better denotes the original proto-Dravidian/Hurrian language from which Semitic, modern Dravidian and Aryan are derived than the earliest form of the Japhetic/Aryan branch of it. The modern opposition between "Indo-European" and "Semitic" is therefore to be reconstrued as a religious rather than a linguistic or racial one, based essentially on the radical opposition of one branch of Semites, the monotheistic and mononationalistic Hebrews, who were mostly Aramean brigands and mercenaries (see below p.43), to the cosmological religion of the other branches of the Indo-European family (see Josephus the Jew, *Jewish Antiquities*, I,1 57 and Philo the Jew, *De Mutatione nominum*, 72-6).

[228] Enlil, the Sumerian god of Wind, is the same as [Skt.] Vayu, [Avestan] Wata, [Germanic] Wotan, who represent the life-breath of the supreme deity in his cosmic anthropomorphic form.

[229] See S. N. Kramer, *Enmerkar and the Lord of Aratta*, Philadelphia: University Museum, 1 952, p.15.

[230] See P. Charvat, *Mesopotamia before History*, London: Routledge, 2002, p.236. The fact that Halafian culture coincides mostly with the Subarian culture (see D. Frayne, "Indo-Europeans and Sumerians: Evidence for their linguistic Contact", CSMS Bulletin 25 (1 993), p.23) makes it reasonable to assume that the proto-Hurrians were perhaps the most ancient practitioners of this ancient religion.

respective sacred literatures. For instance, in Egyptian cosmology, the description of Horus as the one who takes "wide strides" through the several regions of the universe is an exact equivalent of the Indic description of Vishnu's cosmic prowess. Both in Sumer and Egypt the lunar god is called "the great light" in order to indicate its priority to the sun in the order of creation.[231] The designation of the fire-god as "child of the waters" is common to both Sumerian and Vedic literature.[232] The Akkadian term "apsu", the Sumerian "abzu", and the Egyptian "abtu" for the primeval Abyss which is at the base of the cosmologies of all the religions of the area are also related to the Indic word "ap" for water.[233] The fire-god is said to have three births in the Vedas (*KrishnaYajurVeda* I,3,1 4) from Heaven, Earth and the Waters. Similarly, in the Egyptian *Book of the Night* the course of the sun is said to extend through the underworld [Earth], the Waters of Nun, and the Heavens, Nut.[234] The three forms of the supreme Soul, Brahman, Vishnu, Shiva form an indissoluble trinity[235] that appears in Mesopotamia too, as is evident from the frequent invocation of the triad An-Enlil-Ea in the earliest Sumerian cosmological fragments,[236] as well

---

[231] dGishnugal (the great light) is a name of the moon-god Sin in TCL 1 5,1 0,1 51 , since the birth of the moon is, in Sumerian cosmology, prior to that of the sun (see A. Jacob, *Ātman*, p.180).

[232] See M.J. Seux, *Hymnes et Prières aux Dieux de Babylonie et d'Assyrie*, Paris: Editions du Cerf, 1 976, p.251.

[233] The fact that Akkadian preserves the original "p" phoneme whereas Sumerian substitutes "b" for it suggests that Akkadian is indeed closer to the Hurrian and later Aryan languages and argues for the existence of a proto-Akkadian element in Elam/Ubaid along with the Hurrian. It is interesting, in this context, to note that G. Rubio has pointed out that many of the proto-Euphratean words detected in the earliest Sumerian texts from Uruk seem to have been Akkadian and Hurrian "loan-words" (see G. Rubio, "On the alleged 'Pre-Sumerian Substratum'", *JCS* 51 (1 999), p.5).

[234] See E. Hornung, *The Ancient Egyptian Books of the Afterlife*, tr. D. Lorton, Ithaca: Cornell University Press, 1999, p.125; cf. p.66 for similar evidence from "The Book of Gates".

[235] See *Brahmānda Purāna* I,i,4,17ff.

[236] For instance, Nipp.1 0673,1 0652 and Ebeling, TAT, p.1 36 (see H. Wohlstein, *The Sky-god An-Anu*, Jericho, NY: Paul A. Stroock, 1 976, p.4ff).

THE INDO-EUROPEAN ORIGINS OF THE GRAIL

as in oaths and prayers from the time of the Larsa dynasty onwards.[237]

These similarities between the cosmological religions of geographically distant civilisations may be explained either by a mere transmission of religious ideas from one racial group to the other through incidental trade contacts, or else by the attribution of the creation and development of this cosmological world-view to priestly classes which were closely related to an original hieratic group. The fact that priests in the ancient cultures were extremely conservative and not likely to spread their essentially esoteric religions through commercial intermediaries suggests that the latter alternative is indeed the more probable one. And since priests are not likely to have migrated alone from one region to the other, it may be assumed that large sections of the original populations of these geographically distant lands were constituted of branches of one original ethnic group. The conservatism of the ancient religions itself is evidenced in the faithful preservation of the earliest cosmological insights through several generations by the priestly classes. Thus we find that the Assyrian priests writing at a much later stage in the history of Mesopotamian religion still possess the original understanding of the secret significance of the various deities of the Sumerian pantheon that their own religion was based upon.[238]

In order to consolidate our derivation of the romances of the Grail from the same primordial Indo-European cosmological religion, we may attempt to trace the diffusion of the Indo-European tribes in remotest antiquity. As regards the original home of the people who developed the cosmological insights shared by the most ancient religions of the region, the only evidence we have is that of the so-called "Flood" story. The Flood story is a cosmological account of the birth of the universe and its light after the destruction of the

---

[237] See H. Wohlstein, *op. cit.*, p.66ff; cf. H.D. Galter, *Der Gott Ea/Enki in der akkadischen Überlieferung*, Graz, 1983, p.144.

[238] See, in this context, the excellent study by A. Livingstone, *Mystical and Mythological Explanatory Texts of Assyrian and Babylonian Scholars*, Oxford: Clarendon, 1986.

cosmos at the end of a cosmic age (kalpa).[239] The Earthly "boat" which survives the flood bears the seeds of universal life and comes to rest atop a mountain, which is indeed the location in which the light of the universe arises – as the Egyptian evidence makes clear.[240] The story of the deluge however is transferred to a terrestrial setting in the popular flood stories of Sumer, India, and Israel. The "ark", or boat, which sails over the flood, lands on a terrestrial mountain and this mountain is considered to be the originating point of the race itself, since the survivor is described as a primeval king or sage.[241] In the Indian account of the Flood in the *Bhāgavata Purāna*, the boat of Manu, "king of Dravida", comes to rest upon an unnamed "northern" mountain (VIII, 24). In the *Matsya Purāna* we see the same Manu practising penance on Mt. Malaya, a name still used for mountains in general in South India. In the Babylonian history of Berossos, the boat of Xisouthros (corresponding to the Sumerian Ziusudra, the Babylonian Atrahasis[242] and Utnapishtim of the Gilgamesh epic) lands in **Armenia**. According to Nikolaos of Damascus, a contemporary of Augustus,[243] the Armenian mountain on which the boat landed is the Baris mountain, which may be the same as Mt. Ararat (north of Lake Van) mentioned in the biblical Flood story of Genesis 8:3. According to Berossus, the Babylonians moved to different parts of Babylonia

---

[239] See A. Jacob, *op. cit.*, Ch.I. P. Jensen ("Assyrio-Hebraïca", *ZA* IV (1 889), p.272f) was one of the first scholars to point out the similarity of the term "tebitu" in the cosmological verse "sihhirutusu ina elippi tebitim sallum" (Hymn IV to Tammuz, R 30, no.2) to the ship of the deluge.

[240] The Egyptian sun-barque is called the "barque of earth", and the Sumerian "magur" boat which bears the sun is identified with the moon, the moon being the bearer of the seeds of universal life (see A. Jacob, *op. cit.*, pp.1 22,161,189f.).

[241] In a Hurrian fragment of the flood story, Atrahasis, the survivor, is mentioned as being the son of Hamsa. (see H.G. Güterbock, *Kumarbi*, Istanbuler Schriften 16, 1946, p.30f.). In India, the sun is called the "swan (hamsa) in the sky" (see, for instance, *Katha Upanishad*, II,2). So it is possible that Atrahasis, like Manu (Vaivasvata), is the son of the sun (Vivasvant).

[242] H. Usener (*Die Sintfluthsagen*, Bonn: Friedrich Cohen, 1 899) suggested that the right form of this name may have been Hasis-Atra, which seems likely, as the Babylonian version of the Sumerian Ziusudra.

[243] Nikolaos is reported in Josephus' *Jewish Antiquities*, I,93.

THE INDO-EUROPEAN ORIGINS OF THE GRAIL

from Armenia.[244]

In the Ethiopian 'Romance of Alexander', the **Brāhmans** are called the sons of Adam's son, Seth,[245] and Noah was considered a transmitter of the wisdom of Seth.[246] Since Adam is indeed the Cosmic Man and not a human, we may assume that the Brāhmans referred to here are associated with the preservation of the Divine Consciousness of Brahman which arises from the Cosmic Egg and is later conveyed to humanity by the seventh Manu/Noah.[247] As regards Seth, Josephus declares

> that he strove after virtue and, being himself excellent, left descendants who imitated the same virtues. All of these, being virtuous, lived in happiness in the same land without civil strife, with nothing unpleasant coming upon them until after their death. And they discovered the science with regard to the heavenly bodies and their orderly arrangement. [248]

---

[244] See Berossus in W. Lambert and A.R. Millard, *Atrahasis: The Babylonian Story of the Flood*, Oxford: Clarendon Press, 1 969, p.1 36. Berossus, like all authors of terrestrial Flood stories, believes that the antediluvian history is also set on earth, in his case, in Babylonia.

[245] See E.A.W. Budge, *The Alexander Book in Ethiopia*, London: Oxford University Press, 1 933, p.75. The identification of the Brahmans with Seth may be glossed with the reference in the *Brahmānda Purāna* I,i,1 ,8ff. to the fact that the Purānas (or the original Purāna which was later divided into the several extant Puranas) were transmitted by the sage Vasishta (one of the seven sages) to other divine sages Parasara, Jatukarnya, and Vyasa (also called Dvaipayana) and the last then transmitted this divine learning to the mortals Jaimini, Sumantu, Vaisampayana, Pailava, and, finally, Lomaharshana, the Suta. However, a Suta is not a Brahman but the son of a Kshatriya father and a Brahman mother (see, for instance, *Gautama Dharmasūtra*, 4,1 5). We may bear in mind also the reference in *Manusmrithi* to the Dravidians as Kshatriyas (see below p. 147).

[246] See A. Annus, *The Standard Babylonian Epic of Anzu*, Helsinki: The Neo-Assyrian Text Corpus Project, 2001, p.xxix.

[247] See A. Jacob, *op. cit.* , pp.54n,232.

[248] See Josephus, *Jewish Antiquities*, I:70-1 . Mount Seiris may be a corruption of the name of Anzu's mountain Sarsar in the Epic of Anzu where Ninurta regains the tablet of destinies after battling Anzu (see A. Annus, *op. cit.*, p.xxviiiff.).

Josephus identifies the land of Seth as being located around "Seiris", which is also the land of Noah, who is said to have preserved the wisdom of Seth. In the Christian *Opus Imperfectum in Matthaeum of Pseudo-Chrysostom*, the books of Seth were supposed to have been hidden by Noah in the land of Šir, and the so-called "cave of treasures" in which they were hidden is identifiable with Mt. Ararat.[249] In *Genesis* 14:6, the Horites, or Hurrians, are particularly identified with Mt. Seir, and so we may conclude that the proto-Hurrians are identical with the proto-Dravidians of the *Bhāgavata Purāna*, according to which Manu is **King of Dravida**. The Brāhmans who are considered to be the "sons of Seth" must refer to the priesthood of the **proto-Hurrian/proto-Dravidian** population that constituted the earliest Indo-Europeans.[250]

Since the earliest centres of high culture are those of the Canaanites, Hatti, Elamites, Sumerians, and Egyptians, it is possible that Mt. Ararat was the central region from whence the proto-Dravidians travelled to Palestine, Anatolia, Egypt, Mesopotamia and the shores of the Black Sea.[251] In one version of the Sumerian king-list, Ziusudra, the survivor of the Deluge, is also said to have lived in Shuruppak,[252] the last of the antediluvian cities, situated north of Uruk. In the Sumerian Gilgamesh epic, the mountain atop which the boat comes to rest is called Mt. Nimush (or Nisir), which may be in the Zagros.[253]

---

[249] See G.G. Stroumsa, *Another Seed: Studies in Gnostic Mythology*, Leiden:E.J. Brill, 1984, p.117.

[250] However, the Brahman caste seems to have been appropriated at a later stage by the Indo-Aryans (see below p.161).

[251] The northern shores of the Black Sea, in present-day Ukraine, may be identified as the homeland of the Japhetic Aryans (see below p.147).

[252] W-B 62, where Ubar-Tutu(k) the king of Shuruppak is mentioned as the father of SU-KUR-LAM (representing Shuruppak itself), whose son is said to be Zi-u-sud-ra (see T. Jacobsen, *Sumerian King-List*, pp.75f.).

[253] The name of the mountain is sometimes read as Nisir. It is probable that Nimush is the original version of the name in the face of the evidence of the *Bhāgavata Purāna* (cf. M.L. West, *East Face of Helicon*, Oxford: Clarendon Press, 1997, p.492); cf. Ashurnasirpal, Annals II:34 (see Streck, ZA, XV, 272-5). M.G. Kovacs has suggested that it might be the same as Pir Omar Gudrun in southern Kurdistan (see

If so, the region around this particular mountain may have been the home of the originators of the Gilgamesh story. It is noteworthy that the *Bhāgavata Purāna* also begins its long narratives at the hermitage of the "Suta" in the forest of Naimish (*BP* I,1,4), which may indeed be the same as the mountain mentioned in the Gilgamesh epic.

It is possible that one of the earliest regions to be settled by the Noachidian peoples from neighbouring Armenia was *Anatolia*.[254] This is suggested by the great antiquity of the Neolithic archaeological finds at Çatal Hüyük in (ca. 7th millennium B.C.). The civilisation of Syro-Palestine may be even as old as that of Anatolia since settlements in Jordan are traceable from the late 7th millennium B.C. and in Byblos from the 6th.[255]

Following the archaeological finds from Anatolia and **Syro-Palestine** are those from **Susa** in **Elam**. Susa I dates from the sixth to the fifth millennium B.C. [Berossus' history mentions as the first king after the flood Euekhoios,[256] whose name may be a veiled Greek reference to Susa or a "man (=king) of Susa" (Greek "eu" corresponding to Sanskrit "su"), since it does not seem to correspond to the fragmentary name of the first king of Kish in the Sumerian king-list (Ga...ur)]. The earlier settlements in the Elamite highlands than in the neighbouring river-valleys may be due to the fact that it was not originally possible to cultivate land in the swampy plains of Mesopotamia.[257] Speiser

---

The Epic of Gilgamesh, tr. M.G. Kovacs, Stanford: Stanford University Press, 1985, p.11 3).

[254] Though the urban Neolithic achievements at Çatal Hüyük seem to be older than those in Armenia, there is evidence of similar development at the border of ancient Armenia in Jarmo (see D. Lang, *Armenia: Cradle of Civilization*, London: George Allen and Unwin, 1 980, p.61).

[255] See G.W. Ahlstrom, *Ancient Palestine: A historical Introduction*, Minneapolis: Fortress Press, 2002; J. Cauvin, *Religions néolithiques de Syro-Palestine*, Paris: J. Maisonneuve,1 972; S.A. Cook, *op. cit* ; for Jericho, see K.M. Kenyon, *Digging up Jericho*, London: E. Benn, 1957.

[256] Reported by Alexander Polyhistor (see G.P. Verbrugghe and J.M. Wickersham, *Berossus and Manetho, introduced and translated: Native Traditions in ancient Mesopotamia and Egypt*, Ann Arbor, MI: University of Michigan Press, 1996, p.51).

[257] See H. Nissen, *The Early History of the Ancient near East 9000-2000 B.C.*, tr. E.

considered Susa I to be related to similar cultures scattered across the whole of Mesopotamia and Persia, as well as in Armenia, Baluchistan, and a little later in Eridu.[258] He, along with Frankfort, conjectured that the source of this culture may have been in Armenia itself, especially since the farthest northern site to yield pottery of the Susa I type is Mt. Ararat.[259] So it is possible that we have in Elam, as in earliest Anatolia and Palestine, the same Noachidian proto-Dravidian people.

As for the biblical account of the earliest Elamites, we note that the Table of Nations in Genesis 10-11 considers Elam as a son of **Shem**. This suggests that a major constituent of the proto-Dravidian/Hurrian population in Elam may have been proto-Akkadian Semites since the Akkadians are the earliest Semites noted in Mesopotamia.[260] However, these proto-Akkadians may well have been just proto-Dravidians speaking the Akkadian dialect of the "eldest son" of Noah, Shem. The resemblances to Sanskritic vocabulary in Akkadian must derive from the common proto-Dravidian source which produced both Akkadian and, later, Sanskrit. The Akkadian word for the Abyss, "apsu", is related to the "Sanskritic" word for water, "ap". The Akkadian term "sibittu" for seven is also remarkably similar to the Hurrian "šitta" and the Indo-Aryan "sapta".[261] Similarly, the Sanskrit term "hiranya" for "gold" is related to the Akkadian "hurasu", though the source of them both may have been the Hurrian, or proto-Hurrian, "hiyarruhe". The Akkadian word "atmanu" for "sanctum" (Gilgamesh V,249, Anzu I,56) is also cognate with the Sanskritic "atman", meaning soul, and is related as well to the Egyptian Amun (imin), who is called the "inner support" of the entire universe.[262] The Akkadian "atmanu" is the source also of

---

Lutzeier and K.J. Northcott, Chicago: University of Chicago Press, 1 988, pp.55ff.

[258] See E. Speiser, *Mesopotamian Origins*, p.63f.

[259] *Ibid.*, pp.65ff. Speiser placed the "original center" of the First Aenolithic culture "somewhere between Anatolia and the Caspian" (p.66).

[260] See A. Jacob, *Ātman*.

[261] See E.A. Speiser, *Introduction to Hurrian*, p.82. The close relationship between the Hurrians and Indo-Aryans is discussed below p.154.

[262] See A. Annus, *The Standard Babylonian Epic of Anzu*, Helsinki: The Neo-Assyrian Text Corpus Project, 2001, p.xi.

the Sumero-Akkadian term "temmenu"/"temen" for a foundation-stone, particularly that of a temple.[263]

Of the early **Ubaid** culture of southern Mesopotamia, **Eridu**, which dates from the sixth millennium B.C., also shows marked Elamite affinities. As Frankfort pointed out, in Elam "the stage corresponding with al-Ubaid" was found "overlying that called 'Susa I'".[264] According to Speiser, the original name of Ku'ara (near Eridu) in the first dynasty of Uruk[265] - HA.Aki - may be of **Subarian**, or **proto-Hurrian** origin.[266] The very term "subari" or, more precisely, "suwari",[267] is related to Suvalliyat (Suvariya)/Surya, which is also the Hititte/Indic name of the sun-god. Hurri then would be the Iranian pronunciation of the same name, as the Iranian name of the sun-god, "Hvare", suggests. The Subarians (Hurrians) were traditionally identified as a northern highland people, though they may have moved south to Elam as well.[268] The presence of the Hurrians in southern Mesopotamia is attested from the Old Babylonian period since magical ritual tablets of this epoch contain Hurrian language texts.[269]

The wide-ranging extent of the Ubaid culture is evident from the fact that even the most northern city of Nineveh was continuously occupied from the fifth millennium.[270] The earliest sites of northern

---

[263] See *Akkadisches Wörterbuch* III:1 346. This term is carried over into Greek as "τέμενος".

[264] H. Frankfort, *Archaeology and the Sumerian Problem*, Chicago: Chicago University Press, 1 932, p.1 9.

[265] See T. Jacobsen, *The Sumerian King-List*, p.89. It may also be related to the original Akkadian A.a for Ea.

[266] See E. Speiser, *Mesopotamian Origins*, p.38f.

[267] Ibid., p.39n; cf. the letter of Rîb-Aeldi, Prince of Byblos, which refers to the land of Suru, which may be synonymous with Subartu (see A. Ungnad, *op.cit.*, p.50).

[268] According to Landsberger, the pre-Sumerian "Proto-Euphratians" of the south are to be distinguished from the pre-Semitic "Proto-Tigridians" of the north (see B. Landsberger, "The Beginnings of Civilization in Mesopotamia" [1944], in *Three Essays*).

[269] See G. Wilhelm, *Grundzüge der Geschichte und Kultur der Hurriter*, Darmstadt: Wissenschaftliche Buchgesellschaft, 1 982, p.97.

[270] See G. Leick, *Mesopotamia: The Invention of the City*, London: Penguin

Mesopotamian culture are indeed to be found in **Tel el Halaf**, dating back to around 5000 B.C.[271] The powerful influence of the Halafian culture is attested in the imitations of its pottery in southern Armenia[272] as well as in north-eastern Syria.[273] One major distinction of the northern culture is the aesthetically more advanced state of the pottery of the Tel al Halaf region in the north, which is contemporaneous with Ubaid I. The Ubaid I pottery of the delta, dating from even before 5000 B.C., on the other hand, is characterised by a much lower level of craftsmanship and artistry.[274] The Tel el Halaf pottery is marked by bucranium designs[275] which associate it with the seventh millennium shrines of Çatal Hüyük in eastern Anatolia,[276] which may have been established by the earliest proto-Dravidians or Hurrians. However, recently, Oates has shown that, in spite of their qualitative differences, there are generic similarities also between the Samarra and the Ubaid pottery.[277] And Charvat has revealed that the fundamental social and religious forms of later Mesopotamian culture, including that of Uruk, are evident already in embryonic form in the early chalcolithic sites of northern Mesopotamia.[278] **Cremated practices** associated with **fire-rituals** are noticed here[279] and Tell Arpachiyah (TT6) also gives the first evidence of the use of the white-red-black colour triad

---

Books, 2000, p.222. Similarly Nippur, south of Babylon, was inhabited from the fifth millennium (ibid., p.1 43) and Sippar, farther north, is mentioned in early cosmogonical texts, as one of the oldest cities in the land, much like Eridu (*ibid.*, p.1 72).

[271] See J. Finegan, *Archaeological History of the Ancient Middle East*, Boulder, CO: Westview Press, 1979, p.7.

[272] See D. Lang, *Armenia*, p.63.

[273] See G.W. Ahlström, *The History of Ancient Palestine*, p.107.

[274] *Ibid.*, p.9.

[275] *Ibid.*, p.7.

[276] For Çatal Hüyük, see J. Mellaart, *Çatal Hüyük: A Neolithic Town in Anatolia*, London: Thames and Hudson, 1967; also H. Nissen, *op.cit.*, p.35f.

[277] See J. Oates, "Ur and Eridu: the Prehistory", *Iraq* 22 (1 960), p.42, where she suggests a common ancestry for both Samarra and early Eridu.

[278] See P. Charvat, *op. cit.*, pp.92,96.

[279] *Ibid.*, pp.45,90.

which persists from chalcolithic times to Uruk[280] and is representative of the three original castes of the Indo-Europeans, priests, warriors and agriculturists.[281] So we may assume that the proto-Dravidians/Hurrians including proto-Akkadians were present in the north as well as in Elam and Eridu. Since Armenia is the most likely place from which the cultures of both Çatal Hüyük and Tel el Halaf may have originated, it is probable that we are dealing, in the case of the sixth- and fifth millennium pottery of the north as well as the south, with the proto-Dravidian or Noachidian race.

Since Ham is, in the early Jahvist version of Genesis, considered to be the "youngest son of Noah",[282] it is likely that **Japheth** indeed represents the second oldest branch of the Indo-Europeans. Although the earliest attested religions are those of the Semites and the Hamites, the Japhetic Āryans share the same cosmological insights since they are derived from a common source. The Āryans are generally divided into eastern, "shatem" and western, "centum" Āryans. Regarding the **western Āryan** peoples, we must note that, in *Genesis* 9:2, the eldest son of Japheth [the Āryans] is called Gamer, representing the Cimmerians, and he is followed by the Magog[283] (Magi) and the Madai (Medes), Javan (Greeks), Tubal (uncertain),[284] Meschech (uncertain)[285] and Tiras

---

[280] *Ibid.*, p.92. In Greek antiquity, black may have denoted prime matter, red matter and white spirit (ibid., p.93). This corresponds to the three basic energies in Indian philosophy, Tamas, Rajas, Sattva. In Egypt, Osiris is frequently represented with black skin, indicating perhaps his lordship of Earth and of the dead (see R.H. Wilkinson, *Symbol and Magic in Egyptian Art*, London: Thames and Hudson, 1994, p.109).The association of the three Indian castes with these colours is due to the predominance of the sattvic, rajasic, and tamasic elements, respectively, in them.

[281] In India, there are four colours (varnas) since there are four castes (see, for instance, *Brahmānda Purāna* I,ii,1 5,1 8ff.). While white represents the Brahman and red the Kshatriya, the general populace (Vaisya) are distinguished from the servile part of the population (Shudras), the former represented by the colour yellow and the latter by black.

[282] See *The Interpreter's Bible*, I:560.

[283] Gog and Magog are, in *Ezekiel* 39:2 and elsewhere, representatives of the far North.

[284] Josephus (*Jewish Antiquities*, I: 6) identified Tubal with the Iberians.

[285] According to Josephus, *op.cit.*, Meschech corresponded to the Cappodocians.

(uncertain).[286] The Cimmerians themselves are described by Herodotus (IV,14) as having had their initial home "on the shores of the Black Sea". The Cimmerians are probably identical to the most ancient **Celts**, since the **Welsh** (who are a **southern Celtic** people like the Bretons) call themselves, to this day, "Cymry". Diodorus Siculus (Bibliotheca Historica V,32) also states that the Celts living close to the Black Sea are scattered "as far as Scythia" and the **northernmost of these** Celtic tribes are the wildest and most powerful having apparently "wandered across and laid waste the whole of Asia, under the then name of Cimmerians". Diodorus describes the Celts as being tall, blond and well-built, but he may be referring more particularly to the northern Goidelic Celts, that is, the Irish and Scottish. The southern Celts, however, seem to have been more conservative in their tradition since they still bear the original name of the race. Indeed, the priority of the southern Celts appears also in the reference in Parthenius of Nicaea's *Erotica Pathemata* (30, 1-2) to Celtine as a daughter of Bretannus (whose name is borne by the southern Celtic Bretons), who fell in love with Heracles and gave birth to Celtus (who represents the Celts).

We may, at this juncture, consider another branch of the proto-Dravidian stock that seems to have spread through Celtic Europe as a priestly sect, namely the Druids.[287] Apart from the phonetic similarity of "Druid" to "Dravida",[288] we may also notice the mention of "the Dravidas, the Kambojas [who dwelt next to the Gandharas in the extreme north-west of the Indian sub-continent,[289] the Yavanas [Ionians, Greeks], the Sakas [Scythians]" in the *Manusmrithi*, X:43, as Kshatriya (or noble) races that do not perform the sacred rites of the Āryans and do not venerate the Brahmans [even though, as we shall see below, the religious precepts of Brahmanism were indeed learned from the proto-Dravidians][290] and have therefore been relegated to the

---

[286] Josephus considered Tiras as representing the Thracians.

[287] See S. Piggott, *The Druids*, London: Thames and Hudson, 1975.

[288] "v" is, in ancient IE languages, pronounced "u".

[289] It is possible that the Kambojas were an Iranian tribe since Cambyses (6th c. B.C.) was called Kambujiya in Persian.

[290] See below pp.161,249.

status of Shudras, or members of the fourth caste. The list contained here is of Indo-European, and not Indian, tribes and the original Dravidians may well have been related to the Druids.

The Druids may have been the priests of the Cimmerian Celts when the latter moved into Europe, especially Gaul and Britain.[291] In classical texts, the name of the Druids appears mostly in a plural form, as "druidai" (Gk.) or "druidae" or "druides" (Lt.).[292] In Irish, "drai" or "druí" is the singular form of a word meaning "wise man", of which "draod" or "druid" is the plural. The association of the Druids with the Greek word for "oak", first made by Pliny (*Historia Naturalis* XVI,95), is probably a later one due to the importance of tree-worship among the ancient Druids, as well as amongst most of the ancient Hamitic and Semitic peoples, since the sacred tree serves as a symbol of the divine phallus representing the life of the universe.[293]

Piggott believed that the Druidic tradition may go back to at least the second millenium B.C. since it has much in common with the Indo-European language and ideology, especially Sanskritic and Hittite.[294] However, it is quite possible that the Druids were settled in Europe even earlier than the Āryans, perhaps as early as the third millennium B.C. The three-headed god attributable to the Druids in the Marne and the Côte d'Or is possibly related to the three- (or four-) headed god of the Indus Valley of the third millennium B.C.[295] Hence it is not surprising that Clement of Alexandria believed that the Pythagorean and Greek philosophers derived their wisdom from the Gauls and other barbarians,[296] by which he no doubt meant the Druidic

---

[291] The theory of the non-Celtic origin of the Druids is especially supported by the fact that, outside Britian and Gaul, there is no evidence of such priests in other Celtic territories such as the Danube, the Cisalpine and Transalpine Gaul. The Druidic type is perhaps most evident today among the Welsh, whose manner of English pronunciation is remarkably similar to that of the South Indians.

[292] See S. Piggott, *op. cit.*, p.89.

[293] See A. Jacob, *op. cit.*, Ch.XVI.

[294] See S. Piggott, *op. cit.*, p.74.

[295] See the illustration in M. Jansen, *Die Indus-Zivilisation: Wiederentdeckung einer frühen Hochkultur*, Köln: DuMont, 1986. The fourth head of the god is invisible since it is turned backwards.

[296] See S. Piggott, *op. cit.*, p.81.

priestly core of these tribes. Dio Chrysostom (1 st c. A.D.) considered the Druids as being similar to the Persian, Magi, Egyptian priests and Indian Brāhmans.

Among the Gauls, the Druids, along with the "equites", constituted the nobility. The priestly caste of the Celts was itself divided into three orders, "bards", "vates" (interpreters of sacrifices) and "druids" (natural and moral philosophers).[297] These three orders correspond to the three major officiating priests at Vedic rituals, the brahmans, the adhvaryus, and the udgātrs. Like Sanskrit, the Druidic language was an unwritten one, since, as Caesar reports, this guarded the secret wisdom of the Druids from the lay public.[298] It is particularly interesting that the only form of writing that has been associated with the Druids is the cryptic one called "ogam" or "ogham", terms that are related to Irish "oigheam" meaning "secret meaning". The symbolical poetic style of classical Dravidian literature is also called "agam" (meaning "interior") as distinguished from the plainer style called "puram" (meaning "exterior").

The religion of the Druids was clearly cosmological, as is attested in the commentaries of Caesar, who attributed to them much knowledge of the stars and their motion, and of the size of the world.[299] Ammianus Marcellinus declared that they investigated "problems of things secret and sublime".[300] Diodorus Siculus, following Posidonius, maintained that they held that "the souls of men are immortal, and that after a definite number of years they have a second life when the soul passes to another body",[301] which is also the doctrine of the most ancient Dravidians who formulated the tenets of Indian religion. It may be noted however that there is no evidence of fire-worship among the Druids such as became characteristic of the Indo-Āryans and Iranians.[302]

---

[297] Ibid., p.92.

[298] See Caesar, Gallic Wars, VI,14.

[299] Ibid.

[300] See S. Piggott, op. cit., p.101.

[301] Ibid., p.102.

[302] See below p. 156.

Although the Celts are western Japhetic Āryans, the sons of Gamer, in the biblical Table of Nations, include Ashkenaz (the Scythians, who are eastern Japhetic Āryans), Riphath (uncertain)[303] and Thokarmah (uncertain).[304] The Celts and the Scythians are closely associated, as is indicated by Strabo (XI,7,2) who states that the Greek authors called all the northern populations Scythians or Celtoscythians. Asclepiades of Thrace refers to the legendary king Boreas as a king of the Celts (*Probus ad Virgil. Georg.*, II,84) while in other authors he appears as a king of the Scythians, though the Scythians are younger than the Cimmerians. According to Herodotus (IV,3), the Scythians considered themselves as the "youngest of all nations".

The close relation between the later Celts and the Scythians is attested also in the 7th-12th century Irish *Auraicept na n-Éces*, which states that the Scythian king Fenius Farsaid travelled along with Goidel mac Ethéoir to Shinar (Sumer) to study the confused languages at the tower of Nimrod and there devised the Goidelic language as well as the esoteric system of writing called Ogham.[305] The reference to the Tower of Babel suggests that the emergence of the northern Celtic tribes may have occurred in the fourth or third millennium B.C. Fenius is also said to have married Scota, the daughter of the Pharaoh Cingris, and their offspring was Goidel Glas, who represents the Gaelic people. The northern Goidelic Celts (the Irish and the Scots) are thus seen to be contemporaneous with the Scythians who are represented in Genesis as a "son" of Gamer, whereas the Cimmerians (Gamer) or Bretonic Celts are clearly older.

The reference to Babel seems also to be authenticated by the appellation of the Celtic sun-god, Belenus, which must be related to Baal of the Canaanites. The Irish god of thunder, Tuireann, however

---

[303] Josephus (*op.cit.*) identifies Riphath with the Paphlagonians (of north central Anatolia).

[304] It is possible that Tokarmah represents the Tokharians, or the early Germans, who were called Tungri (see below p.48). Josephus (*op.cit.*) identifies Tokarmah with the Phrygians. The 3rd century Hippolytus of Rome (*Chronicle*) identifies the name with the Armenians.

[305] According to the *Lebor Gabála Érenn* (11th C), Fénius Farsaid the Scythian prince travelled to Mesopotamia to help build Nimrod's Tower of Babel.

is related to the Hittite Tarhun (another name of the "weather-god", Teshup) as well as to the Germanic Thor, who is also said to have lived first in Anatolia.[306] The continuance of the solar religion of the Indo-Europeans among the Celts is also glimpsed in the Irish legend that recounts the union of Érin (Ireland) in spring with one of the fabled kings of Ireland, Mac Greine, whose name means "son of the sun" and who is perhaps identifiable with Lug or Lugh, the Celtic equivalent of the storm-god Indra/Thor who represents the power of the sun at its zenith.[307]

The chief branches of the eastern Āryan group are the Iranians, Indians, and Scythians.[308] Of these, the Indians and Iranians seem to have preserved best, in their oral hieratic linguistic tradition, the philosophical import of the ancient cosmology of the proto-Dravidians/Hurrians. This spiritual focus is evident in all of the Indic Vedic and Sanskritic literature, which was originally oral and not committed to writing until relatively recently.[309]

That the **Scythians** themselves derived their limited cosmological understanding and religious practices from their Indo-Iranian kinsmen is clear from their linguistic borrowings such as the word for hemp, which in most Central Asian cultures is derived from the Iranian "bhangha".[310] The predominance of the Iranian language in the regions inhabited by Cimmerians and Scythians, that is, from the Danube to the Dnieper, is evidenced also by the names of the Danube, Dnieper and Dniester, which employ the Avestan term "danu" for river. Indeed, this area corresponds to that inhabited by the Slavs and we may reasonably consider the Scythians as the forbears of the latter.[311]

---

[306] See below p.162f

[307] See R.S. Loomis, *The Grail*, p.52.

[308] The Scythians form an integral part of the Indo-Iranian group, but their spiritual tradition seems to have been less developed (see below p.152).

[309] For the early oral history of Sanskrit, see A.A. Macdonell, *A History of Sanskrit Literature*, Delhi: Munshiram Manoharlal, 1961 , p.20f, and C.K. Raja, Survey of Sanskrit Literature, Bombay: Bharatiya Vidya Bhavan, 1962, pp.11 ,1 68.

[310] See M. Eliade, *op. cit.*, p.400f.

[311] The Slavic word for god "bog" is thus also derived from Iranian "baga" and

The Biblical Table of Nations represents the most ancient Iranians, Indians and Greeks as being as old as the Cimmerians, who were older than the Scythians. The first historical accounts of the Iranians and the Indians, however, suggest that they, like the northern Goidelic Celts, became closely associated with the Scythians, who seem to have borrowed many of the religious elements from their Iranian and Indian neighbours.

One religious practice that links the Scythians to the Indo-Iranians is their custom of soma-drinking which accounts for their ancient designation as "hoamavarga", or "soma-drinking", Scythians.[312] However, Eliade's researches in Central Asian shamanism, which may be a vestige of ancient Scythian religious practice, point to a rather rudimentary practical application of the spiritual bases of the cosmological religion of the ancients in the shamanistic rituals.[313] The use of intoxicants for the acquisition of transcendental states is, according to Eliade, a relatively inferior path in comparison to the inner spiritual discipline advocated by yoga,[314] and the reduction of yogic knowledge to ecstatic flights among the shamans[315] is an indication of a certain degeneration of the wisdom of the ancient Near East in its transmission to the north. As Eliade pointed out,

> let us emphasize once again the structural difference that distinguishes classic Yoga from shamanism. Although the latter is not without certain techniques of concentration, … its final goal is always ecstasy and the soul's ecstatic journey through the various cosmic regions, whereas Yoga pursues entasis, final concentration on the spirit and "escape" from the cosmos.[316]

Sanskrit "bhaga". Indeed the close similarity between Slavic, even modern Slavic, and Sanskrit confirms the continuity of the Scythians in the Slavic race.

[312] So in the inscriptions of Darius I (see P.O. Skjaervo, in G. Erdosy, *op.cit*, p.157).

[313] Cf. M. Eliade's discussion of shamanism among the Scythians, *op.cit.*, pp.394ff.

[314] See M. Eliade, *op.cit.*, p.401.

[315] The term "shaman" may be related to the typical Indian Brāhmanical patronymic "Sharman" (the corresponding patronymics for the Kshatriyas, Vaishyas and Shudras being "Varman", "Gupta" and "Dāsa"; see VP III,10,9).

[316] *Ibid.*, p.417.

The **Indians**, like the Iranians and Scythians, seem to have originally been a nomadic tribe. We may remember Megasthenes' report that

> The Indians were in old times nomadic, like those Scythians who did not till the soil, but roamed about in their wagons, as the seasons varied, from one part of Scythia to another, neither dwelling in towns nor worshipping in temples;[317] and that the Indians likewise had neither towns nor temples of the gods, but were so barbarous that they wore the skins of such wild animals as they could kill ... they subsisted also on such wild animals as they could catch, eating the flesh raw, - before, at least, the coming of Dionysus into India. Dionysus, however, when he came and had conquered the people, founded cities and gave laws to these cities, and introduced the use of wine among the Indians, as he had done among the Greeks, and taught them to sow the land, himself supplying seeds for the purpose ... It is also said that Dionysus first yoked oxen to the plough, and made many of the Indians husbandmen instead of nomads, and furnished them with the implements of agriculture; and that the Indians worship the other gods, and Dionysus himself in particular, with cymbals and drums, because he so taught them ... and that he instructed the Indians to let their hair grow long in honour of the god ....[318]

Since Megasthenes refers to a time when the Indo-Āryans formed part of the Scythian tribes and the settlement of the former in the Indus Valley civilisation precedes the development of Greek culture in the west, it is possible that the Dionysus Megasthenes refers to is not just the Greek god of the Hellenes but his earlier form as the solar god An/Horus the Elder-Osiris.[319] Further, the earliest evidence of the Dravidian solar deity Muruga (Skanda) in South India reveals the

---

[317] The fact that the Scythians did not build temples or worship divine images is mentioned also by Herodotus, *Histories*, I,131.

[318] See Arrian, *Indica*, VII (in R.C. Majumdar, Classical Accounts, p.220f.).

[319] See below pp.188,191,198.

features of a Dionysiac god[320] so that we may be right in maintaining that the civilisation of the Indo-Scythians by the Greeks referred to by Megasthenes is a Hellenisation of an earlier cultural contact between the early Indo-Scythian settlers of north-western India and Elamite Dravidians/Hurrians from the Zagros region.[321]

Literary evidence of the religion of the Indo-Āryans is manifest rather late, in the 16th century B.C., in the northern Mesopotamian kingdom of the **Mitanni**.[322] The original home of the Mitanni remains uncertain. The fact that the Scythians do not exhibit much sophistication in their religious rituals (Herodotus, IV,59) suggests that the Mitanni were not likely to have derived their cosmological insights from their Scythian kinsmen but from their earliest habitation amongst the Hurrians and Akkadians of northern Mesopotamia. It is possible that they may have arrived from the BMAC in Afghanistan (settled from 2200-1700 B.C.), where the evidence of fire-altars confirms the presence of Vedic Āryans.[323] That there was trade between Bactria and North Syria is also proved by the fact that from the 18th c. B.C. north Syrian seals show a typically Central Asian Bactrian camel such as is depicted in the BMAC seals.[324] However, there seems to be little evidence of fire-altars in the Mitanni region itself and it is equally possible that the Mitanni descended directly into Mesopotamia from the Caspian region rather than moving westwards from Afghanistan. The Mitanni themselves may be identifiable with the Medes, and, as Herodotus (VII,69) reveals, the Medes were once universally called Arians,[325] as well as perhaps

---

[320] See below p. 157.

[321] The theory that Āryan is pre-Harappan was put forward by A.D. Pusalkar, "Pre-Harappan, Harappan", pp.233ff.

[322] The original cuneiform spelling of the kingdom used by Suttarna I (early 16th c. B.C.) was apparently "Ma-i-ta-ni" (see I. Gelb, *Hurrians and Subarians*, p.70).

[323] This is the view of A. Parpola, "The Problem of the Aryans", p.369.

[324] *Ibid.*, p.362.

[325] That the name "Mede" may be related to the term Mitanni has been suggested by J. Charpentier, "The Date of Zoroaster"; B. Landsberger and T. Bauer, "Zu neueröffentlichen Geschichtsquellen"; E. Forrer, "Stratification des langues"; and F. Cornelius, "Erin-Manda".

with the proto-Iranians, since several Median words are traceable in Old Persian.[326] It is clear that the Mitanni culture informs both the Indo-Āryan and the Iranian.

The Mitanni exhibit an adherence to an Indo-Āryan, Vedic, and not Zoroastrian Avestan, form of religion along with the Hurrian. The Indo-Āryan culture, as we have seen, may have been a combination of that of the earliest Elamite and Mesopotamian Hurrians who adopted fire-rituals from the northern "Gandaridae" of the BMAC no earlier than the 23rd c. B.C. The first coherent list of Indic gods in the treaty of the Mitanni-Hurrian king Šattiwaza and the Hittite king Šuppililiumas I dating from the sixteenth century B.C. includes the names Mitra-Varuna, Indra, and Nāsatyas,[327] though Indra and Naonhaithya came to be considered as demons by the Zoroastrians. It is important to note that the Hurro-Akkadian version of the Lord of the Waters among the Mitanni is 'Uruwana' or 'Aruna'. In the Vedic *GB*, I,1,7, Varana[328] is indeed the secret form of the name Varuna,[329] and this repeats the penultimate vowel of both (Mitanni) "Uruwana" and (Gk.) "Ouranos". The form "Aruna" is perhaps related to the Hittite term for "ocean" "arunas",[330] which exhibits the vowel-shift of "a" to "u" that resulted in the Vedic Varuna. Further, the Sumerian name of the sun-god Utu may have been conserved in the Vedic Brāhmanas as the secret name of Sūrya, Ud.[331] The fact that some of the esoteric

---

[326] See P.O. Skjaervo, in G.Erdosy, *op.cit.*, p.159.

[327] The text (CTH 51 and 52 (see D. Yoshida, *op.cit.*, p.12; cf. V. Haas, *Geschichte*, p.543) reads "Dingir MešMitraššiel, Dingir MešUruwanaššiel, DIndar, Dingir MešNašattiyana", where the prefix "šiel" is uncertain. The Nāsatyas are the Ashvins.

[328] Following the example of Latin phonology, we may assume that the original Sanskrit of this region also favoured the "u" sound for the phoneme later transcribed with a "v".

[329] "being Varana, he is mystically called Varuna, because the gods love mysticism" (see U. Chouduri, *Indra and Varuna*, p.95).

[330] See G. Wilhelm, "Meer" in *RLA* VIII:3. Wilhelm suggests that this term is not of Indo-European origin [by which he no doubt means that which is properly called Āryan; see p.108n above], but, rather, Hattic.

[331] See *Taittriyopanishad Brāhmana*, I,45,4: "Yonder sun, that same is *ud*, fire is *gi* [cf. the Sumerian fire-god, Girra], the moon is *tham*".

names of the Indo-Āryan deities, Agni (as Agri) and Sūrya (as Ud), are possibly of Sumerian origin suggests that the Sanskrit language itself may have been fully developed only after the establishment of the Sumerian Uruk culture.[332] The priesthood at Uruk too must have included a brāhmanical element that persisted from Ubaid times. It is possible also that the brāhmanical language behind Akkadian "apsu" and Sumerian "abzu" was ultimately proto-Dravidian/Hurrian, which was loaned into Āryan, Akkadian and Sumerian equally.

The presence of Indo-Āryan cultural elements in later Mesopotamia is attested by the occurrence of the divine names Mitra, Gishnu [Vishnu][333] and Sūrya [as 'Suliaat', from Hittite-Hurrian 'Suwaliyatta'][334] in the Sumerian god-list contained in CT 25, which, though dating from Assyrian times, around the seventh century B.C., must reflect a more ancient list of Sumerian deities translated into Akkadian. The description of the fire-god Girra as the "child of the Apsu" in an Akkadian hymn to the fire-god[335] also corresponds exactly to Agni's typical appellation "apām napāt", child of the waters.

It is to be noted that the Āryans designated the Dasyus or non-Āryans as Anagni, the fireless. The reference in *Manusmrithi* X:43-45 to "the Dravidas, the Kāmbojas, the Yavanas [Ionians], the Sakas [Scythians], etc." as Kshatriya races which have sunk to the level of Shūdras on account of their neglect of the sacred rites and the authority of the Brāhmans suggests that Brāhmanism, though based on the spiritual insights of the proto-Dravidians, was formulated by the Indo-Āryans as an exclusively fire-worshipping cult. Although the Āryan religion was based on fire-rituals, there is as yet little archaeological evidence of fire-worship in the north.[336] However,

---

[332] See below pp.166ff.

[333] The lack of the "w" phoneme accounts for the translation of Vishnu into Gishnu in the Sumerian, "g" regularly substituting "w" in that language.

[334] See H.G. Güterbock, "The god Suwalliyat reconsidered".

[335] See M.J. Seux, *Hymnes et Prières*, p.251.

[336] Recently, however, Anders Kaliff (*Fire, Water, Heaven and Earth*) has suggested that Bronze Age and early Iron Age cremation sites in Scandinavia from around 1800 B.C. to 400 A.D. point to the probable use of sacrificial fire and altars in rituals

from 2200-1700 B.C., there is clear evidence of typical Indo-Āryan settlement in the Bactro-Margiana Archaeological Complex (BMAC). The BMAC is not far north of Mundigak, where from 3000 B.C. we notice extensions of Elamite culture resembling that of the Indus Valley.[337] It is difficult to determine whether the Āryan settlements of BMAC represent a continuation of the early Elamite Hurrians of Mundigak or are new immigrants from the Andronovo culture associated with the Indo-Āryans (1800-900 B.C.).[338] The latter is indeed the more probable. The Andronovo culture is itself derived from the Hut Grave and Catacomb Grave culture of 2800-2000 B.C.[339] and the **Sintashta culture** of the southeast Urals (2300-1900 B.C.),[340] which is marked by chariot burials and may have been proto-Āryan rather than proto-Indo-Āryan. The fact that there is clear evidence of fire-worship in the BMAC and little evidence of it in Mundigak suggests that the former is derived from the Andronovo rather than from the Elamite colonies. Elaborate fire altars are evident in the ruins of the BMAC complex which correspond to the Āryan fire-sacrifices. The temples also contain rooms with "all the necessary apparatus for the preparation of drinks extracted from poppy, hemp and ephedra" that may have been used for the soma-rituals.[341] The BMAC may have thus been the centre of cultural contact between the proto-Dravidian/Hurrian peoples of Mundigak and the later Indo-Āryans. It is interesting to note too, in this context, that the

akin to the Vedic.

[337] Herodotus's description of the inhabitants of the various satrapies of Darius suggests that this region in Afghanistan may have been settled by Bactrians (Darius' 12th province) or Sattagydae, Gandaridae, Dadicae and Aparytae (7th province) (cf. J.P. Mallory and V. H. Mair, *The Tarim Mummies*, p.45f.; p.262).

[338] Andronovo type pottery has been found in the early layers of Margiana (see A. Parpola, "The problem of the Aryans", p.363).

[339] The Hut Grave culture apparently separated into the Timber Grave (proto-Iranian) and Andronovo (proto-Āryan) cultures. The fourth millennium predecessor of the Hut Grave and Catacomb Grave cultures may have been the **Yamnaya culture** dating from 3500-2800 B.C. (*ibid.*, p.356).

[340] See J.P. Mallory and VH. Mair, *op. cit.*, pp.260f.

[341] *Ibid.*, p.262.

Avesta (which is geographically centred in eastern Iran) mentions the Māzanian daevas as worshippers of the Indian gods. According to Burrow, Māzana is known in Iranian sources as the territory between the southern shore of the Caspian Sea and the Alburz mountains.[342] It may be related also to Margiana and the Indo-Āryan culture noted there.

It must be noted that there are indeed fire-altars even in the Harappan sites of **Kalibangan**, in Rajastan, and **Lothal**, in Gujarat, which may be dated to around 2500 B.C. Indeed, the Allchins surmise that there were probably also fire-altars in Harappa and Mohenjaro Daro though these have been missed in the mass-diggings conducted at these sites.[343]

In any case, it is clear that fire-worship was maintained particularly by the Āryan branch of the Indo-Europeans. For, fire-worship is also observed among the Prussian-Lithuanian cult of szwenta (holy fire), and the Scythians too worshipped a goddess called Tabit whose name may be related to the Sanskrit 'tapti' denoting heat. The Greeks and Romans also maintained a cult of hestia or vesta.[344] Plutarch (*Numa*, II) informs us that "Numa is said to have built the temple of Vesta in circular form as protection for the inextinguishable fire, copying not the fire of the earth as being Vesta, but of the whole universe, as centre of which the Pythagoreans believe fire to be established, and this they call Hestia and the monad".

On the other hand, we must remember Herodotus' statement that the Iranians did not worship fire originally.[345] In the Purānas, too, Pururavas, the early Aila [=Elamite?] king, is said to have obtained sacrificial fire from the "Gandharvas", who also taught him the constitution of the three sacred fires of the Āryans.[346] Pururavas is

---

[342] See E.Bryant, *Quest*, p.130.

[343] See R. and B. Allchin, *The rise of civilization*, p.183. See also D. K. Chakrabarti, "The archaeology of Hinduism", pp.44f.

[344] See M. Sharma, *Fire-worship*, p.19.

[345] See *Herodotus*, Histories, I,132.

[346] See F.E. Pargiter, *op.cit.*, p.309. In the *Mbh* I, 75, Pururavas is said to have brought the three kinds of sacrificial fire from the Gandharvas.

stated in the Puranas to be an Aila king of Pratishthana. The Ailas themselves are designated as Karddameyas which relates them to the river Karddama in Iran, particularly in the region of Balkh.[347] The kshatriya ruler of the lunar dynasty, Pururavas, is, according to the *Bhavishya Purāna*, Pratisarg 3, the son of Budh, the son of the Moon, Chandra,[348] who himself was the son of the sage Atri born of Brahma. The rise of both Chandra and Pururavas is dated to the Treta Yuga.

Fire-worship was thus perhaps not universal among the earliest Āryan tribes. The fact that the Pururavas are said to have learnt the fire-rituals from the **Gandharvas** suggests that the early Hurrians of Elam and the earliest Iranians did not worship fire and learnt it from a more northerly wave of Āryans who must have, at a very early date, moved eastwards from their Armenian homeland. However, even the Gandharas are included among the Aila [=Elamite?] dynasties in the Purānas, which suggests that these Āryans too were a northern and eastern branch of proto-Hurrians identifiable with the Japhetites. The Japhetic tribes that moved northwards to the Pontic-Caspian steppes created the **Yamnaya** culture there[349] which is considered the major source of the Āryan tribes.[350]

The Gandaridae are also mentioned by Herodotus (III,91) as one of the Indian tribes of the seventh satrapy of Darius I (550-486 B.C.) and can be located near the Bactrians of the 12th satrapy. The archaeological evidence of the early Gandharvas may be that found in the Gandhara Grave culture of the Swat settled from 1700-1400 B.C., which followed the BMAC. The occupants of the BMAC may

---

[347] See *Rāmāyana* VII,103,21ff.

[348] Budh was married to Ila, the daughter of Manu Vaivaswat or Shrāddhadeva.

[349] W. Bernard suggested that the human remains from Period I of Gandhara bore resemblances to those of Bronze Age and early Iron Age crania of 2500 B.C. – A.D. 500 from the Caucasus and Volga region as well as from Tepe Hissar in Iran (see K.A.R. Kennedy, "Have Aryans been identified", p.49).

[350] See A. Parpola, "The Problem of the Aryans", p.356. It is possible that Gandharva is related to Goidelic, the term used to designate the Irish, Scots and Manx forms of Celtic, but there is little evidence of a precise fire-worshipping identity either in the archaeology or in the mythological literature of the Irish except the occurrence of the appellation "Áed" (fire) in the royal names recorded in the mediaeval Irish *Lebor Gabála Érenn*.

have been related to the same family as the later Gandhara. Since the Gandhara culture also bears the first evidence of cremation rituals in South Asia, we may consider them to have indeed consolidated the Vedic customs of the Indo-Āryans. Cremation is evidenced also in the Andronovo culture.[351] At the same time, the neighbouring Bishkent culture, which is contemporaneous with the Gandhara and is related to the northern BMAC type, exhibits also a curious quasi-Scythian custom of inhumation involving the removal of the entrails and their replacement with clarified butter which may have persisted among the Vedic Indians, as is suggested by *SB* XII,v,2,5.[352]

The Pururavas who adopted fire-worship from the Gandharas may thus represent an Elamite branch of the proto-Āryan family, while the Gandaridae, who may have arrived from the south-east Caspian region (since the BMAC culture is apparently derived from the latter)[353] may be a typically Indo-Āryan, north-eastern branch of the same family.[354] That the Indic Vedic culture itself may have been developed after an original formulation at a proto-Indo-Iranian stage is suggested by the greater elaboration of the name of the god Tvoreshtar amongst the Iranians - representing the older religion of the proto-Āryans - compared to the Vedic Tvashtr.[355] Indeed many of the characteristic traits of the rituals of ancient India derive from

---

[351] *Ibid.*, p.366. It is interesting to note, however, that the earliest Neolithic caves of Palestine in Gezer (7th millennium B.C.) already give evidence of a culture that practised cremation. Inhumation appears in these sites only much later in the fourth millennium B.C. (see S.A. Cook, *op. cit.*, p.74). This confirms the possibility that Palestine and Anatolia were first inhabited by proto-Dravidians/Hurrians before they were settled by the Armenoid peoples who practised inhumation. The early neolithic/chalcolithic levels of Yarim Tepe II (7th millennium B.C.), near Assyrian Nineveh, also reveal crematory practices (see P. Charvat, *op.cit.*, p.45). So we may assume that cremation was the earliest funereal mode of the entire Noachidian race.

[352] See A. Parpola, *op.cit.*, p.365.

[353] See J.P. Mallory and V.H. Mair, *op.cit.*, p.262.

[354] It is possible that the Gandharas themselves were later considered as not belonging to the Brāhmanical orthodoxy since, in *Mbh*, Shanti Parva, 12.65, they are classified along with the Yavanas (Greeks), Kiratas, Sakas, etc. as outsiders living within the dominion of the Indic Āryans.

[355] Cf. A. Jacob, "Cosmology and Ethics", p.96.

an Indo-Iranian period as is attested by the similarity of the terms, yajna/yaja, soma/haoma,mantra/manθra, nama/nəmô. Even the term atharvan has only an Iranian etymology âθravâ.[356]

However, it should also be remembered that this fire-worship is employed in a religion which formed the basis of the solar religions of the Sumerians or Egyptians as well. In the Sumerian religion too, the chief solar god An is equated to Girra, the fire-god (in an Assyrian exegetical text)[357] and Re in Egypt is the same as the solar force, Agni. So that it is possible that the adoration of the solar force as divine fire may have been an integral part of the original proto-Dravidian religion that was shared by Semites, Japhetites and Hamites. But the actual fire-rituals may have been preserved more carefully by the Japhetic Indo-Āryan stock that had migrated at a very early date northwards to the Yamnaya and Andronovo cultures whence they moved southwards again later, in the second millennium B.C., towards northern Mesopotamia, Iran and India. The eastward movement of proto-Dravidians-Hurrians (Ailas as well as Ikshvākus) with Elamite forms of the Brahmanical religion may have encountered the more northerly fire-worshipping Gandaridae tribes to form the typically Indian branch of the Āryan family.

Pargiter has suggested that the Dravidian "brāhmanical" institution was also considerably transformed by the Āryans. While the original [proto-] Dravidian priesthood was characterised by the practice of yogic austerities (tapas) which gave them magical powers, the Āryan was preoccupied with the performance of sacrifices, especially revolving around the worship of fire.[358] The Indo-Āryan religion thus seems to have combined the ancient proto-Dravidian wisdom of the Elamite/Mesopotamian Hurrians with more northerly fire- and soma-rituals and horse-sacrifices. And the original proto-

---

[356] See P. Kretschmer, *Kuhns Zeitschrift* 55, p.80; cf. J. Gonda, *Religionen Indiens*, I, p.107.

[357] RA 62-52,17-8 (see A. Livingstone, *op.cit.*, p.74); cf. K170+Rm520rev. (*ibid.*, p.30ff).

[358] See F.E. Pargiter, *op.cit.*, p.308f.

Dravidian or Noachidian wisdom[359] is also best preserved in the cultivated [sanskrit=refined] and inflected language of the upper castes of the Indo-Āryans, though Sanskrit retains several Dravidian elements in it.[360]

Farther west, one of the oldest branches of the Germanic peoples is called the **Alemanni**, a name that may be a corruption of an earlier form as Aryamanni. Although the Germanic tribes may have formed a part of the northern Cimmerian Celtic race, Snorri Sturlusson,[361] the author of the *Prose Edda*, maintains that the Germans obtained their religion from Anatolians who moved into Europe.[362] The first Anatolian (the "Aesir"/Asuras) who migrated into Germany is said to be "Voden" or "Odin", the god of Wind [the original Germanic form, Wotan, is clearly related to the Āryan Wata, a form of the wind-god, Vayu].[363] Odin, however, is said to be a distant descendant of "Tror" or "Thor",[364]

---

[359] That the biblical Noah, a descendant of Adam's son, Seth, represents the wisdom of Seth is evident from the Gnostic tradition (see G.G. Stroumsa, op. cit., p.107). Josephus' *Jewish Antiquities*, I, 70-71 also makes clear the association of the line of Seth with cosmological learning (see A. Annus, *op.cit.*, p.xxvii).

[360] Aurobindho Ghose pointed out that some of the obsolete or "high" Sanskrit words were indeed common Dravidian ones such as "sodara" for brother (instead of the typical Sanskritic "bratha") and "akka" for sister (see A. Ghose, "The Origins of Aryan Speech", *Sri Aurobindo Birth Centenary Library*, vol.10, p.560). Interestingly, the common Germanic word for son, "sohn", is similarly cognate with a high Sanskrit word, "sūnuh", rather than with the typical Sanskritic "putra" (*ibid.*). This confirms the relative lateness of the formation of Sanskrit.

[361] See *The Prose Edda of Snorri Sturlusson*, p.25ff.

[362] This is confirmed by the earliest archaeology of Europe, where the first formation of the earliest Germanic cultures is to be located in thesouth, in modern-day Czechoslovakia, which it may have reached from "the Mediterranean or Anatolia" (G. Childe, *op.cit.*, p.1 01). Geoffrey of Monmouth (*History of the Kings of Britain*, Chs.3-1 6) points to the Trojan origin of even the earliest Britons, since Britain was, according to him, first settled by a great grandson of Aeneas called Brute. It is possible that Brute is related to the Bretannus of the Erotica Pathemata mentioned above p.147

[363] See A. Jacob, *op. cit.*, pp.1 49n,157.

[364] It is possible that the name Thor is derived from the same root thor denoting the ejaculation of semen which is noted in the epithet ' thoreni' applied to Aphrodite as sprung of Zeus' seed in the Derveni Orphic writings (see M.L. West, *Orphic Poems*,

the son of a Trojan king called Mennon or Munon who had married a daughter of King Priam. Thor himself first wandered to Thrace and then to other parts of the world. We will note that Thrace is also the source of the Dionysiac cult.[365] The date of the migration may have been around that of the Trojan War. The seniority of Thor to Odin here only points to the late rise of our universe whose sustaining force Odin is.[366] Wotan/Odin indeed corresponds to Wata, the universal form of the wind-god Vayu/Shiva/Enlil.[367]

Odin's three sons, Vegdeg, Beldeg (Baldur) and Sigi ruled over East Germany, Westphalia, and France, respectively. Further expeditions took Odin to Denmark, Sweden and Norway, whereby he succeeded in spreading the "language of Asia" all over Europe. Thus we see that, although the Cimmerians are, according to the biblical Table of Nations, the eldest son of Japheth, and settled on the northern shores of the Black Sea, from whence the Germanic branch could have moved directly into Europe, mythological literature describes the arrival of the latter in Europe through Anatolia, so that the Aryan languages of Europe are considered to be derivatives of the Anatolian ones. According to Tacitus, Mannus was the ancestor of the Germanic race, and he had three sons represented by the Ingaevones, Herminones, and Istaevones.[368] The first Germanic tribe to have crossed the Rhine and ousted the indigenous Celts were the **Tungri**, whose other name, *Germani*, was used for all the tribes.[369]

---

p.91). If so, this would approximate Thor to Ninurta and Skandha (whose name means "jet of semen"), son of Shiva/Enlil/Wotan (see A. Jacob, *Ātman*, Ch.XIX). The name Thor also seems to be related to Taurit, the Anatolian bull-god who is later identified with Teshup, the son of Kumarbi/Chronos. Teshup is indeed the Hurrian counterpart of the younger Thor who battles the Midgard serpent (see *The Prose Edda*, "The Deluding of Gylfi"). If this etymology be right, the most ancient western Indo-European term for "bull" must be one that is significative of its virility. This etymology would also confirm Sturlusson's claims regarding the Anatolian origins of the Eddic mythology.

[365] See A. Jacob, *op. cit.*, p.133.

[366] See *ibid.*, Ch.XXIII.

[367] See *ibid.*, p.157.

[368] See Tacitus, *Germania*, Sec.2.

[369] In this context, it is interesting to note that one of Hammurabi's inscriptions

The chief god of the Germans is said to be the creator god Tuisto [from Tvashtr/Tvoreshtar/Tartarus].[370] The collective name 'Edda' for the sacred poems of the Germans is also clearly related to the Indo-Āryan 'Veda', rather more than to the Iranian 'Avesta', just as Tuisto is more closely related to the Indic Tvastr than to the Iranian Tvoreshtar. The name of the Germanic Tree of Life, Yggdrasil, also possibly derives from the Āryan deity Indra who was adored in this form.[371] However, in the *Prose Edda*, "Gylfaginning (The Deluding of Gylfi)", the end of the universe, Ragnarök, is heralded by a long winter exactly as in the Yima story of the Vendidad.[372] The Iranian name Yima for the first man is also retained in that of the Germanic "giant" or First Man, Ymir, who is killed by Wotan, that is, by the temporal form (Kala, Chronos) of the breath of the Purusha (Vayu, Wotan).[373] And we have seen that the name, Wotan, is itself derived from the wind-god Wata who is more prominently mentioned in the Iranian sacred literature than in the Indic.[374] This may suggest that the Germanic tribes derived their cosmological information from the Anatolian region at a date before the separation of the Indic from the Iranian Āryans. Furthermore, a trace of the transmission of the early religion to the north through the Armenoid Sumerians and their Anatolian neighbours may perhaps be found in the name of the Eddic Ocean-god Aegir, which resembles the Sumerian Enki (Okeanos) and Egyptian Osiris.[375]

(C.J. Gadd and L. Legrain, *Ur Excavations: Texts*, Vol. I: Royal Inscriptions, London, 1 928, Nr. 1 46, Pl.Q) refers to the "Elamites, Guti, Subartu and Tukriš" together as being peoples whose "mountains are distant and language complicated" (see A Ungnad, *op.cit.*, pp.48f.). It is not certain if the Tukriš were the same as Tacitus' Tungri, and, if so, where they were first situated.

[370] Tacitus, *Ibid.*

[371] See A. Jacob, *op. cit.*, Ch.XXIII.

[372] See *ibid.*, p.65.

[373] See below p.184.

[374] See A. Jacob, *op.cit.*, p.157n.

[375] *Ibid.*, p.170.

Although the Japhetites are a very ancient branch of the Indo-European family, their appearance in history is later than that of the youngest branch, the Hamitic. The Semites, Japhetites and Hamites may have all been early settled in Elam as proto-Hurrians/Dravidians. Following the biblical description of the sons of Noah - the Semites, the Japhetites and the Hamites – we find that the original founders of both Sumer and Egypt are said to be the **Hamites**. Kush and Mestraim, the founders of Sumer and Egypt respectively, are said to be sons of Ham. In the earlier Jahvist version of Genesis 9:1 8, Ham is mentioned as the youngest son, after Japheth.

It may be noted that the most ancient bull cult in Anatolia dating from at least the seventh millenium B.C. is dedicated to a Hattic deity called Taru,[376] who was transformed into the Hurrian-Hittite weather-god Teshup. Heth is said to be a son of the Hamitic Canaan in Genesis 10:1 5. It is not surprising that the same bovine deity is found also among the Canaanites as Baal.[377] Speiser suggested that "Kina-hhi", the term for Canaan, is itself of Hurrian provenance.[378] It is also attested in the Akkadian Amarna texts as "Kinahni". If the most ancient cultures of Anatolia and the Palestine, as well as of Sumer and Egypt, are to be attributed to Ham, it would seem that the Hamites, though described in the original Bible as the "third" son of Noah, indeed played a particularly important role in the diffusion of the most ancient proto-Hurrian/Dravidian tradition, which they seem to have preserved very carefully.[379] Indeed, according to Sankuniathon of Beirut, Kronos (Kala/Shiva) granted Attica to Athena (Anat, consort

---

[376] See V. Haas, *Geschichte der hethitischen Religion*, Leiden: E.J. Brill, 1 994, p.322.

[377] See V. Haas, *op. cit.* , p.320; cf. C.H. Gordon, "Canaanite Mythology", in S. Kramer (ed.), *Mythologies of the Ancient World*, Garden City, NY: Doubleday, 1 961 , pp.1 81 -21 5. In the Bible (Genesis X:1 5), Canaan also engenders the Amorite.

[378] See E. Speiser, *Mesopotamian Origins*, p.141.

[379] See G. Sergi, *The Mediterranean Race: A Study of the Origin of European Peoples*, London: W. Scott, 1909, p.150, where the author maintains that the indigenous peoples of Asia Minor as well as Syria are of the same type as the Egyptians and "derived from the same centre of diffusion". These Hamitic folk form part of the Mediterranean Race (*ibid.*, p.41).

of Baal), Egypt to Taautos (Thoth),[380] Byblos to the goddess Baaltis or
Dione (who may be a consort of El/Kronos himself), and Beirut to
Poseidon and the Kabeiri, or Dioscuri.[381] Of the descendants of the
Kabeiri, it was Chna (Canaan) who changed his name to Phoenix
(Phoenicia).[382] It is clear therefore that the Hamitic Canaanite culture
was a very ancient and widespread one.

According to Genesis 11, the division of languages first occurred in
Babel, in the north - after the settlement of Eridu/Ubaid by the three
sons of Noah. So it is likely that the language of Elam/Eridu as well
as of proto-Akkadian Kish was indeed a form of proto-Dravidian/
Hurrian,[383] whereas the languages of the Uruk period were split into
Sumerian, Akkadian and Elamite. The king associated with Babel
is the Hamitic king, Nimrod.[384] As Nimrod is also called a son of
Kush in Genesis 10:8, it is difficult to discern the influx of any new
racial element into the Hamitic in this biblical statement. Yet, as we
shall see, there is a noticeable difference between an early stratum of
Mediterranean folk and a later brachycephalic, or "Armenoid",[385] one
in the Uruk culture of Sumer, as well as in early Egypt.

In Mesopotamia, the **Uruk** culture (from ca. 3500 B.C.) is
significantly different from the earlier Susaite culture of the Ubaid
period, and we may detect the arrival of the Armenoid, proto-Alpine
founders of Sumerian culture in this period. It must be noted also that

---

[380] According to Malalas, Hermes/Thoth came from "Italy" (see below p. 171n).

[381] The Kabeiri are also identified with the Korybantes and the Samothracians (see
Philo of Byblos, *op. cit.* , p.47).

[382] Ibid.

[383] See E. Speiser (*Mesopotamian Origins*, Philadelphia: University of Pennsylvania
Press, 1930, p.54n) suggests that the very name Agade has the same ending as
Hurrian place-names such as Lub-di, Tai-di, Irri-di, so that it is very likely that
"the available philological evidence confirms the theory that the oldest population of
Akkad had much in common with the Elamitic group".[

[384] According to the Sumerian king-list, it was Enmerkar who was first established
at Uruk (see T. Jacobsen, *The Sumerian King-list*, Chicago: University ofChicago
Press, 1939, p.87).

[385] By "Armenoid" is meant a brachycephalic racial type and not necessarily one of
Armenian origin.

166

the earliest Uruk tablets are from both Kish and Uruk proper,[386] which suggests an extensive north-south migration of the new Sumerians. But the fact that the Sumerian king-list begins its postdiluvian section with the establishment of a kingdom at Kish in the north, which is more likely proto-Dravidian and proto-Akkadian, suggests that the political ascendancy of the Sumerians in Uruk was a gradual one, beginning with political accomodation with the original inhabitants of the north and ending with a final establishment of independence at Uruk.

The cuneiform system of writing emerges in the Uruk period and is transmitted in a simplified form to Elam. That the Sumerians were the founders of the system of notation and writing which developed in the south is made clear by the fact that only Sumerian has the phonemevalues required to make the word for Enlil intelligible.[387] The first numerical tablets found at Uruk are from the Uruk IV period, whereas those in Elam date from the following Uruk III period,[388] showing that the transmission of writing to Elam was relatively late. The earliest tablets also give evidence of a sexagesimal system of measurement along with four other systems varied according to the objects being measured,[389] whereas the Elamites used mostly just the decimal system.[390] The Sumerians seem to have been responsible for both the administrative excellence attested by their invention of writing and the urban civilisation that the Uruk culture, which begins Sumerian civilisation proper, represents.[391]

A noteworthy difference that is evident between the Ubaid and Uruk cultures is their respective customs of interment, with the

---

[386] See J. Bottero, *op. cit.*, p.70.

[387] *Ibid.*, p.80.

[388] See H. Nissen, P. Damerow, R.K. Englund, *Archaic Bookkeeping*, Chicago: University of Chicago Press, 1993, p.5

[389] Thus discrete objects were measured mostly in the sexagesimal system whereas land measures were recorded through the Gan2 system (*ibid.*, pp.27,43,138,131).

[390] *Ibid.*, pp.93-5, pp.75-7.

[391] See G. Algaze, *The Uruk World-System: The Dynamics of Expansion of early Mesopotamian Civilization*, Chicago: Chicago University Press, 1993.

former favoring an extended posture of the corpse and the latter a flexed.[392] We shall observe below that the Beaker folk of Europe also favoured this form of burial. It is to be noted that, while the skulls found in the graves of the Ubaid period are all dolicocephalic and "Mediterranean", those of the subsequent Uruk culture are mixed, showing at first a "predominance of brachycephali" which is gradually replaced by dolichocephali.[393] The brachycephalic skulls of Ubaid signal an Armenoid race, belonging either to the Alpine physical type or to the Uralic,[394] but the new race must have been assimilated into the older population. The pictorial representations of the early Sumerians reveal markedly Anatolian, "Hittite" noses,[395] and the Sumerian language, both the Main Dialect and Emesal, may have contributed to proto-Hittite itself.[396] The earliest Cretans too may have been related to the Anatolian and the Uruk Sumerians.[397] The Sumerians may be a branch of the proto-Dravidians mixed with brachycephalic, perhaps Alpine, or even Uralic, elements.[398] And the language of the Sumerians may be a form of the original proto-Dravidian/Hurrian language modified by that of the new stock.

---

[392] See J. Oates, "Ur and Eridu", p.42; cf. the same flexed position in the Naqada graves studied by DeMorgan (see G.E. Smith, *op. cit.*, p.89)

[393] See H. Frankfort, *op. cit.*, p.9. The recurrence of dolicephalic types suggests a successful absorption of the new brachycephalic type by the indigenous population.

[394] It is possible to detect a similar mingling of proto-Aryan peoples with Ural-Altaic elements in a slightly later period, i.e., in the late Yamnaya culture (ca.2000 B.C.), which reveals a practice of skull deformation in infancy that was indulged in later, in the Iron Age, by the Mongoloid Huns (see J.P. Mallory and V.H. Mair, *The Tarim Mummies*, London: Thames and Hudson, 2000, p.239).

[395] Compare the statues in A. Parrot, *Sumer*, Paris: Gallimard, 1960, and in K. Bittel, *Les Hittites*, Paris: Gallimard, 1976. Cf. also, in this context, C. Autran, *Sumérien et Indo-Européen*, Paris: Librairie Orientaliste Paul Geuthner, 1925, p.1 69: "sous le rapport langue,Sumer représente, en tout cas, l'un des eléments qui, en des temps fort anciens, ont concouru à la formation de l'indo-européen, qu'il est, par suite, un témoin archaique de l'un des dialects pre-indo-européens essentiels".

[396] The "centum" quality of Sumerian is evident in the Sumerian word for "eye", "igi", which is closer to the Germanic "Auge" than to the Sanskritic "aksha".

[397] See below p. 171.

[398] For the relation between Dravidian and Uralic, see S. Tyler, "Dravidian and Uralian: the lexical Evidence", *Language*, 44, pp.1 98-212.

In the Susa II period (latter part of the fourth millennium B.C.), Elam too was "colonised" by the Sumerians, since the pottery of this period is remarkably different from that of the earlier Susa I period and bears a close similarity to that of Sumer.[399] Also, the use of a Sumerian name for the chief deity of Susa, Nin-shushinak, seems to confirm the predominance of Sumerian influence in Elam in the post-Susa I period.[400]

We have already seen that the founding of Eridu may have been due to the Elamite proto-Hurrians (who are probably the same as the eldest branch of the proto-Dravidians), since it precedes the immigration of the "Armenoid" type to Uruk. The fact that there are no written records earlier than the numerical tablets of Uruk IV thus does not mean that the most ancient societies of Susa and Eridu were not highly cultured, since the system of writing itself developed mainly for the purposes of computation and not for the preservation of sacred knowledge which, being esoteric, could not be committed to writing but was passed on from generation to generation in an oral tradition.[401] This suggests that the ancient proto-Dravidian religion may have been preserved in Elam and Ubaid in an oral Hurrian/Akkadian form before it was codified by the Sumerian intellectuals of Kish-Uruk.[402] When we consider the religion of the specifically Sumerian Uruk culture, however, we should not be surprised to find

---

[399] See D.T. Potts, *The Archaeology of Elam*, Cambridge: Cambridge University Press, 1999, p.52.

[400] See P. Steinkeller, "Early Political Development in Mesopotamia and the Origins of the Sargonic Empire", in *Akkad, the First World Empire*, ed. M. Leverani, Padua: Sargon srl, 1 993, p.111 .

[401] See H. Nissen, *Archaic Bookkeeping*, p.21, where Nissen points out that, of the 5000 or so written documents retrieved from Uruk IV and Uruk III, "not one of them is clearly related to religious, narrative, or historical topics ... This fact strongly implies that such text genres were simply not written down".

[402] In this context, we may consider the curious passage in *Genesis* 9:22, which states that Ham "saw the nakedness" of his father Noah and told his brothers of it. This may refer to the public dissemination of the ancestral wisdom among the highly literate Hamitic civilisations of Sumer and Egypt, whereas the other Indo-Europeans preserved it in purely oral form. For the tradition that Noah symbolises the wisdom of "Seth" see p.140 above.

that there is a clear continuity between the temple forms of the earlier Eridu and the classical Uruk types.

In Egypt, too, the original proto-Dravidian/Hurrian culture was modified by the entrance of the Armenoid "New Race". G.E. Smith, in the case of pre-dynastic Egyptians of Naga-ed-der and Giza, and W.M.F. Petrie, in the case of the Naqada "New Race" graves, have shown that the original founders of Egyptian civilization are to be distinguished from an incoming "Armenoid" race. Smith noticed the difference between the indigenous dolicocephalic variety and the alien brachycephalic type both at Naga-ed-der near Abydos and Giza in the Delta, that is, both in Upper and Lower Egypt.[403] This New Race was probably an Armenoid branch of the Indo-Europeans.[404] They may have been characteristically brachycephalic, big boned and fair, whereas the Mediterraneans are dolicephalic, small boned and brown. The "Hamitic" founders of Egyptian as well as of Ubaid Sumer belonged to the earlier Mediterranean type.

The newcomers may possibly be related to the "Beaker" folk, who were widely dispersed in Europe as well as in North Africa in the late chalcolithic era (corresponding to Danube III, ca.2500 B.C.).[405] The "Beaker" folk are brachycephalic[406] and interred in a contracted position in graves aligned in a north-south axis rather than the east-west axis followed by the preceding Corded Ware folk.[407] The beaker folk seem to have been effective traders as well as warriors, the graves

---

[403] See G.E. Smith, *op. cit.*

[404] The Indo-Europeans are traditionally divided into three branches, the Mediterranean, the Alpine and the Nordic. Of these, the Nordic, or Aryan, is represented by Japheth in the biblical Table of Nations. We see that the Indo-Europeans are not identical to the Aryans since they include the Alpine "Armenoid" type identifiable with the Uruk Sumerians as well as the earliest proto-Dravidian/Hurrian Mediterranean type.

[405] See G. Childe, *op. cit.*, (1961 ed.), pp.222-8; cf. R.J. Harrison, *The Beaker Folk*, London: Thames and Hudson, 1980.

[406] See K. Gerhardt, *Die Glockenbecherleute in Mittel- und Westdeutschland*, Stuttgart: Schweizerbart'sche Verlag, 1953; cf. R.J. Harrison, *op. cit.*, pp.160f.

[407] See G. Childe, *op. cit*, p.226; cf. R.J. Harrison, *op. cit.*, p.51.

of the latter being especially richly supplied with funerary goods.[408] Cremations too were performed by this community and may have been reserved for the upper classes or castes, since cremations in Moravia are seen to be especially furnished with beakers.[409] Though it is uncertain where this type originated, some claiming Andalusia as the original habitat and others Germany, Childe believes that they too were of "East Mediterranean stock".[410] The Beaker folk may perhaps be more accurately identified with the Alpine or Armenoid branch of the Indo-Europeans.[411]

This Armenoid type seems to have, already in the fourth millennium B.C., entered the Nile Delta from Palestine and Syria, but, as Petrie points out, the type is equally present in Libya and could have entered Egypt from the west as well. In fact, Petrie notices family resemblances between the "new race", as he calls them, and the Libyans, Palestinians, Amorites, as well as the earliest inhabitants of Mycenae, Cyprus and even central Italy.[412] Crete in its Neolithic period seemed to Sir Arthur Evans to be "an insular offshoot of an extensive Anatolian province".[413] The name of the legendary king Minos of Crete is cognate with Manu/ Menes and this may be due to their racial relation to the "Armenoid" Egyptians of the Delta, and to those farther west, in Libya, in the period immediately following the Neolithic.[414]

---

[408] The Beaker folk seem also to have been associated with the ritual monuments of Britain including those at Stonehenge and Avebury (see R.J. Harrison, *op. cit.*, pp.94ff.).

[409] *Ibid.*, p.55.

[410] *Ibid.*, p.227.

[411] The Alpine type is said to have the same round skull as the Beaker folk except that it has a rounded occipital bone whereas the Beaker type has a flattened occipital bone (see R.J. Harrison, *op. cit.*, p.160).

[412] This may be the reason why Malalas mentions that Hermes/Thoth arrived from Italy to rule Egypt after Mestraim : (see Verbrugghe and Wickersham, *Berossus and Manetho*).

[413] Quoted in G. Childe, *op.cit.*, p.17. Evans also pointed out the similarities between the cod-pieces of the ancient Libyans and those of the early Bronze Age Minoans (see S. Hood, *The Minoans: Crete in the Bronze Age*, London: Thames and Hudson, 1971, p.30f).

[414] See G. Childe, *op.cit.*, p.19; cf. Hesiod, *Catalogues of Women and Eoiae*, 74:

The arrival of the new race is dated by Petrie to around 3200 B.C., that is, at the time of the Uruk culture, the rise of which is also, as we shall see, dependent on the infusion of newcomers into a more indigenous Mesopotamian society. As in Mesopotamia, the arrival of the "New Race" in Naqada coincides with the emergence of a greater complexity of social organisation.[415]

The **Dravidians** who settled in South India seem to have been originally related to the Sumerians. In the Tamil Kallatam of the 10th century A.D., Skanda/**Muruga**, or Subrahmanya ('perfect brāhmanhood')[416], is said to have bestowed the Vedic knowledge on the sage **Agastya**, who then transmitted this wisdom to "South India" having crossed the "Vindhya" mountain range. It is possible that the sage Agastya (also called Maitravaruni since he was born of the Vedic gods Mitra-Varuna),[417] is actually a reference to Akkad,[418] and the transmission of Vedic wisdom to "South India" a modern rendering of the traditional memory of a migration of proto-Akkadians from northern Mesopotamia to the Uruk region of southern Mesopotamia. The reference to the "Vindhya" mountain range suggests that this immigration proceeded from a region north-east of Kish, since there are no high mountains south of Kish. The fact that Agastya is said to have crossed the "Vindhya" mountains in order to reach Uraga suggests that the Kish dynasties included the earliest peoples who arrived from farther north and these we have suggested may have been proto-Dravidian or Hurrian. The presence of a king with the Sanskrit-like name Ūsîwatar (possibly from (Skt.) vishva=universal)

"(Minos) who was most kingly of mortal kings and reigned over very many people dwelling round about, holding the sceptre of Zeus wherewith he ruled many."

[415] See T. Wilkinson, *Genesis of the Pharoahs*, London: Thames and Hudson, 2003, p.185.

[416] The name "Subrahmanya" is first attested in Sanskrit in the Baudhāyana Dharmashāstra (600-200 B.C.) and in Tamil in a poem by Cēntanār *Tiruvicaippa* II,3 (9th -10thc. A.D.)

[417] *Brhaddevata* 30; *Rāmāyana* VII,57.

[418] See above p.115. According to the Sumerian King-List, Akkad is said to have been founded by Ur-Zababa (see T. Jacobsen, *op. cit.*, p.111).

in the 13th dynasty (established at Kish) of the Sumerian king-list[419] also points to a continuing proto-Indic element in the earliest royal lineage of Mesopotamia.

Agastya is said to have learned the "difficult language" of the Tamils from either Muruga or directly from Muruga's father Shiva.[420] The reference in Kālidasa must therefore be to a time when the Uruk Sumerians (proto-Tamils) were still somewhat alien to the Akkadians. What is curious, however, is that the Vedic knowledge typically associated with the Āryans was itself conveyed to Agastya (Akkad) through the god of the Dravidians. Muruga himself is characterised by his affiliation with mountans and hunting, his typical weapon being the spear, 'vel'. According to Zvelebil, he represents "the Dravidian speakers who 'descended' from the mountains of Southern Iran (Zagros)."[421] These Dravidians "finally moved eastward as well into the plains of southern Panjab, the Indus Valley, and finally "down south" throughout the peninsula".

The Dravidians of the ancient Near East may have been **proto-Tamils** as distinguished from the earlier proto-Dravidians. We have seen that the literary references to the sage Agastya and his spiritual instruction of the Tamils suggest that the proto-Tamils are related to the Sumerians of Uruk. Their contemporaneity with the Armenoid rulers of Uruk is suggested also by an episode in the Sanskrit poem of Kalidāsa (5th c. A.D.), Raghuvamsha (VI,59ff.) which refers to Agastya's being the officiating priest of a Pāndya (Tamil) king who is the contemporary of Aja (the grandfather of the Ikshvāku king Rāma), and to the capital of the Pāndya king as being not Madurai, as one would have expected if the scene were set in South India, but rather "Uraga",[422] which seems to refer to the Sumerian Uruk itself, though this would push the origins of the Uruk dynasty to before the fourth millennium B.C., which traditionally marks the start of the Kali Yuga, since Rāma is said to have been born already at the

---

[419] See T. Jacobsen, *ibid.*, p.109.

[420] See K. Zvelebil, *Tamil Traditions*, p.24.

[421] *Ibid.*, p.79.

[422] See G.S. Ghurye, *Indian Acculturation*, p.31.

beginning of the Treta Yuga.[423] Whatever the chronology of the extant literature may be in relation to that of the Yugas, Aja himself seems to be represented in the Sumerian king-list as Aka,[424] of the first dynasty of **Kish**, which preceded the foundation of Uruk. One of the extant Sumerian histories related to "Gilgamesh and Agga" too refers to the initial supremacy of Kish and the north under the king Agga, son of Enmebaraggesi, who demands the submission of Gilgamesh in Uruk.[425] The first rulers of Kish may have been proto-Akkadians related to the **Ikshvākus**, since Ikshvāku itself seems to be identical to **Akshak**[426] in the Sumerian King-List.[427]

If the "solar" Ikshvāku dynasty of the Indian king-lists be representative of the Kish/Akshak civilisation, the other "lunar" dynasty derived from Manu's daughter Ilā, the *Aila*, may well denote *Elam*.[428] These northern Mesopotamians and Elamites may have imparted their spiritual wisdom to the Sumerians of Uruk, whose political ascendancy seems to have been established in the south. Both the Aila [Elamite] and the Ikshvāku [Kish] dynasties are derived from Manu, the proto-Dravidian king (*BP*, VIII,24). If we were to draw up a tentative scheme of first beginnings, we may imagine Noah/Manu as representing an enlightened proto-Dravidian/Hurrian group which branched off into Semitic groups which flourished first in the northern and Elamite mountainous regions and later in

---

[423] See *BP* I,3.

[424] The "centum" quality of Sumerian is also evident in the Sumerian word for "eye", "igi", which is closer to the Germanic "auge" than to the Sanskritic "aksha".

[425] See J.B. Pritchard, *ANET*, pp.44-7. In the Sumerian King-List, Aka is a king of the first dynasty (at Kish), though Gilgamesh follows apparently later in the second dynasty (at Uruk) after the fall of Kish (see T. Jacobsen, *op.cit.*, pp.85, 89-91).

[426] Akshak was later called Upi (Gk. Opis) and may, like Kish, have been situated in the southern vicinity of modern Baghdad.

[427] See T. Jacobsen, *Sumerian King-List.*, p.107. The first king of Akshak is recorded in the King-List as Unzi, though there was perhaps an earlier ruler called Zuzu (*ibid.*, p.181), who is the only historically verifiable king of Akshak. The first Akshak dynasty may have ended by 3400 B.C. (see *RLA* I:64).

[428] It may be noted, in passing, that the Edda ('The Deluding of Gylfi') too records the first human beings as a girl called Embla and a boy called Ask.

northern Mesopotamia, while an Armenoid Indo-European group (perhaps related to proto-Tamil) spread first through north-westerly areas of the Near East and then entered Mesopotamia from the north to finally establish their political supremacy in Uruk.

The original Vedic system of esoteric wisdom elaborated by the proto-Hurrians/Dravidians may have been conveyed, through the mediation of proto-Akkadians, to the Armenoid-proto-Tamil group which had consolidated their power in Uruk as the so-called Sumerians. However, the fact that the historic evidence of the entrance of the modern Dravidians (whom we may call Tamils, to distinguish them from the proto-Dravidians) into *South India* is of relatively recent date, perhaps around the thirteenth century B.C., means that there are only a few dim hints of the Near Eastern origins of the Dravidian peoples in the earliest archaeology and literature of South India. Nevertheless Lahovary believed that the ancestors of the Dravidians emigrated from Mesopotamia to India already sometime in the course of the fourth millennium.[429] Lahovary also notes the important linguistic fact that central and western Dravidian, such as Kannada and Telugu, seem to have remained closer to Basque and the ancient non-Āryan languages of southern Europe than Tamil and Malayalam. "At the same time, lexical and even morphological corresondences with Semitic have been retained in several central Dravidian idioms which are lacking in South Dravidian",[430] which confirms the north-south route of the Dravidian migration into India, and dismisses any theories of an indigenous Indian origin of the Dravidians.

The earliest archaeological evidence (ca. 1200-80 B.C.) of the entrance of the Tamils into South India is from dolmen burial sites in Adichanallur (similar to those in Palestine and Cyprus), where some of the finds such as golden "mouth-pieces", bronze representations of cocks and spear-heads may be related to the worship of Muruga/Marduk/Ninurta.[431] The megalithic graves of the Madurai district

---

[429] See N. Lahovary, *Dravidian Origins and the West*, p.16.

[430] *Ibid.*, p.372.

[431] See K. Zvelebil, *op.cit.*, p. 75f.

dating from around 1000 B.C. also reveal resemblances to the early Iron Age graves of the Caucasus and Sialk Necropolis B.[432]

The Dravidians of South India seem to have been principally characterised by their Shaivite devotion to Muruga. The earliest textual references to Muruga from the Dravidian Sangam literature of the first three or four centuries A.D. bear witness to a Dionysiac god who is capable of infusing women with love-sickness and possessing his devotees in a frenzy.[433] In the Tamil lexicon, *Tivakaram*, dating from the 8th century A.D., we find a full-fledged religion of Muruga/Marduk among the Tamils since it lists all the titles of the god.[434]

---

[432] See B. and R. Allchin, *op.cit.*, p.230.

[433] See K. Zvelebil, *op.cit.*, p.78.

[434] *Ibid.*, p.73.

II. THE SOLAR COSMOLOGY OF
THE INDO-EUROPEANS

What is especially noteworthy in the cosmological orientation of the religions of all the ancient Indo-Europeans is that it is essentially focussed on the significance of the solar force in our universe. This is hardly surprising when some of the proto-Indo-Europeans that we have identified as proto-Dravidian/proto-Hurrian were indeed called Subarians or Suwarians on account of their sun-worship. However, more pertinent to the present study of the original significance of the Grail perhaps is the crucial importance of the divine phallus that bears the solar force and from which the sun emerges. Indeed, we shall, in the course of our study, notice that the ancient religions of the Indo-Europeans were all based on phallic worship. For, in the cosmological scheme of the ancient Indo-Europeans, the entire evolution of the material universe arises from repeated castrations, and preservations, of the divine phallus, first in the Ideal realm of the Purusha, then in the early cosmos of Brahman and, lastly, in the "underworld" of the material universe, where the solar force (as Osiris) is sunk after the second assault, bereft of its vital force.until the latter is revived as the Tree of Life that arises from the underworld and extends to the heavens.[435]

---

[435] See below pp.183ff.

In reconstructing the cosmology of the most ancient Indo-Europeans[436] I shall employ both Āryan and Hamitic sources, that is, the literary evidence of the Puranas, the Vedas, the Brahmanas, the Avesta, the Bundahishn, the records of the religions of Egypt, Sumer, Akkad, Assyria and the Hurrians, as well as the earliest western Āryan theogonies of the Hittites, the proto-Stoic and Orphic Greeks, and the ancient Germans. For, although the prehistory of the cosmos is presented in clearest outlines in the Indic Purānic and Vedic literature,[437] this account achieves a greater elaboration in the Hamitic documents of ancient Egypt and Sumer that focus on the different stages of the development of the sun.

ĀTMAN

The first cosmic hypostasis (Ātman/the Soul) is in the Vedas, *RV* X,129,1, called **the One**, which "breathless, breathed by its own nature: apart from it was nothing whatsoever". Although it is the only Existent, it is nevertheless surrounded by what is called a "**Chaos**" [Abyss] of **dark** and indistinct "**water**" (st.3), which, from the logic of the verse, must be still unformed.[438] This Soul or the One corresponds to the Egyptian Amun (who is also called Atmu, Soul)[439] and is the

[436] For a detailed study of the ancient Indo-European cosmology, see A. Jacob, *Ātman.*

[437] Portions of the Purānas - which constitute the "Bible" of the Indo-Europeans - may indeed have been composed earlier than the Vedas, since the *BrdP* I,i,1,40-41 maintains that they were heard by Brahma before the Vedas. Purānas typically contain discussions of sarga (cosmogony), pratisarga (regeneration of the cosmos), manvantara (epochs of Manu), vamsha (ethnic genealogies) and vamshanucarita (royal genealogies). The cosmic Flood stories in the Puranas are to be found also in the Tamil 'Purānams', which copy the encyclopaedic genre of the Sanskrit models.

[438] These primal entities correspond to the Egyptian Amun-Amunet, Nun-Nunet, Huh-Huhet, Kuk-Kuket (see K. Sethe, *Amun*) as well as the Hesiodic and Orphic Eros, Chaos, Earth and Tartarus (see Hesiod, *Theogony*, 116-120; cf. below p.33).

[439] Hu-Nefer papyrus, (see E.A.W. Budge, *The Gods of the Egyptians*, II:10,15). If the Egyptian Amun indeed represents a corruption of the Sanskritic 'ātman', then it must indicate the presence of an Indic priestly tradition in Egypt at a very early

sole living Being, that which alone "breathes", in the earliest stages of the cosmos, just as Amun is the foundation of the Nun/Apsu. In the *BrdP* too we find that the first form of the deity [at the beginning of a kalpa, or cosmic age] is that of the supreme Soul, Ātman: "This entire dark world was pervaded by his Ātman" (I,i,3,12), with its three essential energies, or 'gunas', called Tamas, Rajas, and Sattva,[440] maintained in perfect balance.

RV X,129,4 goes on to state that from the One (Amun) arose **Desire** (Kāma), the "primal seed and germ of Spirit [Mind]". In *AV* III,21,4, Desire is used as an appellation of **Agni**, showing that Agni/Kāma is originally the desire of the One and the source of the ideal universe. That is why Agni is identifiable with Ātman as the very first form of the deity (**Shiva**). In *AV* XIX,52,1-3, the first hypostasis is said to be Desire (Kāma) itself, and it is said to have created Mind.[441] In *RV* X,90, further, it is stated: "**Fervour [Tapas] creates Rta (the Sacred Order), and Truth**"[442] and from these are produced first Night,[443] and then **the**

---

date, from at least the fifth dynasty, ca. 2500 B.C., when the worship of Amun is first attested. The Vedas do not give evidence of the worship of a god called, simply, Ātman. The concentration on the Ātman is peculiar, rather, to the Upanishads, and the Purānas, which latter are more comprehensive in their cosmogony than the Vedas.

[440] See further below p.181.

[441] Here Mind is equivalent to the Ideal Man/Prajāpati/Brahman, though, at the stage of the Cosmic Man, the latter becomes identified with the Intellect rather than with the Mind, which is represented by the Moon (see below p.17).

[442] We may compare the mention of Amun-Amunet, Nun-Nunet, Atum-Routy, Shu-Tefnut in PT 301, pyr. 446-7 (K. Sethe, *Amun*, p.34f.; cf. S. Bickel, *La Cosmogonie Egyptienne*, p.28n.). This is not an ogdoad but, rather, an order of generations, whereby Amun is represented as the source of Nun, who fathers Atum, etc. Atum's consort Routy is perhaps linguistically cognate with Sanskrit Rta. Routy is represented as a pair of lionesses and identified also with Atum's children Shu and Tefnut in PT 447 (see 'Ruti' in *LÄ* V:321). It is not surprising therefore that Tefnut is regularly identified with Maat, the sacred order (for Routy's relation to Tefnut see S. Bickel, *op.cit.*, p.190). Following the Vedic passage, Shu may particularly symbolise Truth, even as Tefnut symbolises Maat.

[443] In Hesiod's theogony, Night and Erebus are born of Chaos (Nun, Apsu). Night is also said to be the wife of An in Sumerian cosmology (Ebeling KAR I no.38, 9-23), which makes An the same as the Light of Dyaus and Night an aspect of the primal Earth, Prithvi/Ki/Antum.

Waters.[444] We have noted above, from *RV* X,129,1 that the Chaos itself was filled with the waters, so we may infer therefrom that the Waters produced after Night are now formed. Indeed, the Waters are ever moving and infused with Rta, so they are also ever striving for Truth.[445] Actually their name (apā) itself means "action or movement", so that in the *Nighantu*, it is given as a synonym of "karma".[446]

PURUSHA

According to the *BrdP*, the transformation of the Soul, Ātman, into Brahman, the self-conscious, enlightened form of the supreme deity, is accomplished through the power of intense yogic meditation (I,i,5,6). The unmanifest deity begins to be gradually manifested when one of its three constituent energies - Tamas, Rajas, and Sattva - begins to predominate over the others.[447] The first manifest form of the deity caused by the disturbance of the balance of the essential energies is as an **ideal macroanthropos**. The Purusha is said in the *Katha Upanishad* to employ **Prakrti**, or Nature as the first agent of manifestation and this Praktri is the same as **Ahamkara**, or the Ego. All human yogic endeavour is thus directed to a destruction of the Ahamkara (as in the *Bhagavad Gita*, VI) and its desire in order to return to the Ideal state of the Purusha, called Vishnu.[448]

---

[444] These Waters are not the formless cosmic streams of the Abyss/Chaos, but must refer to the substance of Heaven, which is, in an Assyrian exegetical text, (see A. Livingstone, *Mystical and Mythological Explanatory Texts*, p.33) said to be constituted of waters ('ša me').

[445] See U. Choudhuri, *Indra and Varuna*, p.156.

[446] We have here an explanation of the identification of Rta with the later Hindu concepts of "karma" and "dharma".

[447] Cf. Shriram Sharma, *Scientific Basis of Yajnas*, Ch.20: "At the time of the Pralaya, Tamas ruled. The Lord did Ikshana which induced movement in Prakriti made of three gunas originally equipoised." From this Lord, or Yajna Purusha, emerged the manifest cosmos.

[448] See M. Biardeau, *op.cit.*, p.127.

The Ideal Purusha is the intelligible form of the entire physical cosmos (SB XIV, 5,5,18). The process of this primal, and entirely ideal, manifestation of the Lord (Hari) is recounted in the BP II,5. The Lord, desirous of creation arouses, out of his own power of illusion, Māya[449] - aided by **Time** (Kāla-Shiva) - the three forms of divine energy - **Sattva, Rajas, and Tamas**. We see already that Shiva, though representative of the destructive aspect of the deity, is indeed one of the primal agents of cosmic creation, as Time, and, as we shall see, also as the cosmic Ego.[450] In the *Shvetāsvatara Upanishad*, the Cosmic Man is indeed called "the omnipresent Shiva" (III,11), since he is the same as the supreme Soul, Ātman. The aim of the cosmic creation is not only the harmonious order of the physical universe but also its rise to self-consciousness (Intellect/Brahman).[451] When the divine energies are differentiated, the supreme soul assumes three forms, the sattvic aspect being represented by the perfect macroanthromorphic Vishnu, the rājasic by the luminous Brahma, and the tāmasic by the Shiva who will destroy the cosmos at the end of its cycle (*BrdP* I,i,4,5f.). This is a trinity that is "mutually interdependent; these do not become separated even for a moment" (*BrdP* I,i,4,11).

The first result of the disturbance of the equilibrium of the three divine energies during the earliest moments of the cosmic creation is the emergence of **Mahat** (The Great) from Nature (Prakritī/Pārvatī, consort of Shiva), and this contains a combination of Rājas and Tāmas. It is from Mahat-tattva[=principle] that **Ahamkāra (Cosmic Egoity)**, dominated entirely by Tamas, arises. In the *BrdP* III,iv,4,37 Ahamkāra is said to evolve from Mahat, and from the Ahamkāra arise the **Bhūtas** (elements) and the **Indriyas** (senses). The entire material universe is a result of the dull egoistic element of Ahamkāra.[452]

---

[449] For the Vaishnav and Shaivite Āgamic conceptions of Māya, see A. Jacob, *Brahman*, Ch.XV.

[450] We note the creative aspect of Chronos also in the Orphic theogonies, and in the proto-Stoic cosmogony of Pherecydes (see below p.187).

[451] That is why the demon Vrtra that Indra famously battles in the Vedas is at once the demon of material restriction as well as of the unconscious (see J..Miller, *Vision*, pp.62,95,178). V.G. Rele, *Vedic Gods*, pp.56,103, observes the same contest between the unconscious and consciousness within the human microcosm.

[452] These primal cosmic elements of the *BrdP* reappear in the Sankhya philosophical

In the *BP*, the divine Mind, which is the most spiritual aspect of the manifesting deity since it represents the highest level of divine energy, **Sattva**, is ruled by the **Moon**. The second aspect of the deity, his **rājasic**, is said to be dominated by **Brahman**, the creator of the manifest universe and the light that emerge from the Cosmic Egg.

In the *RV* X,90, Purushasūkta, the Purusha is described as first expanding "in all directions, to what eats and does not eat". The Lord as a Cosmic Man, Purusha, is thus finally of colossal proportions as is evident from the dimensions provided in *BP* II,6,36ff. There it is stated that our universe merely spans the distance between the heart and the waist of Purusha. From his hip downwards extend the underworlds of Earth and from his chest upwards the four divine worlds, Maharloka, Janaloka, Tapoloka and Satyaloka. In the *BP* III,6,26 it is stated that the head of the Purusha is Heaven, the feet Earth and the navel the Mid-region.

THE FIRST SACRIFICE: TIME AND THE COSMIC EGG

According to *SB* VI,1,2, the **second phase of the cosmic creation** is accomplished through a **sacrifice** in which the Purusha is the sacrificial victim. The Purusha brings forth as a result the manifest cosmos constituted of the elements of earth, heavens and the mid-

---

doctrine of the **Mahat**, or The Great, as the first evolute from Prakriti. Pure sattvic potentiality, Mahat is the principle of Manas and Buddhi.

The **Ahamkāra** or ego-sense is the second product of the evolution of Nature and is responsible for the self-sense in living beings.

Manas evolves from the sattvic aspect of the Ahamkara. The **Pancha Tanmātras** or five objects (color, sound, smell, taste, touch), which are the subtle form of the Pancha Mahābhūtas (see below), partake of all three gunas.

The **Pancha jnāna indriyas** or five sense organs (eyes, ears, nose, tongue and body) – are related to the sattvic aspect of Manas. The **Pancha karma indriyas** or five organs of action – the hands, legs, vocal apparatus, urino-genital organ and anus - evolve from the rājasic aspect of Manas.

The **Pancha mahābhūtas**, or five great substances – earth, water, fire, air and ether – are the gross form of the Tanmātras representing the tāmasic aspect of the "Ahamkāra". These are the basis of the manifest universe.

region, as well as its constitutents, the sun, moon, winds, humankind, and wild and domestic animals.[453]

Prajāpati or Brahman begins the second phase of this creative activity through three unions. The first union with earth, by means of Agni, results in a **cosmic egg** which becomes the **mid-region** (of the stars, also called "atmosphere") and **wind**. "That which was the embryo inside emerged as the wind ... and that which was the shell became the atmosphere". The second union is with the mid-region by means of the wind and this results in another egg the shell and embryo of which became the **heavens** and the **sun**. The third union with the heavens is effected by means of the sun and this results in the production of another egg. The shell and embryo of this egg became **the quarters** and the **moon**.

The first temporal movement in the cosmos is indeed initiated by the breath of the Lord, or the wind-god **Vāyu** (Enlil/Wotan). Since the breath of the Ideal Man arises in the form of a "rapidly moving wind", we may assume that it is the movement of the Wind that is responsible for the appearance of **Time**. Time may be considered to have not properly emerged until after the infusion of the divine breath/fire into the prime matter of Earth. We must also remember that Time operates on an entirely subconscious level since the Ideal Man does not achieve consciousness, the divine light, until the latter emerges from the cosmic egg formed after the castration and impregnation of Heaven. The elements of Earth and Heaven united in the Ideal Man are thus separated by the temporal aspect of the Ideal Man himself, Time (Chronos/Kumarbi/Enki).

According to *AV* XIX,53,8-9, both Prajāpati (here the creative form of the supreme deity, identical to the perfect light of Brahman who is "as it were the Mind", *KYV* II,6,6) and Fervour are said to be generated by **Kāla**, Time, who must be the same as the Desire (Agni) of *AV* XIX,52,1-3.[454] Desire and the Mind are then said to have created Heaven. Kāla is typically an epithet of Shiva, whose consort is called Kāli. Shiva/Enki as Time is thus closely allied to the Desire (Agni)

---

[453] See H.W. Tull, *The Vedic origins*, p.50.

[454] See above p. 181.

of the supreme lord which serves as the prime motive force in the manifestation of the Deity. The erotic, as well as spiritual and ascetic, aspect of Shiva/Kāla is indeed clearly emphasised in the Shaivite mythologies.[455]

In *RV* IV,18,12, Indra is said to have "slain" his father: "What God, when by the foot thy Sire thou tookest and slewest, was at hand to give thee comfort?" Indra's father is said to be Dyaus in *RV* IV,17,5, though in *KYV* V,7,1, Indra is directly identified with Prajāpati, suggesting that he is not merely a son of Prajāpati but indeed an aspect of him (just as Chronos is an aspect of Ouranos/Aither).

The separation of the Heaven and Earth constituting the Ideal Man by Time is represented in some mythologies as a **castration** of Heaven's phallus, but this mutilation, is, as it were, a "self-sacrifice". The castration of the divine phallus causes its seed to impregnate the Cosmic Man himself resulting in the formation within his stomach of the egg from which the material matrix of the universe, Earth emerges in the form of a lotus suffused by the divine light of Brahman/An.

In *RV* X,90, the sacrifice of Prajāpati/Purusha has the result that "three-fourths" of him remains in heaven as life eternal, whereas one fourth of him descends to the manifest universe as the creation (v.3). The creation itself involves the emergence of animal life, the Vedic hymns, and the castes of men. The moon arises from Purusha's Mind (v.13) and the sun from his eye, Indra and Agni from his mouth and Vāyu from his breath. From his head is formed the sky and from his feet, earth, while from his navel arises the mid-region (v.14). We see that the emergence of the entire universe is due to this original sacrifice.

In the Germanic Edda the cosmic man is described as a giant, **Ymir**.[456] In the Eddic poem 'Vafprúdnismál', Odin asks a god (jötunn) Vafprúdnir to demonstrate his knowledge of the creation of the cosmos. During this catechism it emerges that:

---

[455] See W. O'Flaherty, *Asceticism and Eroticism*, Chs.IVff.

[456] The Germans use the name of the survivor of the Flood, the seventh Manu, Vaivasvata, for the First Man, Purusha.

Out of Ymir's flesh was fashioned the earth,
And the mountains were made of his bones;
The sky from the frost cold giant's skull,
And the ocean out of his blood.[457]

Similarly, in the 'Grímnísmal', it is stated that

Out of Ymir's flesh was fashioned the earth,
And the ocean out of his blood;
Of his bones the hills, of his hair the trees,
Of his skull the heavens high.

Mithgarth the gods from his eyebrows made,
And set for the sons of men;
And out of his brain the baleful clouds
They made to move on high.[458]

Ymir's flesh thus forms Earth, his skull Heaven and his brows Midgard or the mid-region of the stars.

In the "Gylfaginning", the mythical king Gylfi (or Gangleri) is instructed in divine cosmogony by Odin and it is revealed that the Primal Man, Ymir, was formed in the Ginnungagap, the Mid-region of the stars, through the condensation resulting from a mixture of hot air from Muspell, the southern region, and frost from Nihlheim, the northern. This seems to correspond to the combinations of the three gunas described in the Puranic cosmology.[459] Along with Ymir was created a universal cow, Audumbla, that fed Ymir with its milk. It is from these two primal entities that, first, the Titans, called jötunns, are formed and then the gods (Aesir/Asuras), Odin, Vili and Vé. When Odin and his brothers kill their father, the blood that emerges from Ymir's body threatens to flood the universe. So they take the body to Ginnungagap and form the heaven and earth of our system

---

[457] Tr. H.A. Bellows, *The Poetic Edda*.

[458] *Ibid.*

[459] See above p.181.

from his skull and flesh, while his blood is turned into the oceans. The stars are formed out of sparks from Muspell and positioned in the heavens by Odin and his brothers. The habitable region of Earth is called Midgard and Earth itself is surrounded by an Ocean ruled by the Midgard serpent, Jörmungandr.[460]

The supersession of the original Heaven is represented in the early Greek cosomologies, as well as in the Hurrian, as a castration of Ouranos (Dyaus) by **Chronos**. Chronos' attack on Ouranos is an indication of an extremely violent nature that recurs in the character of his stormy son Zeus (Seth/Ganesha).[461] The Hesiodic Chronos is the daring son of Earth and Heaven who responds to his mother's desire to thwart his father's habit of hiding his offspring and not allowing them to become manifest. It is significant that Ouranos' hiding of his children is particularly described as "evil-doing" in Hesiod's *Theogony*, l.158, since Chronos is not the only villainous figure in the early drama of the cosmos. To aid his mother in her distress, Chronos undertakes to castrate Ouranos, whose anthropomorphic form in the Hesiodic account clearly identifies him with the Purusha himself.

In the Orphic cosmogonies, the Cosmic Egg is said to be formed by Chronos out of Aither and the Chasm,[462] Aither apparently corresponding to Heaven and the Chasm to the unformed Abyss of Mesopotamian and Egyptian mythology that turns into Earth.[463] Chronos particularly forms Protogonos, or Phanes [Brahman] in the Cosmic Egg.[464] The proto-Stoic cosmogony of Pherecydes begins with Chronos [Time], Chthonie [Earth], and Zas [Dyaus/Heaven].[465]

---

[460] As Lincoln has pointed out, similar accounts of the dismemberment of a primal cosmic man may be found in Indic, Greek, Germanic, Celtic, Baltic and Slavic texts (see B. Lincoln, *Death, war and sacrifice*, p.168).

[461] See below p. 191.

[462] See M.L. West, *Orphic Poems*, p.70.

[463] See above p.179, cf. A. Jacob, *Ātman*, Ch.VII.

[464] *Ibid.*, p.178.

[465] H. Diels, *Doxographi Graeci*, Berlin, 1879, p.654; cf. Probus, *In Verg. Ecl.*6. Pherecydes calls 'Zas' Aither.

Chronos is said to "generate" fire, wind and water[466] in the five matrices of the gods from Chthonie and Zas.[467] Zas must therefore be identical to Aither and Chthonie to the Chasm.

The egg is surrounded by a serpent which breaks it by squeezing. In Epiphanius' account of Epicurus' cosmology, the serpent encircling the egg is itself constituted of wind.[468] The association of the egg with wind is also made clear in the description of Chronos' giving birth to "Eros and all the winds" in an Orphic poem quoted by Apollonius Rhodius.[469] In the cosmogonies of Hieronymus and Hellanicus, Chronos, who springs from the waters, produces the egg.[470] Again, though there is no reference to the formation of the divine light in a Cosmic Egg in Hesiod, in the Orphic account of Protogonos, Phanes is represented as being born of an egg.[471]

In the Hurrian epic of the Kingship in Heaven, *Kumarbi* is considered Anu's son,[472] and he destroys his father Anu so as to

---

[466] Cf. the Assyrian exegetical text RA 62 52 17-8:
Girra: Anu: fire.
Primeval: Ea: water.
East wind: Enlil: wind.
(see A. Livingstone, op. cit., p.74).

[467] The gods are called the fivefold race in the Vedas (*AV* VII,6,1) as well.

[468] See M.L. West, *op.cit.*, p.202.

[469] *Ibid.*, p.200. Eros is the same as Phanes/Brahman (see below p.190).

[470] See *ER* IV,126.

[471] See M.L. West, *op.cit.*, p.70.

[472] Kumār, in India, is the name of Shiva's solar son, Skanda/Muruga, who is the final ninth form of Agni, the first form being Rudra/Shiva himself. The other forms, according to *SB* VI,i,3, are Sarva, Pashupati, Ugra, Asani, Bhāva, Mahādeva and Īshana, who are embodied in the waters, plants, Vāyu, lightning, Parjanya (the rain-god), the moon and the sun respectively. In the *BrdP* I,ii,10, the identification of the forms of Agni/Shiva with the universal phenomena is somewhat different. There, the first form of Shiva - who is the creation [or phallus] of Brahma - is Rudra, and is said to be embodied in the sun, the second, called Bhāva, in the waters, the third, called Sarva, in the earth, the fourth, called Īshana, in the wind (Vāyu), the fifth, called Pashupati, in the fire, the sixth, called Bhima (corresponding to Asani), in the ether, the seventh, called Ugra, in the initiated brāhman priest and the last, called Mahādeva, in the moon. The order of manifestations in the *SB* is more

assume the rule of the primal cosmos. Kumarbi (Chronos) indeed castrates Anu (Heaven/the ideal Cosmic Man) while dragging him down from Heaven. However, Anu succeeds later in fleeing to his natural abode, that is, Heaven. The manner of Kumarbi's castration of Anu is reminiscent of Chronos' in Hesiod:[473]

> After [Anu] Kumarbi rushed,
> and seized him, Anu, by his feet
> and pulled him down from the sky.
> He bit his loins[474]

In Egypt, Time is posited at the stage of the appearance of **Shu** [Sumerian Enlil]: "[the Command of the supreme god] created Time - When Shu was there to raise the sky" (CT IV,325).[475] However, Plutarch (*De Iside et Osiride*, Ch.12), rightly considers **Geb** [Earth] and Nut [Heaven] to be identical to Chronos and Rhea.[476] So Time is related to Earth as well. In Egypt Re is said to have impregnatied the cow Nut as the Bull of Heaven,[477] who, here, stands for Geb/Chronos, consort of Nut, Heaven.[478]

Geb and Nut are sustained by the force of Shu after their separation by the latter. In the Amduat, the gigantic serpent called the "World-encircler" through whose coils the solar journey is undertaken in the

---

chronological than that of the *BrdP*, which represents them spatially in a series of concentric circles. For we note that the first and last forms, in the *BrdP* account, are constituted by the sun and moon respectively, the second and seventh by the waters and the Mind, the third and sixth by Earth and Heaven, the fourth and fifth by the Wind (Vāyu) and plantal life (Pashupati) - which latter is no doubt to be identified with Soma.

[473] See Hesiod, *Thegony*, ll.173ff.

[474] See H.G. Güterbock, "Hittite Mythology", p.156.

[475] See R.T. Rundle Clark, *Myth and Symbol*, p.76.

[476] It should be noted that the male Geb, in Egyptian mythology, represents earth rather than heaven, as in Greek and Sumerian and Indian mythology.

[477] See E.O. James, *op.cit.*, p.177.

[478] See E.A.W. Budge, *op.cit.*, I:100.

underworld similarly represents Time.[479] The serpent is also the form taken by the Sumerian Enki/Okeanos surrounding Earth, showing the identity between Shu/Enlil and Enki.

THE SECOND SACRIFICE

From the cosmic egg developed in the Cosmic Man arise the lotus formation of **Earth** and the perfect Light of the divine Mind, **Brahman**.[480] The Intellectual Light (Brahman) of the universe represents also the Self-Consciousness of the deity. In the Purānas, Purusha [i.e. as Brahman] is indeed called the mirror of divine self-consciousness, the coming to consciousness of the supreme Self (*BP* VI,5,17).[481]

This perfect light of the cosmos that marks the beginning of the second kalpa called Padmakalpa does not last indefinitely as it did in the first, Brahmakalpa but is destroyed and forced to descend into the underworld whence it emerges later as the sun of our system. The mythological form of the destruction of the first light is to be found in the story of Zeus' swallowing of Phanes in the Orphic cosmogonies. This, as we shall see, is a euphemism for Zeus's swallowing of Phanes' phallus itself.[482] In the Egyptian mouth-opening rituals too, we note

---

[479] See p.240 below.

[480] See p.187 above.

[481] This is also the real significance of the obtuse biblical rendering of the same idea in *Genesis* I:27 as God creating "man" in "his own image". Adam, meaning "man" in Hebrew, is linguistically the same as Purusha. The god who creates Adam is El and not Jahve, for, according to the Phoenician mythology ascribed by Philo of Byblos to Sankhuniathon, the Phoenician counterpart of Chronos was El, son of Ouranos and Ge (see Philo of Byblos, *op.cit.*, p.49; cf. H.G. Güterbock, "Hittite Mythology" in S. Kramer, *Mythologies*, p.160). This El is the same senior god whom the Hebrews too once worshipped in their originally polytheistic pantheon before they transferred their sole allegiance to his son, Jahve, under the tutelage of Abraham. Since El is Chronos, the "man" that he creates is the anthropomorphic Brahman/ Phanes.

[482] See below p. 192.

that the moribund solar force Osiris is depicted as being revived with the "thigh" of Seth (the Egyptian counterpart of Zeus), which is clearly a euphemism for the sexual organ of Horus the Elder which Seth must, like Zeus, have swallowed.[483] In the Indic literature, Ganesha, like his counterparts Zeus/Teshup/Seth, is said, in the *ShP*, to have attacked Brahma after he attacked his father Shiva (just as Shiva/Kāla attacked the primal Heaven of the Purusha). In the *ShP* and the *SP*, Shiva is said to have beheaded his son and then, on Pārvatī's pleading, found an elephantine replacement for it.[484] This may be an incident in the combat between father and son which resulted in the swallowing of Shiva's phallus. For, the trunk of the elephantine head that Ganesha ultimately obtains is clearly phallic. Ganesha is further depicted with a "pot-belly" which contains the entire universe, so the universal power of the Shaivite phallus is reflected both in Ganesha's head and in his stomach.[485]

In the Hurrian epic of the Kinsghip in Heaven, one of the products of the castrated Anu's seed formed in the belly of Kumarbi is **Teshup**, the Weather-god,[486] along with the other gods of the Mid-region who include Tashmishu (Suwalliyat, the sun-god), and Marduk. These are the gods who correspond to Seth, Horus the Elder, and Horus the Younger in the Heliopolitan cosmogony. Teshup interestingly is not merely a son of Kumarbi (Enki), but also of An, since it is the latter's seed that is preserved in Kumarbi when Kumarbi bites off An's genitals.[487] Teshup's mother is said to have been Earth (Text Ib9 of the epic) since

---

[483] Cf. the *Book of Job*, 40:17 where the reference to the tail and thigh of Behemoth are clearly to his penis and testicles (see J.E. Hartley, *The Book of Job*, p.525). Horus is said to have "castrated" Seth as well in 'The Contendings of Horus and Seth' (see below p.45f)

[484] See S.L. Nagar, *op.cit.*, pp.8f.

[485] *Ibid.*, p.115.

[486] Teshup is a later Hurrian form of the earlier Hattian deity adored in the form of a bull, Taru, Taurit (see *KG*, p.134f.).

[487] Kumarbi is himself a chthonic deity. and androgynous, since he gives birth to Teshup and his siblings.

Earth is the consort of Heaven, who is castrated by Kumarbi.[488] Tashmishu[489] who is called Teshup's "pure brother", may be the Hurrian counterpart of the Hittite Suwalliyat (Sūrya).[490] Teshup is indeed regularly coupled with his "pure brother" Suwalliyat, just as the storm-god Adad is with the solar Shamash.

Just as Seth is represented in Egypt as dragging Osiris down, and Zeus swallows Phanes, or his genitals, their Hurrian counterpart uses a sickle (much like that used by Kumarbi to castrate An) to sever the phallus of Heaven, Ullikummi, from off the shoulders of the giant Uppeluri (symbolising the Cosmic Egg) who bears Heaven and Earth. Since Uppeluri represents the Cosmic Egg, the severing of the "stone" Ullikummi from it clearly denotes Teshup's seizure of the phallus of An from it. It is significant in this context to note that the commentator of the Orphic Derveni theogony explains that Zeus indeed swallowed "the sexual organ" (**aidion**).[491] In other versions of the Orphic theogony, Phanes is said to be devoured by Zeus,[492] thereby absorbing the original universe into himself, but we may assume that it is the phallus of Phanes that is thus consumed. From this Orphic evidence we may assume that the Hurrian Teshup too finally swallows this phallus so that the universal life that it contains moves into his own body.[493]

As Seth is given the dominion of heaven in Egypt,[494] so too Teshup's rightful domain as the storm-god is heaven. That Teshup is the equivalent of the Egyptian Seth is borne out by the cuneiform

---

[488] See H.G. Güterbock, *Kumarbi*, p.87.

[489] The Hurrian form hides the Akkadian name of the sun-god 'Shamash' within it.

[490] See H.G. Güterbock, "The God Suwalliyat reconsidered", 1-18. Güterbock considers these names to be indicative of Ninurta and he is right insofar as Ninurta is ultimately the same as his father Enki/Osiris-Horus the Elder, though he is properly the solar seed of his father.

[491] See M.L. West, *Orphic Poems*, p.85. It is not surprising therefore that Protogonos is called both Phanes and Priapus in the Orphic Hymn VI (*ibid.*, p.252).

[492] See M.L. West, *op.cit.*, p88f.

[493] Cf. the similar case of Ganesha above p.191.

[494] See p.222 below.

treaty of alliance between Hattusilis and Rameses II, where Shamash, the sun-god, and Teshup are mentioned in the same way as Shamash and Adad, the storm-god, are in Assyria.[495] (The "vizier" [brother] of Teshup is said to be Ninurta, who must then be identical to Suwalliyat/ Tashmishu.)[496] We see therefore that the sun-god and weather-god are two aspects of the same deity and co-operate in the formation of the sun of our system. Thus the two are often considered as dual deities, as for instance, Shamash-Adad

The Egyptian counterpart of Teshup, Seth, is a son of Geb, and the stormy brother of Osiris. An Egyptian text declares that Seth felled Osiris the sky.[497] This felling of the heavenly light is necessary for the emergence of the solar force in the mid-region, since it involves, crucially, the consumption of the heavenly phallus and its transference into the underworld. Thus, although Osiris is murdered by his "brother" Seth, he is later resurrected in the underworld as his son, Horus the Younger, the sun-god of the horizon.

The birth of the sun is related to the tragic passion which Osiris undergoes whereby the light of Heaven is transformed into the principal light of our solar system. Osiris may have been killed by Seth in the form of a bull,[498] which is also the form of Teshup/Taru.[499] According to Plutarch (*De Iside et Osiride*, 18), Seth (Typhon) not only killed Osiris but also dismembered him and, though Isis succeeded in reassembling his body, his phallus was not to be found since it had been thrown into the river where it was consumed by certain "fish". Osiris' resurrection is thus effected ritually in a mouth-opening ritual which requires the heart and the foreleg of a bull (representing Seth),[500]

---

[495] S. Langdon and A.H. Gardiner, "The treaty of alliance between Hattusili, king of the Hittites, and the pharaoh Rameses II of Egypt", *JEA* 6 (1920), 187.

[496] See above p.192.

[497] Pap. Bremner-Rhind, 5,7,8 (see H. Te Velde, *Seth*, p.85).

[498] See H. te Velde, *op.cit.*, p.86.

[499] See below p.198; cf. p.163n above.

[500] H. te Velde (*op.cit.*, p.89) thinks that the foreleg is Seth's, since, in "other texts", the foreleg of Seth is to be "strictly guarded by Isis and the sons of Horus". It is possible that the foreleg has a phallic significance as well since Zeus is supposed to

for the foreleg represents Seth's genitals. That it is Seth who must revive Osiris is not a contradiction since Seth is indeed the *alter ego* of Osiris.[501] That is why the mutilation of Re is also represented as a self-castration of Re,[502] Seth is indeed clearly a phallic god, since the moon, Toth, who is engendered by the homosexual union of Seth and Horus the Younger, itself needs the stimulation of Seth's phallus to become infused with light and sight.[503]

Seth, the stormy aspect of Osiris himself, is also a god associated with intoxication, and especially the inebriating force of beer: "He confuses the heart to conquer the heart of the enemy".[504] Beer here is the Egyptian equivalent of the Indic Soma.[505] Seth is occasionally also identified with Apop, the serpent that he combats,[506] since the latter represents the gaseous wind which surrounds Earth. The "arm" of Seth is a weapon with which he vanquishes Apop,[507] to secure the passage of the sun-barque. It is important to note also that it is Seth who is finally given rule over Heaven since Osiris/Horus has already been dragged down from Heaven to the realm of Earth[508] whereas Seth remains as a god of thunder and storm in the region above

---

have swallowed the phallus of Heaven (see below p.198). Seth is also represented in the mouth-opening ritual by his metal 'mshtyw', which is mentioned in the chant accompanying the ritual to open Osiris' mouth (*ibid.*, p.88).

[501] That Seth is but Osiris' alter ego was brilliantly suggested by H. Te Velde, *op.cit.*, p.95.

[502] See M.S. Holmberg, *op.cit.*, p.44.

[503] See H. Te Velde, *op.cit.*, p.49f.

[504] Pap. Leiden I 348, rt.13,4; cf., H. Te Velde, *op.cit.*, p.7. The intoxication of Seth is surely related to that of Indra, the soma-drinker, and Dionysus the wine-drinker (see below pp.48n,57). According to a Leiden papyrus, his name represents the intoxicating power of beer. As the god of fermented liquor, Seth is clearly a "Bacchic" god. According to Plutarch, the name of Seth means "the overpowering" (see H. Te Velde, *op.cit.*, p.3ff.).

[505] See below pp.215ff.

[506] See H. Te Velde, *op.cit.*, p.104. Plutarch also considers Seth as the equivalent of Typhon (see *De Iside et Osiride*, 367).

[507] *Ibid.*, p.87.

[508] See H. te Velde, *op.cit.*, p.61.

it, corresponding to the Hurrian "weather-god", Teshup and Zeus Adados.

In the Indic literature, the sacrifice of Prajāpati/Brahman is depicted in sexual terms that suggest a castration. According to *SB* VI,i,1,2, when Prajāpati/Brahman desired to have union with his daughter, Dawn, **Rudra/Shiva** is instructed by the gods to avert this incestuous intercourse,[509] whereupon Rudra pierces Prajāpati with an arrow.[510] The myth of Shiva's attack on Prajāpati for his incestuous intercourse with his daughter Dawn is a repetition of the assault on Ouranos by Chronos in the Hesiodic theogony. However, the seed of Prajāpati forms the solar force, Skanda.[511]

In the Vedas, Prajāpati/Brahman is also called "Purusha" since the second cosmic sacrifice is a duplication of the first ideal one. That the sacrifice of Prajāpati, or Purusha, is a self-sacrifice is clearly stressed in the Vedas. *KYV* IV,6,2, for instance, declares: "Do thou thyself [Vishvakarman = Prajāpati] sacrifice thyself to thyself, rejoicing".[512] In *RV* X,90 ('Purushasūkta'), Purusha is offered as a sacrifice by the gods and out of him are formed the creatures.[513] In *TS* V,2,5,1 the cosmic

---

[509] Cf. *SB* I,vii,4. Since the punishment inflicted on Prajāpati/Brahman (An) in the Vedas is due to his incestuous intercourse with his daughter Usha (Inanna), we should not be surprised to note that, in Sumer, Inanna herself is both An's daughter and consort (see the hymn (A.O. 6458) where (ll.19-20) Inanna is declared An's legitimate consort (H. Wohlstein, *op.cit.*, p.111).

[510] Cf. *SB* I,vii,4. This story is repeated in the Purānas with Brahma substituting Prajāpati (see, for instance, *SP* III,40,1-59; cf. W. O'Flaherty, *op.cit.*, p.126).

[511] See below pp.197f, 208,226f,236.

[512] This sacrifice of Purusha which initiates the creation of the universe is the basis of the oldest Indo-European human sacrifices attested especially in Iran, Germany and Gaul (see Bruce Lincoln, *Myth, Cosmos and Society: Indo-European Themes of Creation and Destruction*, Cambridge, MA: Harvard University Press, 1986), and, to a lesser degree, in India. The description of the Purushamedha in *SB* XIII,vi suggests that, in India, the human victims were not slaughtered, for, according to *SB* XIII,vi,2,12-13, "if thou wert to consummate [the victims], man would eat man. Accordingly, as soon as fire had been carried round them, [the sacrificer] set them free, and offered oblations to the same divinities, and thereby gratified those divinities".

[513] This closely resembles the episode in the Babylonian Atrahasis mentioned above

Purusha is called "the sacrifice". And all the gods are said to extend this sacrifice (*RV* X,10,9,5). **Brahmanaspati** in particular, the chief of the gods and equivalent of Ganesha and Zeus, assumes the title of Lord of the Sacrifice.[514] In *VS* II,13, Brahmanaspati is beseeched to "extend" the sacrifice, whereby is probably indicated the "formal" extensive power of the castrated phallus.[515]

Ganesha is indeed the precise counterpart of the Egyptian and Near Eastern storm-god in India and Skanda's enigmatic "brother".[516] It is interesting that, in the Mesopotamian 'An=Anum' list, Shamash the sun-god and his stormy counterpart dIM are represented as d.Sulaat and d.Ha.ni.is respectively.[517] The latter may well be the same deity as Ganesha in the Indic religion.

Like Seth, Ganesha was apparently considered originally as a malevolent deity called Vināyaka who caused obstacles to men and inflicted barrenness and delirium on them.[518] The cruel aspect of the Sethian cults is reflected in some of the Ganesha cults in India too, which are given to worshipping an obscene image of the god in the course of drunken and sexually promiscuous revels.[519] Further, Ganesha obstructs the sacrificial devotions of the gods (*BrP*) and hinders men from worshipping Soma (*SP*).[520] In the *BrvP*, Ganesha is visited at birth by Sani (Saturn/Chronos, who is the same as Shiva himself),[521] whose maleficious gaze causes Pārvatī's son to lose his

---

p.136.

[514] Cf. *SB* I,vii,4,21-2.

[515] The notion of "extending" the sacrifice also betokens the expansion of the sacrificial symbols into their original cosmic form and force (cf. p.246 below).

[516] Just as Seth is coeval with Osiris as well as with Horus the Younger, his Indic counterpart Ganesha is equally so with Shiva and Skanda, since the latter is but the solar aspect of his "father".

[517] Tablet III, No.269ff; see R. Litke, *Reconstruction*, p.145.

[518] See the Mānavagrihyasutra and the Vājapayagrihyasutra (in S.L. Nagar, op.cit., p.45).

[519] See 'Ganesa' in *Hindu World*, Vol.1, p.378.

[520] *Ibid.*, pp.16, 49, 52.

[521] See above p.184.

head, which is then replaced by Vishnu with the head of an elephant,[522] the form in which he is worshipped today in India. In the *ShP* and the *SP*, it is Shiva himself who beheads his son and then, on Pārvatī's pleading, finds an elephantine replacement for it.[523]

Indra is closely related to Shiva and is an "assistant" of Angra Mainyu (Shiva) in the Avesta. Indra is particularly the tremendous force of solar energy who is characterised especially by his weapon, vajra, which later allows the solar energy to emerge as the light of the universe. Thus he is closely related to Shiva's son Ganesha/Seth, who aids the formation of the sun in the underworld. At the same time, Indra is also related to Skanda/Muruga/Marduk and therefore to Enlil's son, Ninurta or Inurta.[524] The latter, however, is indeed the same as his stormy brother since he too – like his "brother" Teshup (Seth/Zeus) – is described as fighting the dragon and facilitating the development of the sun.

The birth of Indra, the chief of the gods, resembles that of Seth, who is said to have emerged "sideways from his mother".[525] At *RV* IV,18,1-2 Indra is said to have issued sideways from his mother Aditi and, on his birth, his mother hid him (IV,18,5). Although this awkward manner of his birth associates Indra with Seth, as well as with Zeus, Seth represents Ganesha, the son of Shiva, rather than Indra himself. Once again we note a fusion of the force represented by Indra/Shiva with Shiva's violent son, Ganesha, who himself is inextricably related to his solar brother Skanda. Indra, who is closely associated with Shiva, is indeed split into the two forces (or

---

[522] *Ibid.*, p.12f.

[523] *Ibid.*, pp.8f.

[524] This variant spelling is attested in AKF II 128. Among the Kassites, Ninurta is given as one of two Akkadian glosses to the name "Marattaš", which may stand for the leader of the Maruts (see p.200n below). Indra is called "marutvat", accompanied by Maruts, in *RV* I,100,1 (cf. *RV* III,4,6; III,47,1; III,50,1). Dumezil has suggested that the other gloss, Gi-dar, is also probably a corruption of Indar (see G. Dumezil, *Dieux cassites*, p.27; cf. A. Deimel, *Pantheon*, "Nin-ib", p.210). It is possible also that it is to be read as Mitra. At any rate, we note that Indra is identified with the solar son of Shiva, Skanda/Ninurta.

[525] See Plutarch, *De Iside et Osiride*, Ch.12; cf. H. Te Velde, *op.cit.*, p.27.

"sons") which constitute the solar energy, Skanda, and the storm-force Ganesha.

Indra represents the seminal solar force of Shiva which will form the sun. Indra's vital and heroic quality – that of Zeus/Teshup/Ganesha - is emphasised by his frequent epithet of divine 'Bull'.[526] The Bull is also a typical epithet of Teshup of the Hittites, who is a counterpart of Seth/Zeus Adados.[527] Similarly, in Sumer, the term "Bull of Heaven" is used of Girra (Agni), and it also serves as an appellation of Enlil, (CT 24,5,41 and CT 24,41), as well as of Adad (CT XV, 3f.), that is, of the stormy wind-like stages of solar evolution which, finally, are of greater importance in the formation of the sun than the purely luminous element represented by the pure brother of Adad/Seth/Teshup/Ganesha.

In Greece, **Zeus** is the storm-force which swallows Phanes, or his phallus. He thus forces the life and light of Ouranos down into Earth before it can rise up to the sky as the sun. In Homer, Zeus is recognizable as a storm-god, and, according to Diogenes of Apollonia, the Homeric Zeus is the "apotheosis of air [Vāyu]".[528] Zeus is also identified by Herodotus with Teshup's Syrian counterpart, Adad, as Zeus **Adados**.[529] The fact that Phanes is swallowed by Zeus [Adados] renders more easy the identification of the divine pairs, Phanes and Zeus, Horus the Elder-Osiris and Seth, Tashmisu-Suwalliyat and Teshup, Ninurta and Adad, Skanda and Ganesha, for it is due to the absorption of the vital power of Heaven by the storm-god that the cosmic light is reborn in our system as the sun.

---

[526] The adoration of deities in the form of a bull may be traced back to Anatolia, where bovine altars are found in the ruins of Çatal Huyuk from the 7th millennium B.C. The founders of this most ancient culture may have been proto-Hurrians/Dravidians since the Subartu (=Hurrian) culture was widespread in the Near East from very early times (see A. Ungnad, *Subartu*, p.114) and the transmission of the bull-cult to Sumer may have been via Elam, where the temples, like the present-day South Indian ones, bore bull's horns on their tower (see W. Hinz, *Lost World*, p.56).

[527] See G. Wilhelm, Hurrians, p.70.

[528] See A.B. Cook, *Zeus*, I:351.

[529] By the end of the second century B.C., Zeus comes to be identified quite commonly with Adad as Zeus Adados (see A.B. Cook, *op.cit.*, I:549).

We see therefore that the stormy aspect of Kāla/Chronos/Kumarbi, who caused the castration of the Ideal Man and his subsequent impregnation resulting in the Cosmic Egg, persists in the turbulent nature of his offspring. Although this assault forces the light into the underworld, the storm-god also encourages the resurgence of the solar energy in the form of the incipient sun of our system.

THE SOLAR FORCE IN THE UNDERWORLD

In the Egyptian CT, 'Book of the Two Ways', it appears that the course of the solar force of the Heavens is one that takes it into Earth, what is sometimes called the "underworld". Rosetau, for instance, is described as being "at the boundary of the sky" and contains the corpse of Osiris "locked in darkness and surrounded by fire",[530] Osiris' corpse being in the depths of this netherworld. Interestingly, the waters reached by the sun in the second hour of the *Amduat* are called **Wernes**, which is reminiscent of the Vedic Varuna.[531] The waters of Wernes are followed by those of Osiris in the third hour. In the fourth hour, however, the waters are replaced by the desert of Rosetau, or Sokar. In the sixth hour, that is, halfway through its passion, the sun of the underworld reaches the waters of Nun after leaving the desert of Sokar and lies in the waters as the corpse of Osiris. These waters are clearly regenerative, as the Tenth Hour of the *Amduat* makes clear.[532] It is during the sixth hour that the corpse of Osiris is united with the spirit of Re. In The *Book of Caverns*, Osiris, who lies within the earth sphinx Aker at the centre of the underworld, becomes ithyphallic when the spirit of Re passes through the cavern. Since Osiris is but the underworld form of Horus the Elder/Brahman/Ouranos who has been castrated by his son, we see that the sixth hour in the underworld marks the return of his sexual potency. According to the Pyramid Texts, too, Osiris in the

---

[530] *Ibid.*, p.11.

[531] See E. Hornung, *Ancient Egyptian*, p.34.

[532] *Ibid.*, pp.33ff.

underworld is assimilated to Re, the solar force, at midnight.[533] Since it is Zeus/Teshup/Ganesha/Seth who preserves the divine phallus in himself we may also reasonably associate Re with Seth/Indra.[534]

In the Indic literature (*KB* 18,9), the sun is said to enter the waters and there become *Varuna*. This is not just a reference to the setting sun but to the birth of the sun itself in the underworld. Varuna in the underworld is the same as the Heavenly light Brahman/Mitra that has been shattered by Angra Manyu. From the underworld the solar force rises to the realm of Soma (Mind/Moon/Nanna)[535] and then emerges as the rising sun, Sūrya/Horus the Younger/Shamash. Varuna's typical location in the west[536] corresponds to Osiris' typical appellation as the god of the setting sun and of the spirits of the west, or the "westerners". The western region ruled by Varuna is the entrance to the underworld, the realm of Osiris.

The close relationship between **Indra**/Shiva/Agni and Varuna (Osiris) is borne out by more than one passage in the Vedas. In *RV* IV, 42, Indra calls himself Varuna "I am King Varuna". However, Indra is not exactly the same as Varuna but a form of him since, in *RV* VII, 82,5 we read that "In peace and quiet Mitra waits on Varuna, the Other [Indra] awful, with the Maruts seeks renown".[537] In *RV* VI, 68, 2, Indra with the mace used against the dragon Vrtra and Mitra are described as companions with contrary characteristics: "One with his might and thunderbolt slays Vrtra; the other (Mitra) as a Sage stands near in troubles" Mitra is typically the "brāhmanical" god, since he is

---

[533] See E. Hornung, *Conceptions*, pp.93-6.

[534] The solar equivalence of Indra to Re is borne out by *AV* XIII,3,13.

[535] In the *BP* (V,22,8), the moon (Soma representing the nutritive and energetic force of the moon) is located above the sun ("in the north"), just as the twenty eight constellations are situated above the moon one above the other (V,22,11).

[536] See *BP* VI,21,7.

[537] According to the *BP* VI,18,10ff., the Maruts are the sons, not of Aditi, but of Diti, who, like Aditi, is one of the thirteen wives of Kashyapa. They are borne by Diti as Asuras in order to destroy Indra, chief of the devas. However, Indra succeeds in entering Diti's womb and cuts the foetus into seven parts, which multiply seven-fold to form the forty-nine Maruts, who are later converted into devas by Indra and led by him.

originally the same as Brahman. Indra, on the other hand, is the war-like "kshatriya".

In the Germanic poem "Lokasenna" of the *Poetic Edda* we find a description of a feast prepared for the gods by the "sea-god" **Aegir** (who is in fact, the god of Ocean, Enki/Osiris), who is also called Gymir, since he is also the same as Hymir (Horus the Elder), who, as we shall see, is attacked by Thor (Seth). All the gods attend including Loki, the trouble-making Aesir who kills one of Aegir's serving men and thus starts a boisterous quarrel with the other guests. Loki is finally driven out of the party when Thor arrives and threatens him. However he does not leave without cursing Aegir that he shall no longer brew ale. Loki is thus the Eddic equivalent of Seth/Ganesha/Zeus.

The tale continues in an extract from the *Poetic Edda* called "Hymisqvidha" which begins with a scene wherein Aegir, when asked by Thor to brew ale for the Aesir (Asuras/gods), declares that he does not have a cauldron large enough for this purpose. The god Tyr, one of Thor's comrades, informs Thor that they could obtain such a cauldron from his father, the giant Hymir. Tyr and Thor go to Hymir and find not one but eight cauldrons, seven of which break when being taken down. The remaining one serves to cook a heavy meal after which Thor seems to accompany Hymir on a fishing expedition where Thor almost catches the world-serpent Jörmungandr. Hymir then taunts Thor on his inability to break the cauldron, whereupon, spurred by Hymir's wife, who explains that Hymir's skull is harder than the cauldron, Thor smashes the cauldron on Hymir's skull. Hymir laments the loss of his cauldron but allows Thor to take it with him. Thor lugs the cauldron to Aegir who is now finally able to brew beer for the gods. Loki and Thor are thus the same god as Seth/Ganesha/Zeus in their malevolent and benevolent aspects.

The name "Hymir" is itself clearly cognate with Ymir, the Primal Man who is, as we have seen, in the "Gylfaginning" of Snorri Sturlusson's *Prose Edda*, sacrificed by the gods Odin, Vili and Vé (who are indeed Ymir's grandchildren) and dismembered in such a way that the universe emerges from his body.[538] The association of our heavens with Ymir's skull is significant since in the "Hymisqvidha" Thor breaks the cauldron against Hymir's skull, which is supposed to be harder than the cauldron. Thor's assault on Hymir is clearly analogous to Indra's on Dyaus (Heaven) or Zeus' on Phanes. It is also akin to Odin's on Ymir in "Gylfaginning". What is more significant is that the assault results in Hymir's being robbed of his "cauldron", in order that Aegir/Gymir may have it. We have seen that the sacrifice of Phanes/Brahman entails the castration of this Cosmic Man the transference of his life-force symbolised by his phallus to the manifest world. Aesir's initial complaint of not possessing a cauldron large enough for the gods is indeed a complaint of his own impotence. Thor's obtaining of a cauldron from Hymir for Aesir is thus an account of how Thor obtained the phallus of Hymir in order to revive the same god submerged in the underworld as Aesir with it. This is the same as the revivification of the moribund Osiris in Egypt with the "phallus" that Seth/Ganesha/Zeus had swallowed after the attack on Horus the Elder/Brahman/Phanes.

ASHVATTHA - THE PHALLIC TREE OF LIFE AND AXIS OF THE UNIVERSE

The reviving potency of Osiris in the sixth hour of the *Amduat* betokens the rise of the universal life contained in the phallus of Heaven (Horus the Elder-Osiris) into the Mid-Region of our universe between Heaven and Earth. We know also that the divine phallus was absorbed by Zeus/Teshup/Seth so that the entire universe moved into his "stomach". This suggests once again that Seth is indeed the life-force of Osiris. The rising phallic force of this deity is often represented as a "**tree**" of life.

The universal tree has its roots in the Abyss or the underworld, while its trunk represents Earth and branches the Mid-region of the "atmosphere". Atop its branches, in Heaven, will emerge the

---

[538] See above p.185f.

full-fledged sun. In the Indic sacred literature, the 'ashvattha' fig-tree is considered to be inverted, so that its roots grow upwards and its branches spread downwards.[539] That the tree is an analog of the phallus is made clear by the reference in *LP* 17ff. to the phallus too as an endless column of fire which fills the universe, and at the top of which is Brahma in the solar form of a swan (hamsa)[540] and at the base of which is Vishnu in the form of a boar.[541] The sun-god (Sūrya/Āditya) is indeed the final manifestation within our universe of the original light of the cosmos, Brahman, which appeared above the "lotus" Earth.

In India, as in Sumer, the tree of life is the axis of the universe[542] comprising the three regions of earth, the mid-region, and the heavens, which are dominated respectively by the three forms that the solar energy assumes in our universe as well as in the primal cosmos - Agni, Vāyu, Āditya. Agni is, in *KYV* V,5,1, called "the lowest of deities", while Vishnu (i.e. as Āditya) is the highest. In the *Maitrāyana Upanishad* VI,4, the tree (called metonymously "Brahman") is called "three-footed", and from the evidence of the Germanic Edda we may consider these feet or roots as not restricted to heaven but as equally embracing Heaven, Earth and the Mid-Region.[543]

---

[539] *Katha Upanishad*, VI,1.

[540] The swan is Brahma's vehicle since it is the sun that conveys the Brāhmanical light to our system as the sun. The association of the swan with the sun in Indic mythology is the basis of the reference to swan-knights in the Germanic (see below p.274).

[541] The representation of Vishnu as a boar corresponds to Vāyu as the life of the universe since Vāyu, the breath of the Purusha, seeks out Earth in the form of a boar and mates with it (cf. *KYV* VII,1,4: "This was in the beginning the waters, the ocean. In it Prajāpati become the wind moved. He saw her, and becoming a boar he seized her. Her, become Vishvakarma, he wiped. She extended, she became the earth, and hence the earth is called the earth [lit. the extended]"). For the persistence of the boar imagery in the German mythology see above p.122n.

[542] The significance of the Grail as the axis of the universe has been noted also by Julius Evola, *Mystery of the Grail*, Chs.17,18.

[543] Moslem literature too retains the image of a downward tending cosmic tree which reaches to the lowest heaven. A similar tree growing from the lowest depths of Hell, however, grows upwards (See A.J. Wensinck, "Tree and Bird", pp.33,35).

Just as the Sumerian Enki does, so too Varuna, in *RV* I,24,7, "sustaineth erect the Tree's stem in the baseless region [the Abyss, apsu]", for Varuna is the Lord of the Abyss, or the underworld. The roots of the tree arise from deep within the Abyss, while the trunk represents Earth. The branches of the Tree of Life represent the Mid-region of the manifest universe and the sun which arises from atop them rules this region as well. The passage from the *Maitrāyana Upanishad* mentioned above further makes clear that the "branches", which represent the Mid-region of the manifest universe, contain "space, wind, fire, water, earth and the like". The summit of the tree, that is, the highest point of its branches, represents Heaven, the domain of the gods. The highest of the three heavens serves as the seat of the gods (*AV* V,4,3,4). There the Ādityas enjoy their nectar of immortality,[544] while Yama (*RV* X,135,1) is ruler of the lowest heaven. According to *AV* V,4,3, the original location of Soma, which infuses the entire Tree, is in the highest heavens.[545]

The tree of life holds Heaven and Earth together and is also identified with **Indra**,[546] who, as we have seen, was also identified with the Ideal Man, Purusha.[547] Indra is called "the Bull" who has drunk the powerful Soma:

> 6. This Bull's most gracious far-extended favour existed first of all in full abundance.
> By his support they [the Ādityas] are maintained in common who in the Asura's mansions dwell together.
> 7. What was the tree, what wood,[548] in sooth, produced it, from which they fashioned forth the Earth and Heaven?

---

[544] The first of the Ādityas, Mitra-Varuna, are the lords of rta, or the me's, of the universe, the waters in which they were born being the seat of these me's.

[545] See the references to the realm of Soma in Schroeder, Ch.IV

[546] Indra is the mystical name of Indha, which, according to *SB* VI,i,1,2, means "the blower", a name that relates Indra to Vāyu.

[547] See above p.185.

[548] This particular curiosity with regard to the "wood" of the tree is clearly addressed to the erect phallus as well. See the reference to the drum made of this wood, below p.231.

These Twain [earth and heaven] stand fast and wax not old for ever: …
… He is the Bull, the Heaven's and Earth's supporter.[549]

In *RV* III,31, Indra develops into a universal tree as a result of his consumption of Soma and this Soma-inspired growth holds Earth and Heaven together:

> 11. For [Indra] the Cow [Aditi], noble and far-extending, poured pleasant juices, bringing oil and sweetness.
> 12. They [the kine] made a mansion for their Father [their protector, Indra], deftly provided him a great and glorious dwelling/ With firm support parted and stayed the Parents [Heaven and Earth], and sitting, fixed him there erected, mighty.
> 13. What time the ample chalice [of soma] had impelled him, swift waxing, vast, to pierce the earth and heaven.

Indra is always closely associated with the "Soma" or seminal fluid of the universe and he is called the "lord of the seed".[550] Indra is said to have imbibed the sap of life, Soma (seed), in the dwelling of Tvashtr,[551] who is the formative aspect of Dyaus. Soma is described in *RV* III,48,2-3 as that milk which Indra's mother, Aditi, "poured for thee [Indra] in thy mighty Father's dwelling./ Desiring food he came unto his Mother, and on her breast beheld the pungent Soma."[552] At *RV* III,I,7, the infant "Agni" is said to be nourished by the "milch-kine" (solar rays) which are present in the seven cosmic rivers which issue out of the mountain when Indra destroys the serpent Vrtra. The "cows" (the water of Aditi) are said to be impregnated by the "bull". At *RV* I,84,15 the "milch-kine" are said to have recognized their lord

---

[549] *RV* X,31.

[550] *MBh I*, 57, 1-27.

[551] This is the god worshipped by the Germans as Tuisto (see above p. 164).

[552] That soma is ultimately the same as (Ger.) samen/seed, which infuses Indra as the "Tree" of Life, is clear from this reference to Indra consuming soma at his mother's breast, since, according to the *Bundahishn* Ch.XVI,5, the woman's milk is produced by the male seed just as blood is produced by the female.

as Tvashtr's Bull in the mansion of the moon, the moon being the heavenly body in which the Soma will be finally stored.[553]

Indra's intoxication with Soma is also the source of the Dionysiac and Bacchic wine-rituals. Soma thus represents the creative potency of fire which is responsible for the formation of our universe and its light but must nevertheless be controlled in order to allow the sun to emerge as the ruler of the universe. In this context, it may be noted that, in the Brāhmanas, the moon (SB I,vi,4,18) as well as Soma (SB III,iv,3,13) is called Vrtra,[554] the serpent, which we shall see is also infused with Soma and Agni. The moon, which is always associated with Soma, is indeed considered to be a form of Agni as Kāma (Desire).

It has been suggested, also, that, in the human microcosmos, the Tree may be manifest as the central nervous system.[555] Since the base of the spinal cord is the seat of unconscious, as well as of sexual, activity, it is indeed the task of spiritual man in the yogic system to rise to supraconsciousness by mastering the "serpent".[556] The tree which sustains the microcosmos as well as the macrocosmos is, indeed, filled with the seed of desire which, when it succeeds in producing the clear light of consciousness (Brahman) in enlightened man, at once prompts the destruction of the tree itself as an illusion.[557]

In Mesopotamia, the solar deities Tammuz and Dionysus and Ninurta are all admired as a Tree of Life, which is indeed symbolic of the entire universe at the head of which appears the sun. Shamash and Tammuz, representing the sun of heaven and the sun of earth,

---

[553] See below p.215f.

[554] See A.K. Lahiri, Vedic Vrtra, pp.181,183.

[555] For an understanding of the tree within the human microcosm as the structure of the entire nervous system itself see V.G. Rele, op.cit., pp.26f. The two hemispheres of the brain are considered by Rele as symbolic of the two heavens, while the base of the spinal cord represents Earth.

[556] See below pp.220ff

[557] This characteristic Indo-European spirituality is recovered in the West in the philosophy of Arthur Schopenhauer (especially in his masterwork, Die Welt als Wille und Vorstellung, 1819), who inspired Richard Wagner especially in the formulation of his last works including Parsifal.

ALEXANDER JACOB

are indeed represented as the guardians of the Tree of Life.[558] In the Sumerian poem, "Enki and the World-Order", the roots of the cosmic tree are generated by Enki in the Abyss. Enki is called (l.3) the son of Enlil (Shu) and of An (Horus the Elder), though he is the same as both. Enki is said to have planted the "**me** tree" or the tree of life in the Abzu. This tree, called a "**kishkanu**" (Sumerian "gishkin") tree in an Akkadian hymn to the "tree of Eridu", extends from the depths of the apsu, where Enki dwells, to the heights of heaven, and represents at the same time the pathway of Enki to mankind.[559] In the 'Epic of Gilgamesh' (IX,164ff) too, the hero finds a tree of "cornelian"and "lapis lazuli" at the eastern end of Earth, from whence the sun, Shamash, ascends to the heavens.[560] The protective shade of the tree is said to spread over the entire universe. At l.69 of "Enki and the World-Order" Enki is called the "great light who rises over the great below", as well as the "great lord of Sumer".[561]

Enlil's son Ninurta is also admired as the axis of the universe or tree of life. That the tree of life is a symbol of Enlil's warrior son, or "strong arm",[562] Ninurta, is made clear in the epic *Lugal e* (l.189), where Ninurta is called "the cedar which grows in the **Abzu**" (l.189)[563] as well as "the great **Meš** tree" (l.310).[564] Ninurta is also called the "**date-palm**"

---

[558] See S. Langdon, *Tammuz and Ishtar*, p.31.

[559] See 'The Poem of Erra', I,150; cf. M. Rutten, "Les Religions Asianiques", p. 98f.

[560] See A.J. Wensinck, "Tree and Bird", p.3. In *Daniel* 4:10-17, Nebuchadnezzar describes a dream of a similar cosmic tree, and so too does Ezekiel in *Ezekiel* 31:3 (cf. A.J. Wensinck, *ibid.*, pp.25f.).

[561] Sumer itself is most probably the name of the "primordial hill" of the central island of Earth, through which the solar force of the universe emerges since Sumer is called "the great mountain, the land of the universe" in l.192. Sumeru ('Holy Meru') is also a name of Mt. Meru in *BrdP* I,ii,15,42. The names of the other lands around Sumer – Ur, Meluhha, Dilmun, Elam-Marhasi, and Martu - which Enki blesses in the poem of "Enki and the World-Order" may have similar cosmological significances.

[562] See J. Van Dijk, *Lugal ud*, p.29. The strong arm of Ninurta is itself personified as Adad/Sarur (see below p.233).

[563] *Ibid.*, p.75.

[564] *Ibid.*, p.90.

in the An=Anum god-list, Tablet I, dLugal.giš.gišimmar (ŠA6).[565] The mešu tree is like the kishkanu tree since, in the Irra myth,[566] its roots are said to be in the Ocean and its top touches the heavens. The mešu tree is called the "flesh of the gods" (*Poem of Erra*, I,150), since, as we have seen, its trunk represents 'earth', the material substance of the universe.[567]

We have noted that Indra is infused with the powerful seminal force of Soma, It is not surprising that Ninurta, like Shiva's son, Skanda, represents the seed of Enlil.[568] Ninurta is, like his father Enlil, also said to be a great "mountain" [i.e. phallus] which extends from earth to heaven. According to KAR 142,I,22ff, Ninurta's seminal force appears in seven forms as dIB (Urash),[569] Nin-urta, Za-ba-ba,[570] Na-bi-um, Ne-iri-gal, Sa-kud and Pa-bil-sag.[571] The Dilmunite[572] name of Nabium/Nabû, d.En-sa6-ag, in the myth of "Enki and Ninhursag", also contains a reference to the date-palm, just as the date-palm branch engraved on the left side of a Rimum inscription also hints at this metaphorical name of Nabû.[573] Urash or Lord of Earth is the same as Enki. Nabû is particularly the force within the moon (Soma). So we may assume that the last three names refer to the three stages of the manifesting sun as Agni-Vāyu-Āditya.[574]

---

[565] See R. Litke, *op.cit.*, p.46.

[566] See E. Ebeling, KARI, 168, Rs.I, l.28ff.

[567] See above p.202.

[568] So in the myth "Lugal-e" (see T. Jacobsen, *Treasures*, p.131).

[569] Urash refers to Enki as Lord of Earth, or the underworld, where Varuna/Osiris lies before his development as the sun.

[570] This is also an appellation of Marduk (See K. Tallquist, *Akkadische Götterepitheta*, p.364).

[571] See K. Tallquist, *op.cit.*, p. 421.

[572] We have seen already that Dilmun itself signifies the spot at which the sun rises, and is the paradise (the lower heavens) to which Ziusudra, the survivor of the cosmic flood (Yima/Manu), is sent at the end of his life.

[573] See K. Al-Nashef, "The Deities of Dilmun", p.346.

[574] See above p.203.

According to the Iranian *Greater Bundahishn*, Ch.XIV, the First Man, Gayomard gave birth autoerotically to the twins Mashye and Mashyane, who grew up "in the semblance of a **tree**, whose fruit was the ten races of mankind" (10). We have seen that the Tree of Life represents the life of the universe in the Mid-Region between Earth and Heaven. Gayomard is the same as Brahman/Prajāpati/Horus the Elder, who is struck down by Ganesha/Zeus/Seth and forced into the underworld.

In the Avesta (Rashn Yasht, XII,17), it is stated that, in the centre of the Vouru-kasha Sea (the Abyss), stands "the **tree of the eagle** … that is called the tree of good remedies … on which rest the seeds of all plants".[575] At the base of the tree is a "lizard" created by Ahriman to destroy the tree. However ten fish save the tree by continually swimming around it.[576]

In the Eddic mythology, the name of the **Yggdrasil** ash-tree may be phonetically related to the Vedic Indra.[577] We may note the similarity of the description of this tree in "Voluspa" and "Grimnismal" to those in the Vedas, and in Mesopotamian and Egyptian cosmological literature:

---

[575] Yasna 42,4 also mentions a sacred [unicorn] beast which stands in the Vouru-kasha sea; cf. *Bundahishn*, XIX, which refers to a three-legged ass with one horn, and the Indus seals with their many representations of a beast resembling a unicorn bull.

[576] See *Bundahishn*, XVIII,2. These piscine forms reappear in the story of the fish which saves Manu during the flood (see below p.241).

[577] See above p.155n for the use of the suffix 'šiel' with Indic divine names among the Mitanni. The popular interpretation of Yggdrasil, however (see, for instance, R. Cook, *op.cit.*, p.23), is as "steed of Odin", from Ygg, one of the names of this god meaning "the terrible" (see 'Grimnismal', st.54). The tree is associated with the horse in the Odin myth as well as in shamanistic rituals which depict the "ride" or "ascent" of the shaman to heaven (see M. Eliade, *Shamanism*, p.467). Indeed, the Vedic term "ashvattha" for the fig-tree itself contains the word for horse "ashva" (see J. Miller, *op.cit.*, pp.249f.). The conflation of arboreal and equestrian symbolism is perhaps related to the original conception of the universe as a phallus and of the sun that illuminates it. In fact, in the royal horse-sacrifice of the Indo-Āryans, the horse is equated with the sun itself since it is said to be produced from the "left eye" of Prajāpati (*SB* XIII,iii,1,1) and the sacrifice of the horse is meant to restore this eye to its proper place. The eye is here clearly a reference to the sun.

> I know an ash-tree stands called Yggdrasill,
> a high tree, soaked with shining loam.[578]

and:

> Three roots there grow in three directions
> under the ash of Yggdrasil;
> Hel lives under one, under the second the frost-giants,
> the third humankind.

> Ratatosk is the squirrel's name who has to run
> upon the ash of Yggdrasil;
> the eagle's[579] word he must bring from above
> and tell to Nidhogg below.[580]

Like the Indian tree, the Yggdrasil also grows downwards, since one of its roots is said to be based in the heavens, where the gods (Aesir/Asuras) hold court. Under this root is the well of Urd.[581] In one region of heaven called Valaskjalf (the hall of the slain) is to be found the seat of Odin, called Hlidskjalf, whence he surveys the nine worlds covered by the tree [there being three heavens, as well as three mid-regions and earths].

The second root reaches the Ginnungagap (the Abyss), where the "frost ogres" dwell. This region represents the waters from which the sun is finally born (just as it is born also from Heaven and from Earth). Here is to be found an oracular spring guarded by the sage **Mimir**.[582] Since the base of the tree, as we have seen,[583] is borne by Ea/

---

[578] Voluspa, 19, in *Poetic Edda*, p.6. The "shining loam" is the same as "soma", the life-giving sap of the cosmic tree.

[579] The eagle represents the sun (see above p.209, below p.229n).

[580] Grimnismal, 31-32, in *Poetic Edda*, p.56.

[581] "Gylfaginning" ("The Deluding of Gylfi"), 15, in *Prose Edda*, p.42f.

[582] A spring is found also at the base of the sacred oak of the Pelasgian Zeus at Dodona (cf. E.O. James, *op.cit.*, p.29). For the references to Mimir in Schroeder, see above p.58f.

[583] See above p.58.

Varuna we may quite reasonably identify Mimir with this deity. Mimir must then be the Germanic counterpart of the Babylonian Mummu, who in the poem *Enuma Elish* I, is called a "vizier" (or son) and is in fact an aspect of Apsu (Varuna). Mummu is also a name given to Marduk as creator of heaven and earth (see below p.230). Mimir's power of creation is particularly ideational according to Damascius' summary of Babylonian cosmogony, where he is described as τὸς νοητὸς κόσμος, the ideal cosmos.[584] Hence Mimir's characterisation as a wise god.

Mimir is indeed said to be one of the Aesir in Chapter 4 of "Ynglingasaga",[585] where it is recounted that, in the war between the Aesir and the Vanir, a truce was agreed upon whereby the Vanir sent their gods Njörðr and Freyr to the Aesir and the latter sent to the Vanir Hoenir and Kvasir. Later the Aesir sent Mimir to the Vanir and the latter sent Kvasir to the Vanir. However the Aesir Hoenir, who was made a chieftain of the Vanir, proved to be lacking in independent judgement and reliant on Mimir, so the Vanir seized Mimir, cut off his head and sent it back to the Aesir. Odin preserved the head of Mimir magically so that it would reveal secret knowledge to him. From our study of the felling of Phanes and An and Horus the Elder, we may presume that this mutilation is an euphemism for castration. In the "Völuspá" (29) of the *Poetic Edda*, Odin pledges his eye (that is, the sun) to Mimir in exchange for the latter's wisdom, while Mimir himself drinks mead from this eye, which lies in his well.[586] In "Gylfaginning" (15), Mimir is said to imbibe mead from this eye using the horn Gjallarhorn which the god Heimdallr will use to announce the Ragnarök, the end of the gods. Mimir's imbibing of mead is a depiction of his reviving potency and Heimdallr, whose "horn" he uses, is thus identifiable with the soma-strenghtened Indra and

---

[584] See A. Heidel, "The meaning of Mummu in Akkadian literature", *JNES*, 7, no.2, April 1948, p.101.

[585] This is the first saga in Snorri Sturlusson's collection of historical sagas, Heimskringla.

[586] Cf. p.237 below secret knowledge of the universe and the growing force of the sun are again juxtaposed.

beer-drinking Seth, and Heimdallr's "horn" itself is similar to Indra's "vajra" which represents the renewed creative vigour of the moribund solar force in the underworld.[587]

The third root ends in Hel, or Niflheim, which is Earth as well as the land of the dead, the underworld. At the base of this region dwells the serpent Nidhogg[588] in the well called Hvergelmir.

We may assume that between Niflheim and heaven is the realm of Ymir, which is the Mid-region of the material universe. In Indic literature, the lower heavens is ruled by Yama, who is also the king of the dead.[589] That the Nordic tree represents the axis from which the sun is born is further made clear in the verses that refer to "Arvak and Alsvid", two horses which "must pull wearily the sun from here".[590]

SOMA

It is interesting to note that, in the *Skanda Purāna*, the fig tree (which symbolises the life of the emergent universe as the phallic Tree of Life) at the centre of the cosmic streams is said to be unshaken by the "doomsday hurricane".[591] In the Nordic Edda too, the Yggdrasil which is destroyed at Ragnarök will inevitably revive the creation after this destruction since it contains within its trunk all the seeds of life.[592] This plenitude of life within the tree is also symbolised by the Moon, which bears the **seeds** of universal animal life, according to the *Bundahishn*.[593]

---

[587] See p.197 above.

[588] The name "Nidhogg" means "striker that destroys" (cf. *Prose Edda*, p.43). It is interesting to note that the serpent is said to be situated at the bottom of Niflheim rather than of the Abyss, as in the other mythologies.

[589] See below p.240.

[590] 'Grimnismal', 37. The name of the shield of the sun, "Svalin", in 'Grimnismal', 38, may be derived from the same root ("svar") which gave Suwalliyat/Sūrya.

[591] See S. Shastri, *op.cit.*, p.65.

[592] See "Voluspa"; cf. R. Cook, *The Tree of Life*, p.12. Cf. the similar power of the Grail-stone below p.267f.

[593] See below p.216.

In Sumer, the moon is the first son of Enlil's and called **Nanna/ Nannar** (the counterpart of the Indo-Iranian Soma/Haoma). The **moon** is the first son of Enlil to be raised to the upper world while Nergal remains in the underworld as a substitute for it. Nanna, as the great light, has priority over the rising sun, Utu (Shamash). Hence the moon is considered the elder or the great light in Sumer (Gishnugal), as well as in Egypt.[594] The moon is also referred to as Magur8, referring to the "makurru" ship of Ninurta as he rises as the sun.[595] Since the barque is the barque of earth, we may assume that the life of Earth, i.e. of the entire material universe, is that which is concentrated in the moon. Thus, before the sun is free to rise into the Mid-region of our universe, the moon is established therein bearing within it the life of the universe. In all the cosmologies that we are studying, the moon bears the seeds of life. While the "moon" bears the seeds of universal life, the sun which is borne by it bears the seed only of man.

The form of Nanna's Akkadian counterpart, **Sin**, like that of Indra, is that of a bull. In Hurrian and Middle Assyrian ritual literature, Sin is typically associated with the impregnation of a cow,[596] which may represent the material substance of the earth. Like Soma, Sin is particularly associated with the sources of life, which he guards as a "herdsman" of "cows".[597] The myth of "Nannar's journey to Nippur", for instance, relates how Nannar milked his cows, poured their "milk" into churns and gave his father Enlil the best of his pure products.[598] One of the attributes of Enannatum, the high-priestess of Nannar is indeed "the bearer of the life-giving egg",[599] since the high-priestess is

---

[594] See below p.219.

[595] See K. Tallquist, *op.cit.*, p.443; cf. Maqlu III,123ff.

[596] See N. Veldhuis, *A Cow of Sin*, Groningen: Styx Publications, 1991; cf. V. Haas, *Geschichte*, p.316. The complaint of the cow in the Iranian Yasna 29 is also for a protector, whom she obtains in the form of Zarathustra/Ziusudra, the first man.

[597] The moon bears the seed of the murdered Bull of Heaven (representing all animal life), or Hoama, in the Avesta (Fargard XXI, 9). The seed of the waters, of the earth and of the plants, on the other hand, is stored in the stars (Fargard XXI, 13).

[598] See T. Jacobsen, *Treasures*, p.127.

[599] en-sal-nunuz-zi dNannar (SAK 206 b2,1; see A. Deimel, *Pantheon*, p.236f).

considered to be the spouse of her god, who represents the generative potency inherent in the moon.

Again, in a Sumerian 'ersemma' hymn to Nannar, we find the following verse emphasising the intoxicating quality of the life-force stored in the moon:

> When you, father Nanna, rise to the shining sanctuary,
> Father Nanna, when you travel on the high flood as on a ship,
> When you travel there, when you travel there, when you travel there,
> When you travel there, when you pour out the intoxicating drink, when you travel there,
> When you feast yourself lavishly on the intoxicant that has been poured out, …

We may compare this to the Vedic hymn to Soma (also called Indhu) who represents the life-force or seed stored in the moon as well as the vital essence of the sun's light:[600]

> These rapid Soma-streams have stirred themselves to motion like strong steeds,
> . . . .
> Immortal, cleansed, these drops, since first they flowed, have never wearied, fain
> To reach the regions and their paths.
> Advancing they have travelled o'er the ridges of the earth and heaven,
> And this the highest realm of all (*RV* IX, 22)

and

> Swift Soma drops have been effused in streams of meath, the gladdening drink,
> For sacred lore of every kin.

---

[600] The association of Soma with the moon which is typical of Indo-Āryan mythology is thus also observable in the mythology of Nanna among the Sumerians.

Hither to newer resting-place the ancient Living Ones [Soma drops] are come.

They made the Sun that he might shine. (23)[601]

Just as Nannar is said to have milked his cows, Soma too is described as rich in cows that have been milked: "Down to the waters Soma, rich in kine, hath flowed with cows, with cows that have been milked" (*RV* IX,107,9).

Soma is the seminal life-force of the universe and the Purānas equate it with the **tears** which are shed by the creating god. In the Purānas (*PP* V,12,1-13; *MP* XXIII,1-10) these tears are received by the sky to form Soma. We may note, at this juncture, a popular legend which recounts the insemination of Pārvatī by Agni. When Shiva, her husband, sees her writhing in pain with the fiery seed of Agni (here the underworld god), he sheds tears, and from his tears is produced a "little man who used a torch and incense to smoke Agni out of the body of Pārvatī".[602] In *MP* 23,1-10, Atri, one of the seven sages created by Brahman, sheds tears from which Soma is formed as a young boy.[603] The homunculus in the first account may thus represent the infant moon.[604] Shiva is also frequently represented with the moon arising from his head just as Thoth does from Seth's.[605] The moon contains the Soma with which Shiva/Indra/Seth himself is infused.

The animal life of the universe, as we note from the Iranian evidence below, is stored in the moon. According to *RV* IX,42,1, Soma

---

[601] The conception of the moon-god as a cow-herd is carried over into the mythology of Krishna (who is considered one of the later incarnations of Vishnu), since Krishna is descended of the *lunar* Aila dynasty (see *BP* XIV,XXIV).

[602] See A. Miles, *Land of the Lingam*, London, 1933, p.219f. (cf. W. O'Flaherty, *op.cit.*, p.107).

[603] Cf. PP V,12,1-13.

[604] Interestingly, in Egypt, mankind itself is formed from the tears of Re (CT 1130 VII 465a, CT 714 VI 344f-g; see S. Bickel, *op.cit.*, p.199). Re sheds tears when his eye (the sun) goes out from him. This must refer to its manifestation in our universe. In an Orphic hymn to Helios too, it is stated that "Thy tears are the race of suffering mortals" (see M.L. West, *Orphic Poems*, p.213).

[605] See W. O'Flaherty, *op.cit.*, p.50.

is considered as the progenitor of the sun. This is no doubt due to its chronological priority to the sun. The moon itself is said to be formed by the infusion of Soma into the waters (*SB* IV,vi,7,12). Soma then engenders the sun in floods along with the other stars. Soma here is clearly identical to Indra/Ninurta filled with Soma. Indeed, in *RV* IX,5, Soma is hymned as the bull and the "self" of Indra himself.

Soma is commonly understood to be an intoxicant pressed from the soma plant and consumed by the Āryan priests during the ritual.[606] The Scythians, as we have noted, are indeed called "haomavarga Sakas", or soma-drinking Scythians,[607] and archaeological finds at the BMAC in Afghanistan include vessels stained with plant-juice. But the real significance of Soma in the Āryan literature is as the life-force of the macroanthropos. Indra's establishment of the solar force in the heavens is due to the potency derived from the Soma within him.

In the Iranian *Bundahishn*, the seed of the Bull (representing all animal life)[608] slaughtered by Angra Mainyu is purified and stored in the moon,[609] just as the seed of the slaughtered First Man (representing all human life) is stored in the sun.[610] The Bull is thus, in the Greater Bundahishn,[611] likened to the shining Moon just as, in Egypt, the seed of Horus reappears on Seth's forehead as the moon, Thoth. Similarly the First Man is likened to the shining sun (where his seed will be purified). In the Haoma-sacrifice, **Hoama** is represented anthropomorphically, for the pressing of the soma plant in this sacrifice is represented as a slaying of a primal god, Haoma

---

[606] The Vedic sacrifice involving the extraction of soma is called "kratu", while that without it is a "yajna".

[607] So in the inscriptions of Darius I (see P.O. Skjaervo in G. Erdosy, op.cit., p.157). Herodotus (VII,64) mentions that Saka was the name given by the Persians to the Scythians. The Behistun inscription (ca.522-486 B.C.) of Darius the Great refers to the Sakas in its Babylonian section as "Gimmirai" (Cimmerians), showing that they were closely related to the Celts in spite of the fact that the latter were western, centum Āryans.

[608] The seed of the dead Bull stored in the moon is the same as the life of the universe preserved after the "deluge" by the first man, Yima/Ziusudra/Manu.

[609] See *Bundahishn* X, 1-2; cf. *Fargard* XXI,9 and *Sirozah* I,12.

[610] *Bundahishn* XV.

[611] See RC. Zaehner, *op.cit.*, p.40.

or his anthropomorphic form **Duroasha** (or Frashmi), in order to extract his productive essence.[612] Duraosha is said to have been in existence even before Vivanghvant, the solar father of Yima (Manu Vaivasvata).[613] Yima is said to be the one who corrupted the Haoma rite by burning the sacred plant (Yasna XXXII,8). Haoma is declared to have been prepared for the corporeal world first by Vivanghavant (the sun) (Hom Yast IX, 3), and fourthly by Pourushaspa,[614] father of Zarathustra. Duroasha is sacrificed so that the vital force of Haoma may be expressed in the world. In the haoma-sacrifice, therefore, the pressing of the soma plant thus symbolises the extraction of the life-force of Haoma/Soma.

Haoma is considered by the Zoroastrians to be not only a source of immortality but also a destroyer of the Daevas (I,6). But the chief of the Devas in the Vedas is Indra, who, as we shall see, kills Vrtra, the serpent in the Ocean encircling Earth. The Iranian counterpart of Vrtra, Verethra, is killed by a figure called Weretraghna, who is the same as Vishnu. But Vishnu is only the expansive aspect of Indra. The Zarathustrian opposition to Indra is due to his role in the castration of his father, Heaven, with whom Haoma may be identified.

The moon god is no less important among the Egyptians than among the Mesopotamians and Indians and Iranians. Indeed it is in Egyptian mythology that we get the clearest account of the birth of the moon. Horus the Younger is said to have been violated by his "uncle" Seth, the storm-god, with the result that Horus is sexually excited and emits his seed. We have seen above that Seth, the stormy aspect of Osiris himself, is a god associated with intoxication, and especially the inebriating force of beer, which serves as the Egyptian counterpart of the soma.[615] Isis, however, contrives to collect the seed of Horus on lettuce which Seth, a lover of lettuce, subsequently eats. "Pregnant" with the seed of Horus, Seth then "gives birth", significantly from his

---

[612] See E.O. James, *op.cit.*, p.26.

[613] Yasna IX,17,27; X, 21; XLIII,5.

[614] It is not clear if Pourashaspa is the same as the Indic Pururavas who are said to have derived fire-worship from the Gandharvas (see above p.158).

[615] See above p.194.

forehead, to the golden disk of the moon, called **Thoth**.[616] Thoth is also identified with the moon-god Aah-Tehuti,[617] and he and Re, as the moon and the sun, are considered the two eyes of Horus (the Elder).

In some versions of the story of Horus and Seth,[618] Seth too, in seducing Horus, emits or "loses" his seed, an action which may have been interpreted as loss of sexual power or castration. The eye of Horus and the testicles of Seth are related to each other in a causal connection of light and life. In the town of Saka, Seth as a bull undergoes self-castration and, in the Pap. d'Orbiney, Seth (called Bata in Saka), castrates himself in order to avoid the sexual advances of his sister-in-law, and then goes into exile in foreign lands.[619] This story may also be related to similar legends of Shiva/Indra in the Indian Purānas[620] and of Attis in Syria.[621]

The phallic importance of Seth, however, is not diminished in this story of seduction and punishment since, even though the moon (Thoth) that is created from the union of Horus and Seth is called the "eye of Horus" (being formed of his seed), it is the "finger"[622] of Seth which is finally required to instil light in it.[623] The "finger" may have a phallic connotation and the force of light is intimately connected to that of life,[624] which Seth, like Indra, eminently embodies. Indeed, as Hornung perceptively suggested, it is possible that Seth is indeed identical to Heka, the Egyptian

---

[616] See H. te Velde, *op.cit.*, p.43f.

[617] E.A.W. Budge, *op.cit.* I, 412.

[618] For instance, Pap. Jumilhac (see H. te Velde, *op.cit.*, p.41).

[619] See H. te Velde, *ibid.*

[620] See A. Daniélou, *Shiva and Dionysus*, p.62.

[621] Cf. the reference to Lucian, *De Dea Syria*, see p.247 below.

[622] The typical depiction of the young Horus (Harpocrates) with a finger in his mouth, generally considered an indication of his infant nature, may also be a suggestion of the phallic violation of Horus by Seth.

[623] PT 48 (see H. te Velde, *op.cit.*, p. 49).

[624] See H. te Velde, *op.cit.*, p.51.

god who represents the magical source of light,[625] just as Ganesha is identifiable with Brahmanaspati. And finally, after the separation by Re[626] of Horus and Seth locked in sexual union, the two gods are reconciled, as Horus the sun, representing the light of earth in the Mid-region,[627] and Seth, the stormy life-force embodied in the thunder of the higher region of heaven. In historical terms, Horus and Seth were united as the rulers of Lower and Upper Egypt.

Moreover, in Pap. Hearst XIV, 2-4, Isis brings the moon "to her son [Horus, the incipient sun] to purge his body [after his sexual initiation by Seth]" in order to purify "the evil[628] which was in his body"[629] We have noted that, in the Avesta, the seed of the bull of heaven (Osiris) which is killed by Angra Mainyu (Seth) is concentrated and purified in the moon. We see that the moon is considered in Egypt too as a purificatory body and note once again a similarity between the Egyptian and Iranian theologies.

In the Theban cosmology, **Khonsu** is the moon-god, counterpart of Nanna. Khonsu is called the "great light,[630] just as, in Sumer too, the moon is called Gishnugal, the great light, since it is elder to the sun. Indeed, Khonsu is not merely the moon but also a twin of the solar force in the underworld, Horus the Younger.[631]

In Hermopolis, Amun engenders the moon-god Khonsu through his union with Mut/Hathor. Mut is particularly a form of Hathor in

---

[625] See E. Hornung, *Das Amduat*, I, 81, cf. II, 98; also H. Te Velde, *op.cit.*, p.177.

[626] Pap. Boulaq 17; in the "Contendings of Horus and Seth", it is Thoth who separates his "parents" Horus and Seth (see H. te Velde, *op.cit.*, p.61).

[627] Though the sun is primarily situated in the Mid-region, it begins as a light of earth, that is, in the underworld.

[628] This may refer to the animal life in the universe which comes to be stored in the moon, since the Zoroastrians generally consider the material universe as a corruption of the Ahura Mazdean.

[629] See H. te Velde, *op.cit.*, p.48.

[630] See K. Sethe, *op.cit.*, pp.31,114. In Sumer, too, the moon is called Gishnugal, the great light (since the moon is senior to the sun, Utu).

[631] The underworld sun and moon, Nergal and Sin, are called the 'great twins' (mashtabbagalgal) in Sumer (see A. Jacob, *Brahman*, p.68).

the underworld, where the moon is born.[632] Amun's pneumatic virtue is similar to that of the Heliopolitan Shu/Enlil. Khonsu, son of Amen-Ra and Hathor/Mut, like Enlil's "son" Nanna and the Vedic "moon"-god Soma, is a repository of the vital power of generation. Thus Khonsu is a god of fertility who causes women to conceive, cattle to become fecund, and the germ to grow in the egg.[633]

THE BATTLE AGAINST THE SERPENT

The rise of the solar force in the underworld into the Mid-region of our universe as the sun is not possible until the serpent at the foot of the Tree, in the depths of the Ocean, is destroyed. This serpent, which represents the force of Earthly constraint, is destroyed not by the solar god himself, since he is at first moribund in the underworld (as Osiris) and then puerile, as the incipient sun (Horus the Younger), but rather by the storm-god (Seth, Teshup, Zeus) who was initially the adversary of his solar counterpart, Osiris. The vital force which fells the fiery sky or solar force and causes the latter to descend into the "underworld" is, thus, not an entirely inimical one since it is the same that will destroy the serpent, separate the earth from heaven in our universe and allow, first, the moon and, then, the sun to rise to the Mid-region of the stars.

It is interesting to note that Osiris in the "underworld" is enfolded, as if in mummy bindings, by the serpent Nehaher ("the Fearful Face").[634] In the *Amduat* the eleventh hour marks the encirclement of the corpse of the dead Osiris (representing the solar light) in the coils of the serpent called "the World-Encircler".[635] Even though the latter is normally considered inimical to the solar light, the serpent preserves Osiris' corpse and is gradually cast off as Osiris revives and emerges in the twelfth hour as the light of the universe from the mound of

---

[632] See E.A.W. Budge, *op.cit.*, II:29.

[633] See E.A.W. Budge, *op.cit.*, II:35.

[634] *Ibid.*, pp.167ff.

[635] See E. Hornung, *op.cit.*, p.41.

Earth. Indeed Osiris (as Enki/Okeanos) is himself identified with a serpent, as the following PT 1146 makes clear:

> I am the outflow of the Primeval Flood,
> He who emerged from the waters,
> I am the "Provider of Attributes" serpent with its many coils …[636]

The serpentine Ocean (Okeanos) coiled around Earth is thus a primordial form of the deity of the primordial waters (Osiris/Enki). Osiris is indeed sometimes represented as encircling the underworld.[637] Sito the serpent that surrounds the primeval Hill is also called "son of Earth", as Osiris also is.[638] The serpent first holds together the corpse of Osiris and then accompanies the emergence of his son, the incipient sun, Horus the Younger.[639] Thus, when Osiris dies and descends into the underworld, his decaying corpse (represented as a mummy) is depicted in the *Book of Caverns* as being held together by Nehaher.[640] This contrast between the two aspects of the serpent is highlighted in the last scene of the *Book of Caverns*, which depicts a serpent within a mound of earth that helps regenerate Osiris as Horus the Younger along with another serpent encircling the solar beetle (Khepry) that is cut into pieces.[641] In the *Amduat* too, while Apop is destroyed in the seventh hour, in the eleventh and twelfth hours the emergent sun itself appears within the bounds of the serpent called "World encircler".[642] From the *MP* we learn that this serpent of the Abyss indeed serves as a rope that is tied between the boat of Manu [representing Earth] and the horn of the fish so that the boat may be drawn to its resting position atop Mt. Meru, the mountain at the centre of the earth from which the sun rises.[643]

---

[636] *Ibid.*, p.50.

[637] See R.T. Rundle Clark, *op.cit.*, p.249.

[638] *Ibid.*, p.240.

[639] See E. Hornung, *op.cit.*, pp.33ff; cf. R.T. Rundle Clark, *op.cit.*, pp.167ff.

[640] Cf. R.T.Rundle Clark, *ibid.*, p.169).

[641] See E. Hornung, *op.cit.*, p.90.

[642] *Ibid.*, pp.33ff.

[643] See S. Shastri, *op.cit.*, p.28; cf. p.239 below.

In the tenth and eleventh hours of the *Book of Gates*, the solar odyssey is marked by the battle against the serpent **Apop**.[644] Apop itself is said to have originated from the spittle of Re's mother Neith in the primordial waters and taken the form of an enormous snake that revolted against Re. That Apop is, in his origin, related to Re is not surprising since we shall see that Vrtra too, like Agni, is born of Tvashtr. Vrtra is also infused with Agni.[645]

In fact, Apop is on occasion identified also with *Seth*, just as Ninurta[646] and Marduk are symbolised as dragons themselves. Ninurta in Sumer and Marduk in Babylon too assume the stormy aspect of the son of Chronos, even though they are the same as Enki/Osiris. Marduk and Shamash are invoked together in prayers (C.A.H., pl.i, 226b), exactly as Adad (Seth) and Shamash are. We have seen that Seth represents the passionate element just as the serpent does the lingering earthly aspect of the solar force. The serpent's obstruction of the emergence of the latter in the universe however can be combatted only by the storm-god himself. Once again the contest is an internal one, just as the sacrifice of the Cosmic Man, as well as that of the First Man, was also a self-sacrifice. Seth overcomes Apop using his characteristic rage (nšn),[647] corresponding to the Indic 'manyu' and Iranian 'mainyu' which, as we have seen, are associated with Shiva/Indra.[648]

In the Heliopolitan myth of the sun too, Seth, though the murderer of Osiris, the divine Light, helps Horus the Younger fight Apop on the barque of Re in order to ensure Re's emergence as the solar light.[649] The barque itself is called the "barque of the earth" in the *Book of the Gates*.[650]

The serpent at the base of the cosmic tree essentially represents the tāmasic force which is a persistence of the dull material aspect of the deity which brought about the first cosmic manifestations

---

[644] See E. Hornung, *op.cit.*, p.64.

[645] See *AV* III,21,1.

[646] BE XXIX 1, rev.iii, 9; see J.V. Kinnier Wilson, *op.cit.*, p.17.

[647] See H. te Velde, *op.cit.*, p.101.

[648] See above p.197.

[649] See H. te Velde, *op.cit.*, Ch.4.

[650] See E.T. Hornung, *Ancient Egyptian Books*, p.60.

through its Māya, or power of illusion, which was also represented as the serpent Sesha on which the Ideal Man (Vishnu) reposed.[651] Thus, in *BP* V,25,1, the serpent Sesha is described as being the tāmasic or Māya-associated aspect of the supreme lord which sustains this universe by the magical effect of sympathy. In the Indian system of Kundalini Yoga, the *Kundalini serpent* (which is analogous to Vrtra)[652] is represented in the microcosm as the force of vitality as well as of sexuality coiled at the base of the spinal cord.[653] The aim of the yogic discipline is, as Cook puts it,

> to awaken this sleeping force and get it to climb the spinal tree, piercing the various spiritual centres (chakras) along its way, until finally it is released [like Brahman from atop the petals of the lotus in the Puranas or the sun from atop the sycamore in Egypt] from the Sahasra Chakra, the Thousand-petalled Lotus, at the top of the head. At this point the heavy material forces of the earth and the waters, ... take flight... The mythical eagle Garuda carries off Kundalini in its beak; heaven and earth, light and darkness, spirit and flesh are finally, ecstatically united.[654]

The sublimation of the serpentine force marks the rise of the soul, Ātman, to its original brilliance as the divine Consciousness, Brahman.

In the Vedas, **Vrtra** is a serpentine cosmic phenomenon represented as being located within a turbulent wind. Vrtra is a demon of resistance which prevents the "mountain" from ejecting its

---

[651] See *VP* I.2.64-65.

[652] See V.G. Rele, *op.cit.*, p.104.

[653] See R. Cook. *op.cit.*, p.25. The fact that the serpent provides Adam and Eve with sexual awareness in Genesis reveals the ultimate reliance of the Hebrew Bible on proto-Indic sources, even though the spiritual significance of the story of the cosmic man is entirely ignored by the priestly redactors of the Bible.

[654] See R. Cook, *ibid.* That this process is akin to a sexual orgasm is not surprising considering the significance of the phallus even in the macrocosmic creation. The "flood" which accompanies the emergence of the sun in our universe (see below pp.79ff) is thus naturally related to the waves of pleasure that suffuse our mind in sexual ecstasy.

life-giving seed. In *KYV* II,5,2, Vrtra is said to be called Vrtra because "he enveloped these worlds".[655] In *TS* II,iv,12,2, Vrtra is said to have grown and enveloped the three worlds.[656] Indra is the hero chosen by the gods to defeat the dragon, Vrtra, when all of the Ādityas, Vāsus, Rudras and gods were paralysed by the monster (*RV* 10,48,11). Indeed, Indra's freeing of the waters from the restriction imposed on them by the dragon Vrtra is associated with the creation of our heaven and earth, which are formed out of Vrtra's body (*RV* I,36,8).

In *BP* VI,9,18, Vrtra is said to cover the universe in darkness, which is not surprising considering that his father Tvashtr is the same as Tartarus, who, according to Hesiod (*Theogony*, 820-22), is the parent of Typhon.[657] And, as Plutarch noted of the Greek hydra, "Typhon is the element of the soul which is passionate, akin to the Titans, without reason, and brutish, and the element of the coporeal which is subject to death, disease and confusion".[658]

Indra also succeeds in freeing the "cows" from the "vala", a rocky enclosure in which they are hidden by the evil **Panis**.[659] The "cows" in the vala myth (10.67,1-12) symbolise the radiant solar energy, since *RV* I,164,3 suggests that this is the secret name of the rays of the dawn.[660] In *RV* X, 108, 5, the "cows" are described as "flying around to the ends of the sky". The Panis themselves are described in *BP* V,24,30 as serpentine, Asuric creations of Diti and Danu and inhabit Rasātala, the sixth of the seven subterranean regions of the material universe bordering on the last, called Pātāla, below which lies the serpent

---

[655] The etymology of the word, however, is more accurately preserved in the Avestan "Vrθra" meaning "resistance" (see A.K. Lahiri, *op.cit.*, p.73).

[656] It is in order to combat this control of the three worlds by Vrtra that Vishnu expands through these worlds with his three gigantic steps (see below p.83) and thus allows Indra to hurl his thunderbolt against the monster (see A.K. Lahiri, *op.cit.*, p.195).

[657] Cf. p.194n

[658] Plutarch, *De Iside et Osiride*, p.197.

[659] In the Vrtra myth (RV I,32,11) the waters confined by Vrtra are compared to the cows confined in the vala by the Panis. However, the Panis are here called 'Dasyus' and not 'Dānavas', as in BP.

[660] H.-P. Schmidt, *Brhaspati und Indra*, p.222.

Sesha. The Panis are thus related to Sesha/Vrtra and particularly associated with the primordial frigidity that obstructs the emergence of the solar rays in our system. It is interesting that "vala" is the same term that is used in the Avesta ("vara") for the ark which bears Yima during the flood which accompanies the birth of the sun.[661] This ark, as we shall note later,[662] is representative of the life of our universe in the Mid-region. And we have seen that the barque of Re is also the "barque of earth".

It is apparent thus that the separation of primal Heaven from Earth by Kāla/Chronos is repeated in the underworld ("earth") by Indra in order to allow the rise of the solar energy from there into the Mid-region of the stars. In *RV* VII, 23,3, it is stated that "Indra when he had slain resistless foemen, forced with his might the two world-halves asunder". In *RV* VI,8, this act of separation of heaven from earth, normally attributed to Indra, is ascribed to Mitra (Horus), since Mitra is but the early form of Indra as the sun:[663] "Wonderful Mitra propped the heaven and earth apart, … He made the two bowls [i.e. earth and heaven] part asunder like two skins".[664]

Vishnu is also credited with the accomplishment of this feat (*RV* VII,99,3), for we have seen that Indra and Vishnu bear the common epithet Vrtrahan/Weretraghna, in the Vedas and the Avesta. Vishnu represents the expansive and sustaining form of Agni much like Vāyu (Shu). In *RV* VII,99, Vishnu (like Marduk in *EE*, and Shu in the Heliopolitan cosmogony, who sustains the separated heaven and earth) is said to firmly support the two halves of the universe, heaven and earth, while he holds fast earth among the waters (Okeanos)

---

[661] The Vedic vala myth is thus a cosmological archetype of the Flood story. The animals saved from the deluge in the later Sumerian and Indo-Iranian Flood stories, as well as in the account of Noah in the Hebrew Bible derived from them, are - unlike the elements of solar energy symbolically referred to in *RV* as "cows" - real animals, and therefore associated with the seeds of all animal life borne by the Vedic Cow [Earth], as well as by the Iranian Bull.

[662] See below p.239.

[663] See below p.238.

[664] This recalls particularly the brutal image of Marduk's splitting of Apsu's consort, Tiamat (Aditi), into heaven and earth in (*EE* IV,137).

which surround it by fixing it with "pegs". According to *SB* XI,viii,1, the "pegs" are "mountains" and "rivers": "He sets this [earth] firmly with the help of mountains and rivers". These mountains and rivers may not be terrestrial, since, as we have noted above, the source from which the material universe as well as its light arises is itself a mountain, while the rivers may be the seven streams flowing through the universe.[665] The universe is said to have been spread out through Vishnu's sacrificial fervour. It is thus spiritual intensity which apparently causes spatial expansion. But if we consider the phallic significance of Marduk's violation of Tiamat[666] as well as of the Soma sacrifices in India,[667] we may be justified in endowing the term "expansion" with the connotation of "erection" as well.

In *RV* V,85, the separation of the heavens from the earth normally attributed to Indra is associated with Varuna, who is (like Indra and Shiva) said to have spread forth the earthly element "as a skin to spread in front of Surya" and "standing in the firmament hath meted the earth out with the sun as with a measure". In *KYV* I, 2, 14, Varuna is called the bull that "hath stablished the sky, the atmosphere/ Hath meted the breadth of the earth" (I, 2,8), for "All these are Varuna's ordinances".

The slaying of Vrtra not only forms heaven and earth out of the latter's body but also allows the elevation of the sun to the mid-region between them: "As you, Indra, killed Vrtra with power, you raised the sun in heaven to be seen" (*RV* I,51,4).[668] In the *AV* IV,10,5, the sun is said to be "born from the ocean, born from Vrtra".[669] According to *RV* X,121,7, it is Indra's deliverance of the waters from the grasp of Vrtra and their subsequent outflow which allow the waters to give birth to Agni (i.e. his third form as the sun). The waters, which are clearly related to seminal fluid, flow out as seven cosmic streams which are called "mothers" (*RV* II,12,3; X,17,10; VIII,96,1), who guard the birth

---

[665] See above p.205.

[666] See below p.229.

[667] See below p.253.

[668] See A.K. Lahiri, *op.cit.*, p.103.

[669] Cf. *SB* V,v,5,1-5.

of Shiva's solar son, Skanda (Muruga/Marduk). The vital solar energy rises from the depths of the Abyss in this flood, since Indra/Soma is said in *RV* IX,42,1[670] to engender the sun in "floods" along with the other stars.[671] Thus the flood is the result of the splitting of the universe as well as the condition of the creation of its light. Indra is therefore the hero who facilitates the birth of our universe as well as releases the solar energy from the icy forces of resistance represented by the Panis and Vrtra. The final identification of Indra with the sun of the heavens is also witnessed in several passages of the *RV*.[672]

In the Sumerian epic *Lugal e*, the outflow of waters resulting from Indra's defeat of Vrtra is reflected in Ninurta's causing a flood that accompanies the emergence of the sun. Like Indra and Adad, Ninurta is considered the "strong arm" of Enlil - who himself has a stormy character and both threatens the heavens and devastates the "lands that offer resistance".[673] However, Ninurta is also the solar force, and one of his seven forms is indeed Nergal, the sun of the underworld.[674] In the *Lugal e* epic, Ninurta is represented, much like Indra in the Vedas, as battling a monstrous creation (hidden in a mountain) of unseparated earth and heaven called **Asakku** (who may be a form of Antum, Earth itself),[675] which constrains, through its frigid force, the

---

[670] Soma is the potency imbibed by Indra (see below p.231).

[671] See *RV* II,19,3:
"Indra, this mighty one, the dragon's slayer, sent forth the flood of waters to the ocean,
He gave the sun his life, he found the cattle".

[672] See, for instance, *RV* VIII,6,24,30; I,83,5; III,39,7; VIII,69,2; X,55,3; X,111,7. The solar imagery associated with Indra is noticeable also in *RV* I,84,1, where his particular virtue (indriyam) is said to fill the deity as the sun's rays fill the darkness.

[673] See the hymn to Enlil, in A. Falkenstein, *Sumerische Götterlieder*, p.98 (cf. p.73n below for the term "resistance"). As Assmann has pointed out (*op.cit.*, pp.42,53), the resistance that is offered by Apop is both a physical withholding of light and life and a symbol of evil itself which has to be destroyed so that Maat (Rta), the divine order of the cosmos may be established; cf. the 19th Dynasty hymn to Amun where it is stated that each of "those who transgress [this] written order is a rebel against Re" (A. Barucq and F. Daumas, *op.cit.*, p.229) cf. p.232n.

[674] See above p.208.

[675] Cf. the liturgical commentary O175 where Asakku is equated with Antum (F.

solar energy (the life-giving "waters") contained in the mountain.[676] The defeat of Asakku as well as of the Mountain which Asakku has dominated results in the separation of Heaven and Earth and a flood of cosmic waters which threatens to destroy all life in the cosmos.[677] Ninurta therefore constructs a dam out of the stony and metallic materials of the corpse of Asakku. This dam is called "hursag", or the foothills, and Ninmah, Enlil's wife and Ninurta's mother, is thus, at the end of the *Lugal e* myth, called Ninhursag, or Lady of the Foothills, which represent the earth of the material universe to which Ninurta has now directed the waters of the cosmic streams.

The mountain rising from the foothills passes from Earth to the Mid-region of the universe, and the seed of the "primordial hill", Ninurta himself,[678] will finally emerge atop it as the sun of the heavens. Indeed, in the epic, Ninurta, having accomplished his great deed, finally assumes his natural role as the sun by boarding a barque, a vehicle that will be familiar to us from the Egyptian solar theology:

The Hero had crushed the Mountain; when he moved in the steppes, he appeared as the [S]un (?),

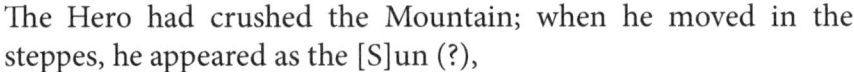

Ninurta went joyously towards the "magur", his beloved boat,
The Lord set his foot on the Makarnunta'e (boat).[679]

Thureau-Dangin, "An acte de donation", 144ff). Ninurta's destruction of Asakku then would be comparable to Marduk's destruction of Tiamat (see below p.78f). This is confirmed also by the other correspondences between the Ninurta mythology and the Marduk (see W.G. Lambert, "Ninurta Mythology", 55-60; cf. also J. Day, *God's Conflict*).

[676] In KAR 142 seven Asakku demons, sons of Anu - corresponding perhaps to the seven forms of Ninurta (see above p.208).

[677] This cataclysm which precedes the emergence of our sun is similar but not identical to the destruction of the cosmos at the end of a cosmic age.

[678] Ninmah is said to have borne Ninurta in the Mountain itself (*Lugal e*, ll.390ff).

[679] J. Van Dijk, *Lugal e*, p.137 (my English translation of van Dijk's French). The term 'utuaula'/ 'ut-tu gis-gal-a' used for Ninurta in *Lugal e* as well as in the Genouillac god-list (H. de Genouillac, "Grande liste", p.100) may refer either to the tempestuous storm which Ninurta sails over in his sun-barque or to his own stormy nature.

Ninurta's defeat of Asakku releases the life-giving seminal waters for the vivification and illumination of the universe.[680] Ninurta's mighty battle against the mountainous "regions of resistance"[681] is conducted with the aid of the mace fashioned for him by Ninildu that is identified with the storm-wind, Rihamun.[682] But since Ramman and Adad are identifiable with Seth, we see again that Ninurta, who is identical to Suwalliyat (Horus the Younger) and his stormy aspect are but the same deity. The storm-wind is necessary for the destruction of the serpentine force of resistance which itself is contained in a windy "mountain".

In the *EE* IV, the son of Enki,[683] Marduk, is the valiant warrior who defeats the watery dragon **Tiamat**, and her second consort, Kingu, in battle. Marduk, like Indra and Seth, is represented as a dragon-slayer,[684] since Tiamat has the monstrous dragon-form of the serpent at the bottom of the underworld of Earth.[685] Tiamat therefore is a counterpart of Vrtra. Both Asakku and Tiamat offer the same obstruction to the rise of the solar force. Indeed, Marduk himself is said, in *Šurpu* IV, 1-3, to have vanquished Asakku. Just as Ninurta in *Lugal-e* does, so also Marduk "fixes a bolt" and stations a watchman around the corpse of Tiamat so as "not to let her waters come forth".[686] It is interesting to note that Marduk combats Tiamat with a collection of winds which "disturb the inwards parts of Tiamat", as well as with the "thunderbolt, his mighty weapon" and his chariot "the storm".

---

[680] See S. Kramer, "Review of A. Hendel", pp.70ff.

[681] See J.V.Kinnier Wilson, *op.cit.*, p.51.

[682] Similarly, Indra's thunderbolt, or Vajra (which, in *RV* III,30,17, is characterised as a "burning weapon"), is said to have been fashioned by Tvashtr, the creative aspect of Varuna (Enki)

[683] See, for instance, Codex Hammurabi. I, 1-26.

[684] The account of Marduk's battle with the dragon is preserved in CT XIII, pl.33f. Rm.282 (cf. *Enuma Elish*, pp.118ff.).

[685] For the imagery of the fight between the eagle, representing the solar force, and the dragon, representing the primeval watery element, see A.J. Wensinck, "Tree and Bird", pp.46f.

[686] Cf. *Proverbs* 8:29: "[God] gave the sea his decree that the waters should not pass his commandment"; and *Job* 26:10.

This is precisely similar to the use of Rihamun by Ninurta in his battle against Asakku.

In the *EE*, it is by dividing the corpse of Tiamat into two parts that the division of heaven and earth in our universe is effected. The Assyrian ritual text K 3476 rev. l.9 reveals the phallic role of Marduk in this aggression: "Marduk, who with his penis … Tiamat".[687] The separation of heaven and earth resultant on the destruction of the serpent facilitates the rise of the sun to its position between them. After his control of the waters of Tiamat, Marduk is indeed able to construct the three heavens distributed among An, Enki and Enlil (*EE*, IV). Marduk's splitting open of Tiamat's body into two in the *EE* is also remarkably like the description, in the Tamil *Akam*, 59, ll.10-11, of Murugan's "vel" cutting "in two the side of **Sura's** [Asura's] body".[688]

In the "Gylfaginning" of the *Prose Edda* too, the **Midgard serpent** is represented as encircling the earth.[689] The god who battles the serpent like Seth and Zeus is Thor, who is called "son of earth [Geb/Enki/ Varuna]" in the Eddic "Lokasena", 58. In the "Gylfaginning" (34), the Midgard serpent, Jörmundgandr, is described as one of the children - along with the Fenris Wolf and Hel - of the Aesir god Loki. Odin took the Midgard serpent from Loki and cast it into the ocean, where it now encircles the earth. Hel was cast into Niflheim while the Fenris-Wolf was finally bound with a tight silken cord. In Ch.46, Thor travels to the castle of Loki, called Utgard Loki, and engages in a series of sports that are seen to be cosmic events. First he tries to drain the contents of a horn that is in fact connected to the Ocean and therefore difficult to exhaust. Then he attempts to lift up a cat from the ground which is in fact difficult to do since it is the Midgard Serpent. The last contest is to wrestle with an old woman who proves to be indomitable since she is in fact Old Age.[690] Furious at being duped in this way, Thor attempts to kill Loki and destroy his castle but they are no longer to be seen. Then

---

[687] See A. Livingstone, *op.cit.*, p.123.

[688] See K. Zvelebil, *op.cit.*, p.80.

[689] *The Prose Edda*, Ch.47; cf. " Gylfaginning".

[690] These three contests seem designed to adumbrate to Thor the pathetic condition of Aegir/Enki/Okeanus/Osiris without his "cauldron" (see above p.201).

Thor sets out to obtain the cauldron of the giant Hymir and catches the Midgard Serpent, as depicted in the "Hymisqvidha".[691]

THE FLOOD

The rise of the sun to the heavens is accomplished by **Indra**. In *RV* IX,86,22, it is stated that the consumption of Soma, the "seed", or life-force, of Agni, by Indra results in the rise of the sun to its place in the universe: "Sinking into the throat of Indra with a roar, led by the men, thou madest Surya mount to heaven". Indra's establishment of the solar force in the heavens is thus due to the potency derived from his consumption of Soma. In *RV* IX,42,1, Soma, identified with Indra, engenders the sun in floods along with the other stars. The floods are thus in all probability caused by the ejaculation of the divine phallus.

In the Vedas, **Indra's arm** or "fist" is represented also as a drum (*RV* VI,47,30-1). At V,20,3 the vehemence of the ritual war-drum is called "Indra-like". In ancient Mesopotamia, too, the hide of an ox was used to make the ritual war-drum, and the sound of the drum is said to represent the voice of god. More importantly, the drum is also identified by the Assyrian exegetes with "Indagara", a name resembling the Indic Indra and probably representing **Adad**/Ramman (CT 24,10,14), the storm-god, whose control of thunder-claps may account for the identification.[692] As we have noted above, Ramman (Adad) is the storm-force of Ninurta, in his battle against monstrous creations such as Asakku. The celebrated fight of Indra against Vrtra in the Vedas is conducted with a special weapon called "*vajra*" which is forged by Tvashtr and this weapon may be understood as being the "storm-flood" of Adad.[693]

---

[691] See above p.78.

[692] See A. Livingstone, *op.cit.*, pp.179,184. Nindagud, which is read 'Indagara', is identifiable with Adad (see A. Deimel, *op.cit.*, p.225). The phonetic resemblance of Indagara to Indra is indeed remarkable. It must be noted that Anu is also identified with the drum in BM 34035 (Livingstone, *op. cit.*, pp.173,184). For Adad, see A.R.W. Green, *Storm-God*, Ch.I.

[693] See below p.233.

Just as Adad is an exceptionally stormy aspect of the primeval cosmic wind respresented by Enlil, in the Avesta, **Ram** represents the same aspect of Vāyu.[694] The Avestan 'Ram Yast', which is addressed to the same stormy deity as Adad/Ramman, is, significantly, about Vāyu, who represents the "breath" of the supreme deity and the second power in the solar triumvirate Agni-Vāyu-Āditya. Vāyu is Indra's close companion in the Vedas, and Ramman is thus a continuation and intensification of the force of Vāyu through which the sun is engendered.

In Babylon, the storm-god is attested as **Rihamun** (the howler).[695] And Adad, Ramman, Rihamun are typically called the "Bull of Heaven".[696] In the exegetical god list `Anu ša amēli', this god is described as representative of thunder, lightning, storm, etc., which evokes the peculiarly stormy nature of this cosmic god. Adad is called the stormy aspect of Marduk also in CT 24,50,10b,[697] Marduk being a form of Ninurta.[698]

That the storm that Adad represents is identical to the flood which forms the sun is made clear in several sacred Sumerian texts, including the epic *Lugal e*. When Ninurta undertakes a mighty battle against certain mountainous "regions of resistance",[699] Enki calls

---

[694] The Ram Yasht is in fact a celebration of the god Vāyu. The Avesta (Yasht 14, Yasht 8) also uses the form Wata to denote the more corporeal form of the god of wind Vāyu (cf. *RV* X, 136,4 which refers to "the steed of Vāta, the friend of Vāyu"). The name Wata is also reflected in the Hittite divine name, Huwattassis, god of Wind (see E. Laroche, Recherches, p.69). The Germanic Wotan/Odin is etymologically related to Otem/Atem (breath) and mythologically to Vāta/Vāyu.

[695] From the Babylonian "ramamu" = to howl, scream (see H. Zimmern, "Religion und Sprache", p.445).

[696] See P. Jensen, "Adad-Mythus", *RLA*, I:26.

[697] "ilAdad=ilMarduk sa zu-un-nu".

[698] See above p.69. Ninurta (Lord of Earth) is indeed the name of the moribund solar force (Enki=Lord of Earth), while his Babylonian counterpart Marduk actually bears a name ("sun-calf") that is more suited to the incipient sun.

[699] See J.V. Kinnier Wilson, *op.cit.*, p.51. Kinnier Wilson's interpretation of this battle in geological, rather than cosmological, terms is entirely unfortunate. The terms resistance and rebellion applied to the hostile forces which the gods combat are uniformly attested in the literature of Sumer, Egypt and India; cf., for example, the

to Nin-ildu, "the great carpenter [or demiurgus] of Anu",[700] who is the counterpart of Tvashtr, to fashion the mighty mace of Ninurta. **Ninurta's "arm"**, or weapon, is itself represented as a separate deity called **Sarur**. The stormy nature of this mace is revealed in Gudea's Cylinder B, where the mace of Ningirsu [Ninurta as lord of the flood] is described as being the "fiery stormwind". This fiery storm wind is indeed deified as the storm god Ri-ha-mun or Adad. Adad is also called "the most powerful of the Weapons" of the "rebel lands", that is, of the Anunnaki, who are typically located in the underworld.[701]

That the stormwind is related to a cosmic flood is suggested also by the Sumerian term 'amaru' for weapon, which may be interpreted as "flood", as a hymn to Nergal makes clear:

So strong was his Weapon, its upward rising was unopposable,

In its aspect as a storm, it was the great Flood which none could oppose;[702]

From the reference to the floods which Soma engenders in *RV* IX,42,1 when liberating the sun,[703] also, we may identify this flood as being

---

Egyptian references in AeHG no.30: "I beat the donkey. I punish the rebels/ I have destroyed Apophis in his attack"; and the hymn in the Medinet Habu sun-chapel: "... who drives off the rebel in his hour, and burns the enemies of Re" (Medinet Habu VI 421B). In the Vedas, the name of the serpent Vrtra itself suggests resistance (see A.K. Lahiri, *op.cit*, Ch.2).

[700] Ninildu is an aspect of Enki's as the "fabricator" and equivalent to Nudimmud (see A. Jacob, *Ātman*, p.165).

[701] See A. Falkenstein, "Sumerische religiöse Texte", *ZA* 55 (1962), p.36; cf. J.V. Kinnier Wilson, *op.cit.*, p.62.

[702] See Kinnier Wilson, *op.cit.*, p.53. Kinnier Wilson also suggests that the cause of the flood in Atrahasis may originally have been not the "noise" caused by man, but rather "the noise of the rebel gods, which will have disturbed [Enlil] – even as it disturbed Apsu in *EE* I,25ff." (*ibid.*, p.112). The rebel gods may be the Sumerian counterpart of the Iranian "daivas" and the Indic Asuras. In *BP* VIII,24,8, the reason for the flood at the end of the sixth Manvantara (which precedes the formation of the light in the seventh) is that the 'Asura' Hayagreeva (much like the Anzu bird) stole the Vedas from Brahman.

[703] See above p.231.

the cosmic storm in which the incipient sun is formed and borne aloft. Ramman is, again, called "bel abubi", lord of the deluge.[704]

It is important to note that, in the *Atrahasis* epic as well as in *Gilgamesh* (Tablet XI), it is the wind-god **Enlil** (Shiva) who causes the flood. In the Babylonian epic of Erra, **Marduk**, the counterpart of the solar force, Ninurta/Muruga,[705] takes the place of his father Enlil in causing the flood:

> I got angry long ago: I rose from my seat and contrived the deluge,
> I rose from my seat, and the government of heaven and earth dissolved.
> And the sky, lo! shook: the stations of the stars in the sky were altered, and I did not bring [them] back to their [former] positions.
> ....
> The offspring of the living diminished, and I did not restore them
> Until, like a farmer, I should take their seed in my hand.
> ....
> I changed the place of the mesu tree and of the elmesu ...[706]

In his stormy nature, Marduk is very similar to Seth, Teshup, Zeus, who are both the storm-force and the solar force at the same time.[707]

THE THIRD SACRIFICE: THE TREE

The solar force which has been forced into the underworld by the storm-force has now to be gradually cleansed of its material elements. The third sacrifice, that of the Tree of Life itself, thus effects a spiritual purification which allows the sun to acquire its tremendous power in our universe. This purification is inextricably allied to the more

---

[704] H. Zimmern, *op.cit.*, p.448; p.555.

[705] For Marduk as one of the epithets of Ninurta, see K. Tallquist, *Akkadische Götterepitheta*, p.422. Ninurta is also called Madanu, one of the epithets of Marduk (*ibid.*).

[706] Tr. L. Cagni, The *Poem of Erra*, p.32. For Muruga's similar destruction of the cosmic "mango" tree in the Tamil *Kantapurānam*, change to 'see below p.236.'

[707] Marduk's solar role is highlighted by the fact that he is considered "the one inside Shamash" (VAT 8917 rev. l.5; see A. Livingstone, *op.cit.*, p.82f.).

general *contemptus mundi* and asceticism which underlie the theology of the solar religions, especially the Indic and the Dionysian-Orphic, as well as the Pythagorean-Platonic.[708]

We have seen that the Tree of Life may represent both the infrastructure of the material universe and the internal nervous structure and erotic energy of microcosmic man. The material universe being considered a result of the illusion of the divine Māya and incomparably inferior to the original Cosmic Light and Intellect, it is the duty of the yogi to detach himself from it by "cutting down" the Tree of Life. The Tree is itself thus represented as being cut down, or displaced, in some of the legends of the mythologies under consideration. Since the "tree" is an analogue for the divine phallus itself and its seminal power, Soma, the exhortation to cut it down in these mythic accounts is clearly one to asceticism as well. In the *SP* I,1,21,82-99, Kāma, who is Shiva's own erotic aspect and burnt down by Shiva in the form of a tree, is called the "evil at the root of all misery".[709] Here the contest is plainly between the ascetic Shiva and the erotic passion which engenders and sustains the illusion of the universe.

We have seen that the serpent at the bottom of the Abyss from whence the tree emerges is identifiable with the Māyā of the supreme deity as well as – microcosmically – with the Kundalini serpent at the base of the spinal cord. In the *MBh* ('Bhagavad Gita'), too, Krishna counsels Arjuna to cut down the ashvattha tree since the tree represents the world of sense-experience, **samsāra**.[710] The injunction to cut down the tree therefore signifies the severing of the illusion of Egoity (Ahamkāra) which lies at the base of the axis of the universe through a mastery of the sexual force (Kāma, Desire) that is represented by the Kundalini serpent.

---

[708] For the Orphic religion see W.K.C. Guthrie, *Orpheus and Greek Religion*, p.156f. It is interesting to note that according to Hecateus of Abdera Orpheus introduced the mysteries of Dionysus and Demeter into Greece which were modelled on those of Osiris and Isis in Egypt (see M.L. West, *Orphic Poems*, p.26). For the Pythagorean doctrines see J.A. Philip, *Pythagoras*, p.137f. We have also noticed the ritual castration in the cult of the Syrian Attis end of last line: change to (see below p.247).

[709] See W.D. O'Flaherty, *op.cit.*, p.159.

[710] See E.O. James, *op.cit.*, p.257.

The baneful aspect of the material manifestation of the cosmos is to be found also in the Dravidian version of the *SP, Kantapurānam*. Here, the mango tree situated in the midst of the ocean is the second form taken by the demon Sūrapadman who himself is concealed in a mountain (exactly as Asakku is in *Lugal-e*,[711] or Vrtra in the Vedas). The first form assumed by Sūrapadman is a monstrous multiform mockery of the Purusha characterised by a thousand arms and legs,[712] corresponding no doubt to the Vedic Vishvarūpā.[713] The son of Shiva born especially for the martial purpose of defeating the Asura Sūrapadman is Muruga, or Skanda, the counterpart of Marduk/Ninurta. Muruga destroys Sūrapadman's first form by revealing his own true, and eternal, form as the Purusha. Sūrapadman's second form, that of the "mango" tree, is also cloven into two by Muruga.

Just as Muruga in the Dravidian version of the myth is said to have cloven the "mango" tree,[714] Marduk too is said to have altered the position of the tree, in the *Poem of Erra*, I,148.[715] We note that Muruga/Marduk/Ninurta oppose the Tree though they themselves represent the Ideal form of it as the divine phallus.

The Sumerian kishkanu tree bears three inimical creatures in itself which have to be overcome before the light of the universe may be released. The Anzu bird nests in its upper branches (representing an obstacle to the emergence of the sun of heaven or its first inchoate form),[716] a serpent at its base (representing the dragon of resistance that the underworld sun has to combat), and a wind-demon, Lilith,

---

[711] The lilith demon in the Sumerian tree of life may also be a counterpart of the same phenomenon.

[712] See D. Handelman, "Myths of Murugan", p.143.

[713] See A. Jacob, *Ātman*, p.216.

[714] See D. Shulman, "Murukan", p.32.

[715] See L. Cagni, *The Poem of Erra*, p.32.

[716] In the Epic of Anzu, the bird is said to be a source of the waters which may bear the sun. However, the bird becomes traitrous to Enlil, and causes the waters to flood uncontrollably and steals the tablets of destinies from Enlil (*Epic of Anzu*, I). Thus it is killed by Ninurta, who then retrieves the tablets of destines from it.

in its trunk.[717] In the myth of the "huluppu" tree, Gilgamesh (Nergal) destroys all these creatures, the bird, the wind-demon and the serpent.[718]

In Germanic mythology too the tree serves as the locus of the great self-sacrifice of the god Odin/Wotan/Wata to himself, which may be a repetition of the original killing of Ymir, the First Man:[719]

> I know that I hung on a windy tree[720]
> nine long nights,
> wounded with a spear, dedicated to Odin,
> myself to myself.[721]

It is as a result of this sacrifice – akin to the ordeals of Marduk and Tammuz and even the Christ[722] – that Odin achieves mastery of the magical runes. The reference to runes indeed draws us to the incident in the "Ynglingasaga" and "Völuspá" where Wotan is said to have acquired secret knowledge from Mimir in exchange for the reflected sun in his well.[723] So this knowledge is no doubt related to the esoteric sources of light, Heka/Brahmanaspati,[724] and the sacred "brāhman" prayer. The description of Yggdrasil as a "windy" tree reminds us of Wotan's own nature as wind-god (Enlil/Vāyu/Wata) as well as of the Purānic accounts of the deluge which accompanies the birth of the sun, where Manu/Mārkandeya/Shiva are, like Wotan, depicted as the only ones that achieve knowledge of the true nature of the universe.[725] Further, this episode is intrinsically akin to Shiva's burning of his erotic aspect Kāma in the form of a tree.[726]

---

[717] We have seen that the trunk of the tree represents Earth (see above p.202).

[718] See D. Wolkstein and S. Kramer, *Inanna*, p.9.

[719] See above p.185f.

[720] We see that the description of the tree as being "windy" is connected to the lilith demon in the Sumerian mythology.

[721] 'Havamal', 138.

[722] See A. Jacob, *Brahman*, pp.33, 84n.

[723] See above p.211.

[724] See above p.218.

[725] See A. Jacob, *Ātman*, p.59.

[726] See above p.235. The sacrifice preceding the birth of the sun is certainly also

VISHNU

After the purification of the solar force from the underworld elements which long encumber it, the sun is finally free to rise to its present life-giving position in the heavens. The energetic expansive force of the solar deity is called **Vishnu**.[727] Vishnu's major contribution to Indra's cosmic accomplishment is the three gigantic steps with which he traverses the three worlds [i.e. Heaven, Earth and the Mid-region][728] that have been covered by the serpent Vrtra. Vishnu thereby "establishes the spaces" (*AV* VII,25,1) and his encompassing the three worlds represents the pervasiveness of the solar energy in the manifest universe.[729] The three steps of Vishnu are called 'devāyana'[730] (the path of the gods), 'pitrāyana'[731] (the path of the fathers or manes), and 'paramapada' (the supreme step). The first of these, as we have seen, may correspond to the pathway of Enki (Lord of Earth) to mankind described in the Sumerian hymn discussed above.[732] *RV* I,154 describes the highest point in the manifest universe as the region of Vishnu (representing his 'paramapada'). Again, in *KYV* V,5,1, Vishnu is said to be the highest form of Agni (=Varuna).

In *AV* XIII,3,13 the different forms of the sun of our system are described in a way that recalls the Egyptian solar gods:

This Agni becomes Varuna in the evening; in the morning, rising he becomes Mitra; he, having become Savitar, goes through the

---

related to the passion of the Christ on the Cross. The identification of the Christ with Apollo that we witness in early Christian art, as for example in the pre-Constantinian necropolis under St. Peter's basilica, was possible because of the original solar significance of the Christ story (see, in this context, T. Harpur, *Pagan Christ*).

[727] We note the same name in the Sumerian god-list CT 25,25,8 as ᵈGišnu.

[728] See *RV* I,154-6; *AV* VII,26,1.

[729] In *RV* I,154,4 Vishnu is said to uphold Earth, Heaven and the Mid-region; cf. *RV* VI,49,13.

[730] *RV* I,72,7; 183,6; 184,6.

[731] *RV* X,2,7.

[732] See above p.207.

atmosphere; he, having become Indra, burns through the midst of the sky.

Here **Varuna** is the counterpart of the Egyptian Osiris, **Mitra** of Harakhte, and **Indra** of Aton-Re.[733] **Savitr** is an advanced aspect of Mitra as the "inciter" who spurs the full development of Sūrya.[734] However, the terms "morning" and "evening" do not refer to terrestrial time but rather to solar. And the "sun" which is adored in several forms, as the rising sun, the risen, the mid-day sun and the setting sun, is not really the star itself, but rather the changing solar energies that characterise it in these several phases.

ĀDITYA

The final perfection of the manifest universe is the establishment of the sun in the Mid-region between Earth and Heaven. The sun is fixed in our heavens by Indra (*RV* II,21,4). In *RV* IX,63,8 Indra is said to make the sun move by yoking ten coursers to it. In *RV* I,24,8, the path of the sun in the system is said to be ordained by Varuna, who is but a form of Agni/Shiva/Indra and the counterpart of Osiris. The sun is also set in motion (*RV* VII,86,1) and established in its course (*RV* VII, 87,1) by Varuna. At *RV* I, 115,5 the sun of the Heavens, Sūrya, is said to be the manifest form of Varuna and Mitra. When the sun sets, it is said to become one with Varuna (*KB* XVIII,9). This is the same as the identification of the setting sun with Osiris, "chief of the western [gods]" in Egypt.

MANU VAIVASVATA

The son of the sun who accompanies the formation of our earth is Manu Vaivasvata or Manu of the Sun (Vivasvant), who guards the seeds of life borne in the ship of life that sails on the flood and is anchored on Mt. Meru, the central mountain of Earth. According to the *Sūrya Siddhānta*,

---

[733] See above p.238.

[734] The falcon associated with the Avestan Mithra and the Egyptian Harakhte is an attribute of Savitr, who precedes the Mitra phase of the solar development (see above p.238).

Ch.I, 22, Manu is said to have appeared in the 28th Chaturyuga of our [Padma] Kalpa.[735] And, in the *Mahābhārata,* Shantiparva, it is said that Manu manifested himself in the Treta Yuga. This seventh Manu, Manu Vaivaswata is responsible for the transmission of the seeds of life to Earth as well as for the mortality (Yama) of the forms that spring from these seeds. Though Manu is differentiated in *RV* from **Yama,** who is considered to be another son of Vivasvant,[736] Yama bears the same epithet of "Shrāddhadeva"[737] (lord of Faith) which Manu also does in *BP* VIII,24. So it is likely that we are dealing with an *alter ego,* especially since the flood hero of the Avesta, Yima, has a twin called Yama.[738] Manu's "half-brother" (or *alter ego*), Yama is indeed ruler of the lower heavens, according to *RV* I,35,6, and the sun and moon themselves are located in the mid-region between Heaven and Earth.

In Egypt, we note that the Hymn in the temple of the Great Oasis declares that the sun "appeared on the back of the Earth",[739] while in the Egyptian Book of the Gates, the solar journey is undertaken in a barque which is called the "**barque of the Earth**".[740] Earth, we have seen, represents the "trunk" of the Tree of Life and is the source of the gods, whose "flesh" it constitutes. The **ship of life** associated with Manu is thus the manifest universe in the highest regions of which appears the sun. This Earth is surrounded by the serpent of the Ocean to which it is bound. In both the *Book of the Gates* and in the *Amduat,* the solar journey through Earth is indeed undertaken within the coils of the World Encircler, the gigantic serpent representing Time.[741]

---

[735] See E. Burgess, *Translation of the Surya-Siddhanta,* 1860; cf. *VP,* I,3: "Twenty-eight times have the Vedas been arranged by the great Rishis in the Vaivaswata Manvantara in the Dvápara age, and consequently eight and twenty Vyásas have passed away; by whom, in their respective periods, the Veda has been divided into four."

[736] In *RV* X, 10ff, Vivasvant engenders, Yama, as well as Yama's twin sister and wife, Yami, by mating with a daughter of Tvashtr.

[737] See *HW* II:615.

[738] Cf. p.272 below.

[739] *Ibid.,* p.80.

[740] See E.T. Hornung, *op.cit.,* p.60.

[741] *Ibid.* In the *Enigmatic Book of the Underworld,* the *ouroboros* serpents represent

Manu saves himself in the ship when it is tied to the "horn" of a fish[742] and is borne by the latter to the heights of "the northern mountain", which, not being specified as a Himalayan one, may well be an Armenian one.[743] In the *BP* VIII,13 too, the First Man, Manu is warned of the deluge by a fish.[744] In the *MBh*, the divine identity of the fish is revealed to be that of Prajāpati/Brahman, since the fish declares to the "seven sages" – who, unlike in the *SB* version of the story, accompany Manu in the ship – "I am Brahma, lord of progeny [Prajāpati] … I in the form of a fish have delivered you from this peril".[745] The fish goes on to state that Manu should create all creatures including "gods, asuras, and men and all the worlds and what moves and what does not move [i.e. animal and vegetable life]."

It is important to note that Manu is the divine ancestor of the race that is to inhabit the earth. In the *SB*, Manu is described as offering a sacrifice after the flood recedes, and from this sacrifice arises, first, a "daughter" Idā [a variant of Ilā],[746] from whom is derived the human race. Ida is another form of Ila, and Ila, according to Purānic legend, is supposed to have married Chandra, the Moon, (or sometimes Budh [Intellect], the father of the Moon, or sometimes even Manu himself, her father). **Ila** is the originator of the Lunar dynasty of kshatriyas, while Manu's son, **Ikshvāku** continues the Solar line of his father.[747]

---

the birth and end of time (*ibid.*, p.78). In the Nordic Eddas, the Midgard serpent is called the "encircler of Earth" ('Voluspa', 60). Since the "magur" boat in Sumer is identified with the moon, we see why Vrtra (the serpent corresponding to the Egyptian "world-encircler") is identified with the moon (see above p.57)

[742] See *SB* I,viii,1,5.

[743] See above p.139.

[744] It is also possible that the "horn" of the fish has another source. We may recall the image of Re emerging as the sun by holding on to the horns of the Cow Mehet-Ouret. The Indic imagery may be a transformation of the Egyptian.

[745] *MBh* II,187,2ff. (tr. S. Shastri, *op.cit.*, p.9); cf. H. Usener, *op.cit.*, p.28ff.

[746] Ilā and Idā are interchangeable in the *BP* (Ilā: IX,16,22) and other Purānas (Idā: *BrdP* III,60,11, VP 85,7) In *SP* (Vaishnava Kānda), it is a name of Narmada, the mighty river (and consort) of Shiva (see S. Shastri, *op.cit*, p.72).

[747] Cf. p. above. Interestingly, Ida is one of the principal nadis of the body in the

yogic system (see A. Jacob, *Brahman*, p.161) and is considered a lunar channel, whereas Pingala is the corresponding solar channel. These two nadis seem to be microcosmic counterparts of the lunar and solar dynastic lines of Ida and Īkshvāku respectively. The central nadi is called Sushumna and this must correspond to Manu (man) himself. For the references to Idaea/Ida in Greek and Germanic mythology see below p.274.

III. THE SOLAR RITUALS OF THE INDO-EUROPEANS

The religious rituals of the Indo-Europeans are based on the original sacrifice of the Ideal cosmic macroanthropos, Purusha, as well as on its repetitions in the manifest cosmos and in the underworld, for it is these sacrifices that result in the formation of the sun.[748] The primary aim of the Vedic ritual is thus to restore the disintegrated Purusha and, especially, his solar energy. As Gonda pointed out with regard to the construction of the Vedic fire-altar,

> In building the great fireplace one restores and reintegrates Prajāpati, whose dismemberment had been the creation of the universe, and makes him whole and complete. At the same time and by means of the same ritual act, the sacrificer, who is identified with Prajāpati (cf. *Shatapatha Brāhmana* VII,4,15) constructs himself a new social personality and secures the continuance of his existence.[749]

---

[748] For a detailed study of the ancient Indo-European rituals, see A. Jacob, *Brahman*.

[749] See J. Gonda, *Prajāpati's rise to higher rank*, p.16f.

The three Haviryajnas,[750] the Agnihotra, Darshapūrnamāsa (New- and Full-moon) and Chāturmāsya (triannual) sacrifices are also explained in *SB* VI,3,35 as cosmic restoratives:

35. After Pragâpati had created the living beings, his joints (parvan) were relaxed. Now Pragâpati, doubtless, is the year, and his joints are the two junctions of day and night (i.e. the, twilights), the full moon and new moon, and the beginnings of the seasons.

36. He was unable to rise with his relaxed joints; and the gods healed him by means of these havis-offerings: by means of the Agnihotra they healed that joint (which consists of) the two junctions of day and night, joined that together; by means of the full-moon and the new-moon sacrifice[751] they healed that joint (which consists of) the full and new moon, joined that together; and by means of the (three) Kâturmâsyas (seasonal offerings) they healed that joint (which consists of) the beginnings of the seasons, joined that together.

The sacrifice of the Purusha which initiated the formation of the universe was most probably imitated in the ancient Indo-European religions by a **human sacrifice**.[752] Human sacrifice is indeed archaeologically evidenced in the early Bronze Age (fourth millennium B.C.) Luhansk site in the Ukraine which forms part of the Yamnaya culture associated with the Āryans.[753] It is attested among the ancient Germanic peoples too and discernible (in Caesar's writings) among the Celts , as well as among the Scythians, and Thracians.[754]

---

[750] The sacrifices following the Vedas (Shruti) are called Shrautasūtras and divided into Pākayajna, Haviryajna and Somayajna sacrifices (see A. Jacob, *Brahman*, pp.187ff). Haviryajnas normally involve oblations of ghee (clarified butter) into the fire.

[751] The Darshapūrnamāsa sacrifice.

[752] See above p.195n.

[753] See above p.195n.

[754] K. Rönnow, ("Zur Erklärung des Pravargya") has pointed to the significant evidence of human sacrifice among the Germans, Celts, Scythians and Thracians and suggested that it must have been practised even by the Greeks and Indians, in

The primary purpose of a sacrifice is however **self-sacrifice** and the sacrifice of a human involved in the proto-Vedic Purushamedha[755] must originally have been conducted as a substitute for the sacrifice of the sacrificer himself, since the sacrificer is, in all Vedic sacrifices, identified with the victim. As Heesterman states, "self-sacrifice is an all-but-ubiquitous theme in the ritual brāhmana texts, the victim as well as the other offerings being regularly equated with the sacrificer".[756] That is why the victim in the Purushamedha was originally exclusively a brāhman or a kshatriya,[757] since only these two castes were qualified to act as representatives of the Purusha and to conduct sacrifices.

The sacrificial victim is also always a male since only his energy can substitute for the **phallic force** of the Purusha that fills the universe with its life. We have observed in our survey of the cosmological bases of sacrifices that the entire evolution of the material universe arises from repeated castrations, and preservations, of the divine phallus, first in the Ideal realm of the Purusha, then in the early cosmos of Brahman and, lastly, in the material universe, as the Tree of Life that arises from the underworld and extends to the heavens.[758] If what is most important in the Purusha is his phallic power, as is evident also in the Hesiodic account of the castration of Ouranos by Chronos,[759] it is probable that the sacrifice originally focussed on the victim's phallus, as we observe, for example, in the veneration of the penis of a slaughtered stallion among the ancient Nordic peoples.[760] Similarly, in the Equus October ceremony in ancient Rome a race-horse was slaughtered and its tail (standing no doubt for its penis) was brought to the regia.[761] In ancient Egypt, the castration of Re is represented

---

spite of the dearth of such evidence among them (see B. Lincoln, *Myth, Cosmos and Society*, p.172).

[755] See above p.244.

[756] J.C. Heesterman, *Broken world*, p.173.

[757] See *Sānkhāyana Grhyasūtra* 16,10,9.

[758] See above pp.202ff.

[759] See Hesiod, *Theogony*, I, 170ff.

[760] See above p.269.

[761] See J. Mallory and D.Q. Adams, *Encyclopedia of Indo-European Culture*, p.330.

as a self-castration. Hu, intellectual expression, and his consort, Sia, intuition, are said in a New Kingdom commentary on the *Book of the Dead* to be "the blood which fell from the phallus of Re, when he was going to mutilate himself".[762] Since the castration of Re corresponds to the castration of Anu in the Hurrian epic of the Kingship in Heaven, and the castration of Prajāpati by Shiva, we may assume that this event precedes the formation of the Cosmic Egg which, in the Purānas arises, from the seed of Prajāpati/Shiva. This may also have been the source of the practice noticed in some rituals of the Dionysiac religion that may have involved self-mutilation.[763]

Over time, however, the human victim was substituted with animals that equally represented the energy of the divine phallus, thus a horse or a bull, and finally with lesser animals such as sheep and goats. Indeed, at the time of the composition of the *SB*, the most common substitute was the goat (*SB* VI,2,1,39). In all cases, however, the original significance of the sacrifice as a self-sacrifice is never forgotten, as many of the processes of the Vedic sacrifices as well as many of the accompanying Vedic chants reveal.[764] *SB* I,3,2,1, for instance, identifies the sacrifice (also frequently called Vishnu) with the Purusha:

Now the sacrifice is the man. The sacrifice is the man for the reason that the man spreads (performs) it; and that in being spread it is made of exactly the same extent as the man: this is the reason why the sacrifice is the man.

The term "spreads" commonly used in Vedic literature for sacrificial action may well be a reference to the erection of the phallus which produces the sun. The spiritual purpose of a sacrifice is to control the sexual energy and convert it into spiritual energy directed to the attainment of the ideal "sattvic" state of the Purusha, that is, as the solar deity Vishnu.

---

[762] See M.Sandman-Holmberg, *The God Ptah*, p.42.

[763] See below p.247.

[764] See *Prānāgnihotra Upanishad*, 17ff.

We have noted above that the phallic sacrifice of the ideal Purusha is repeated in the manifest cosmos, for such a sacrifice is necessary for the transference of the divine power to our solar system.[765] The second sacrifice involves the destruction of Brahman/Prajāpati by his son Ganesha/Indra (Zeus/Seth) and the swallowing of the divine phallus by the latter so that the whole universe and its light moves into his body. Then Seth in turn is seen, for instance in the Egyptian mouth-opening ritual, to have been castrated or killed, for a bull representing Seth is slaughtered and its thigh is used to revive the dead Osiris.[766] In the town of Saka, Seth as a bull undergoes self-castration and, in the Pap. d'Orbiney, Seth (called Bata in Saka), castrates himself in order apparently to avoid the sexual advances of his sister-in-law, and then goes into exile in foreign lands.[767] This is clearly the source of the rites of the Phrygian Attis rites mentioned in Lucian's *De Dea Syria*.[768] In the mouth-opening cerermony performed on divine statues, too, the "thigh" represents the divine genitals[769] – which, according to the Orphic cosmogonies, Zeus (Seth) is said to have swallowed after they had been severed from Ouranos by Zeus' father Chronos.[770] So it is not surprising that Seth's genitals ("thigh") are brought forward to revive the moribund Osiris with its life and light. According to the series entitled 'The Contendings of Horus and Set', too, the conflicts

---

[765] See above pp.190ff.

[766] See above p.191.

[767] See H. te Velde, *Seth God of Confusion*, p.41.

[768] Attis was said to have been castrated by Cybele (the Phrygian counterpart of the Cretan Rhea, consort of Cronos) (see Lucian, *De Dea Syria, The Syrian Goddess*, tr. H.W. Attridge and R.A. Oden, Missoula, MT; Scholars Press, 1976, p.23). According to A.B. Cook (*Zeus*, I:292ff.), Zeus, Pappas and Attis were Phrygian terms used for a god who, like Osiris, was reborn as his son. For the relation between Attis, Adonis and Osiris, see *De Dea Syria*, pp.13ff. Though not apparent, Attis' life resembles that of Dionysus, the sun-god who is also killed and resurrected. When the cult was transferred to Rome, Cybele was celebrated as Magna Mater deorum Idaea and the cult involved the famous taurobolium in which initiates were drenched in the blood of a bull as a form of cleansing and rebirth.

[769] See above p.191.

[770] See above p.190.

between the two gods include the violation of Horus the Younger by Seth and the castration of Seth by Horus.[771] All these incidents focus on the importance of the divine phallus now as the life of the emerging universe as well as its light.

Just as the death of Osiris is followed by his revival in our universe as the sun, the Indo-European religious sacrifices too betoken not only a self-sacrifice of the sacrificer but also a **solar rebirth** that they allow the sacrificer to undergo as a brāhman, or one who has realised the solar virtue of his soul. In the Indian horse-sacrifice, Ashvamedha, for instance, the horse represents the sun which has been lost and must be recovered. Thus *SB* XIII,3,1,1 declares:

> Prajâpati's eye swelled; it fell out: thence the horse was produced; and inasmuch as it swelled (ashvayat), that is the origin and nature of the horse (ashva). By means of the Asvamedha the gods restored it to its place; and verily he who performs the Asvamedha makes Prajâpati complete, and he (himself) becomes complete; and this, indeed, is the atonement for everything, the remedy for everything.

This is the same significance that attaches also to the Osirian funereal rites, especially the mouth-opening ritual.[772] For the assault on the solar force by Seth is referred to as the damage or robbing of the "Horus eye" [the sun] which must be restored to Horus the Elder/ Osiris.

By transfiguring the sacrificer into the solar force, the sacrifice simultaneously bestows **immortality** on him. The nectar of immortality that sacrificers seek for by toil and penance is indeed Soma (*SB* IX,5,1,8). The underlying motif of the Soma sacrifice is one related to the pressing, or killing of the Purusha, as *SB* II,2,2,1 suggests: "in pressing out the king [Soma] they slay him". This may have a special phallic connotation as well since the soma juice is akin

---

[771] *Book of the Dead*, Ch.113; see S. Mercer, *Horus Royal God of Egypt*, p.74; cf. H. Te Velde, *op.cit.*, p.58.

[772] See above p.190f.

to the seminal power of Prajāpati which serves as the source of the sun. Thus the sacrifice, though representing the death of the sacrificer, also signifies the production of Soma, the nectar of immortality. The sacrificer's spiritual rebirth is essentially akin to that of the solar force Agni that we have observed above.

SB III,6,2,16 further reveals that "even in being born, man, by his own self, is born as a debt (owing) to death. And in that he sacrifices, thereby he redeems himself from death." The sacrificer is said to have two bodies, one material and the other ritual/spiritual. Through the sacrifice he mounts to heaven to get a **divine body** and, on earth, he gives his material body to the gods. Thus his material body is sacrificed after purifications such as shaving the hair, cutting the nails, etc. (*TS* VI,1,1,2), although the sacrifice of his material body is, as we have noted, performed with a substitute victim.

The ultimate aim of the original Indo-European sacrifices, modelled after the cosmic sacrifice of the Purusha, however, must have been the **liberation of the self** from the illusions of the material fabric in which it is entangled and the direction of the energy of man into the divine consciousness. This is indeed the principal aim of yogic ascesis as well, which, according to Heesterman, is an internalisation of the sacrifice. However, since yoga is likely to have preceded fire-sacrifices since it is the basis of the cosmic vision that informs both, it is more probable that the fire-sacrifices were a later externalisation of yogic practice rather than that the latter was an internalisation of the former.

As examples of the Vedic sacrifices we may observe here the chief public ritual, the royal consecration, **Rājasūya**, and the most important of the soma sacrifices, the **Agnishtoma**.

The **Rājasūya** is the elaborate ceremony in which a **king** is consecrated and divinised. The Rājasūya sacrifice,[773] like the Ashvamedha or horse-sacrifice, is certainly one of the most ancient, and public, of Vedic sacrifices. Indeed it may have served as the prototype of the other Vedic household sacrifices that similarly aim

---

[773] The Rājasuya is described in *SB* V (cf. also *KYV* I, 6). For a good description of it, see J. Gonda, *Religionen*, I, pp.163ff.

at the divinisation of the sacrificer. At the Rājasūya consecration, the rebirth which the king undergoes during the ceremony represents his rebirth as the solar force. During the ceremony the king is also identified with King Soma, who is also ritually killed in the soma-pressing during a soma sacrifice. The whole rite indeed marks the rebirth of the king as the cosmic Prajāpati/Brahman/Indra/Sūrya whose solar course is represented in the chariot drive section of the ritual.[774] The king also represents the sattvic power of the Purusha as Vishnu, since he is reborn with a divine consciousness after his sacrificial death.[775] The royal power is essentially a charismatic one derived from the solar force and not from the actual social control of peoples and lands. That is why the office of the king is an immortal one passed on from father to son in the salutation "The king is dead, long live the king".[776]

The royal consecration is preceded by one year of rites characterised by the chaturmāsyas (four-month sacrifices) or a dīksha of this duration and it is followed by another year of dīksha-like observances and a new inauguration. During the ishtis (sacrifices with burnt, vegetable offerings) for Mitra and Brhaspati, the king representing the sun engenders himself, "performing by himself the cosmic process of ripening and birth".[777] The sacrificer is presented with a bow representing the vajra, the weapon used by the solar force Indra to slay Vrtra. The sacrificer then raises his arms standing on the throne as "a personificaton of the cosmic pillar resting on the navel of the earth (the throne) and reaching up to the sky".[778] This is clearly a phallic gesture since the priests chant "Rise up, ye two arms, that we may live, besprinkle our pastures with ghee [i.e. semen]."[779] The king does not lower his arms until after the

---

[774] See J.C. Heesterman, *Royal Consecration*, p.149. The queen is during the royal consecration identified with Aditi, the Earth (*SB* VI,5,3,1; XIV,1,3,25).

[775] See below p.252.

[776] See A. Michaels, *op.cit.*, p.280.

[777] *Ibid.*, p.51.

[778] *Ibid*, p.101.

[779] *Ibid.*

chariot race. Then the king mounts the dishāh (quarters) of space by making a step in each of the five directions [the four cardinal points plus the centre] and thereby attains the heavens. At one stage (*SB* V,4,2,6) the king also takes the three solar steps of Vishnu to indicate his lordship of the three worlds.

Then begins a chariot race whose circuit begins and ends at the same place, for the "sacrificer goes ... from the Ocean to heaven and back to the Ocean again, as does the sun," since the wheel of the chariot is at first attached to the cāvāla representing the Ocean.[780] This is followed by a raid on "1000 cows", representing the solar rays, which the king must acquire. In the invocation to the Navagvas "our (ancient) fathers" are said to have helped Indra in winning the 'cows' of the Panis". As Heesterman suggests, the invocation seeks to "win back the sun from the waters".[781] Through the race and the raid the king sets in motion the vāja – or fertility powers through the cosmos.[782]

The unction (abhisecanīya) rites mark the king's rebirth out of the sacrifice [of Prajāpati]. The sixteen or seventeen liquids used in the unction represent the primal 'sweet' waters of Varuna, from which the sun arose.[783] Indeed the Rājasuya is also called Varunasava. For the prince becomes Varuna (*Maitrāyani Samhita* IV). Since the term 'rājasūya' means "generating royalty" it is probably derived from this particular unction ritual. Heesterman suggests that the king is first reborn as Soma, representing the creative power of Brahman, for brāhmanical power is in *JB* II,203 equated with a means of procreation (prajanam brahmā).[784] However the true brāhmanical virtue is the rājasic one represented by Agni while Soma is rather

---

[780] *Ibid.*, p.134.

[781] *Ibid.*, p.187.

[782] The chariot race resembles the course run by the Pharaoh in Egypt during the Sed festival, which was a royal jubilee normally marking thirty years of a pharaoh's reign (see W. Kaiser, "Die kleine Hebseddarstellung").

[783] See above p.226.

[784] J.C. Heesterman, *op. cit.*, p.76.

the sattvic aspect of the supreme divinity.[785]

The king's throne in the enthronement section (*SB* V,4,4,1ff) represents Varuna's watery seat and the womb of both the sun and earthly royalty. On the throne the king is proclaimed a brāhman. It is interesting to note also that, after being hailed as a brāhman (i.e. as one endowed with brāhmanical consciousness) by the four priests, the king is identified with Savitr, Mitra, Indra and Varuna – which are, as we have seen, the four universal phases of the sun.[786] The king is born in the centre of the universe as its lord. On birth, he is symbolically beaten with wooden sticks to remove the covers of the embryo and free him from death.

In the section devoted to a dicing game we are offered a ritual representation of the ordering of the universe, for, in *AV* IV,6,5, Varuna's ordering activity is likened to the throwing of the dice by the player, and the number of dice corresponds to the points of the compass plus the zenith. However, the king does not take part in the dicing game. On the contrary it is the king's royalty that is to be won by the players.[787] In the final bath, avabhrtha, the king is finally cleansed and regenerated.

In the Dashapeya sacrifice of the Rājasūya rituals, which is undertaken on the tenth day and is an Agnishtoma sacrifice (*SB* V,4,5), the aim is to make the king ascend to the heavens. This sacrifice includes a ceremony in which the sacrificer is joined by ten brāhmans (or sometimes by a "thousand" participants) in drinking soma to suggest the permeation of the universe by the king's soma essence. The king makes his subjects and the universe partake of the vital liquids which have rolled off his body during the unction.

The concluding Sautrāmani sacrifice (*SB* V,4,8ff) is dedicated to the Ashvins who refilled Indra with Soma after he once happened to emit it all out. This sacrifice therefore highlights the importance

---

[785] Cf. *KB* 9,5: "Agni is the brahman power, Soma is the royal power"; also *BAU* I4,11: "the brahman is the womb of royalty".

[786] See above p.238f. J.C. Heesterman, who points to this peculiarity in the rājasūya sacrifice (*op.cit.*, p.160), does not see the solar significance of this episode.

[787] *Ibid.*, p.156.

of the conservation of the soma power of the king. In the additional "Truth-messenger" ishtis, homage is paid to the solar deities, Savitr, the Ashvins, (who carry the sun-maiden Sūrya in their chariot),[788] and Pūshan, who is a son of the Ashvins. At this stage the king establishes satya, truth, in the cosmos.

The significance of **soma** in the Vedic sacrifices is clearly due to the fact that the energy required for the revival of the solar force is provided by the seminal power of Soma. In a yajna, Agni (the sun) is said to consume Soma (the moon) as his food, or sustenance. Soma represents the male energy of a man, bull, or horse since the sacrifices originally involved the offering of animals particularly chosen for their virile energy. This is related to the vital importance of the phallus of the Purusha in the cosmic evolution and it is the brāhmans' duty to sustain the phallus-like universe and its light through their sacrificial rituals. And in the soma rituals, the soma plant, which is itself a phallic Purusha symbol, is pressed with a phallic 'lingam' stone, since Soma represents the divine semen. The deity who is imbued with Soma is, as we have seen, **Indra**.[789] That is why the sun in its fullest development is also identical to Indra.[790]

The twin horses of the sun, the **Ashvins**, are also of special importance in the Vedic sacrifices. *RV* IV,45, addressed to the Ashvins, makes clear the relation between the energy obtained from Soma and the rays of the sun borne in its "chariot":

1. Yonder goes up that light: your chariot is yoked that travels round upon the summit of this heaven.
Within this car are stored three kindred shares of food, and a skin filled with meath is rustling as the fourth.

2. Forth come your viands rich with store of pleasant meath, and cars and horses at the flushing of the dawn,
Stripping the covering from the surrounded gloom, and spreading

---

[788] See A.A. Macdonell, *Vedic Mythology*, p.50f.

[789] See above p.205.

[790] See above p.238.

through mid-air bright radiance like the Sun.

3. Drink of the meath with lips accustomed to the draught; harness for the meath's sake the chariot that ye love.
Refresh the way ye go, refresh the paths with meath: hither, O Aśvins, bring the skin that holds the meath.
…
5. Well knowing solemn rites and rich in meath, the fires sing to the morning Aśvins at the break of day,
When with pure hands the prudent energetic priest hath with the stones pressed out the Soma rich in meath.

6. The rays advancing nigh, chasing with day the gloom, spread through the firmament bright radiance like the Sun;
And the Sun harnessing his horses goeth forth: ye through your Godlike nature let his paths be known.

The fourth "skin" bearing mead that is referred to in the first verse is to the bliss that forms the essence of life, while the other three "shares of food" are more normal forms of physical and intellectual energy.

In the *Agnishtoma*, which is a Jyotishtoma or laud of light, the declared aim is the attainment of Indraloka, the heaven of the gods.[791] The Agnishtoma is an elaborate sacrifice lasting five or six days which can be performed only by a **householder**. However, the same focus on Agni (the fire) and Āditya (the sun) is to be noted here as in the simpler Haviryajna, Agnihotra.[792] As *JB* I,240, declares:

He (Agni) becomes established in yonder sun with twenty-one Trivrts [chants] and yonder sun in him with nine Twenty-onefolds. Thus the two become established in each other,[793]

and I,241:

---

[791] For a good account of the *Agnishtoma*, see J. Gonda, *Religionen*, I, pp.152ff.

[792] See A. Jacob, *Brahman*, p.189.

[793] See H.W. Bodewitz, *op.cit.*, p.134.

yonder sun goes home (sets) towards this one here. This one here goes out towards (or visits) yonder one. ... These two deities are dwelling together. One obtains dwelling together with these two and they obtain dwelling together with him. They continuously remove all evil in these worlds.

On the first day, the **Dīksha** or "consecration" takes place. The Dīksha represents the death of the individual and the beginning of his rebirth in a divine state. The sacrificer is shaved and, from that moment on, his food is restricted. He keeps his hands as much as possible in the form of a fist, indicating his status as an embryo. After the Dīksha, the soma is purchased and is brought in like a king on his chariot. It is installed on a throne and addressed as Varuna.[794]

Then there may take place a special **Pravargya** ceremony to which the sacrificer's wife is not admitted. The Pravargya represents the perfection of the force of the sun (*SB* X,2,5,4) and is mainly addressed to the Ashvins, the twin solar horsemen or charioteers. It may be performed by an aspirant only after a long period of tapas which will contribute to "the strengthening of the sun".[795]

The rite involves a phallic Mahāvīra pot representing the sun. What is to be especially noted is that, as Buitenen has revealed, the Mahāvīra is a **phallic symbol**:

> The Mahāvīra with its semi-human, but also semi-phallic shape, its round cap with a small receptacle from which a narrow channel runs down to its base, filled with hot white liquid that overflows, might well be viewed as the male member of creation overflowing with the semen that fecundates nature. Thus the Aitareya Brāhmana 4,5: "... The gharma is the penis...the milk the semen. This semen is ejaculated into the fire, which is the divine womb, for the sake of procreation. [The sacrificer] is born from the divine womb, the fire, out of the oblations".[796]

This is credible insofar as *SB* XIV,1,3,11 also declares that the sap

---

[794] See above p.252.

[795] See J. van Buitenen, *Pravargya*, p.41. The Pravargya is described in *SB* V.

[796] J.B. van Buitenen, *Pravargya*, p.34.

from the head produces plants. The Mahāvīra also denotes **Indra**, as Buitenen's citation of the *brahma jajñānam* hymn suggests:[797]

> 'Having come forth, [the Mahāvīra], the Father, propped up the two large ones – heaven which is the seat and the region of the earth. By begetting, he reached from the bottom to the top, as Brhaspati, the god who is the sovereign of this'.

Here we recognise Indra plainly as the extended phallic Tree of Life, atop which shines the sun in the heavens.[798] *SB* XIV,3,2,24 further equates the Pravargya with the three manifest forms of the solar force as Agni, Vāyu, Āditya.[799] The gharma (hot milk) oblation poured into the pot symbolises the solar force that is "boiled" within the divine phallus in order that it achieve its full power.[800]

This is followed by 'upasad' days which precede the **soma pressings**. On the second of these days, the mahāvedi is erected. The sacrificer now opens his fist and unbuckles the belt which he received during the dīksha representing power (*SB* III,2,1,10). Then, on the 'great night', the instruments for the pressing are prepared. The soma is pressed and offered on the same day, in a series of three pressings, the Prāthasavana (Morning Pressing), Mādhyamdinasavana (Midday Pressing), and the Trtītyasavana (Third Pressing). The soma juice is poured into a receptacle filled with water and purified with a woollen filter. The brahman priests drink after the gods have been offered the juice. The gods addressed are the dual deities Indra-Vāyu, Mitra-Varuna, and the two Ashvins. The morning pressing refers to Indra's defeat of Vrtra and the midday pressing to his destruction of the "vala" which confines the solar energy.[801] At the midday pressing, the sacrificer symbolically distributes parts of his body to the priests, his

---

[797] *Ibid.*, p.35.

[798] See above p.202f.

[799] See above p.203. Agni is the first form of the sun in the underworld, Vāyu (Wotan) the power infusing the Tree of Life, and Ādiyta the manifest sun.

[800] See J.B. van Buitenen, *op.cit.*, p.31.

[801] See Jamison and Witzel, p.39. In Iran, the demonic Apaosa is killed by Tistria at midday (Yt.8.26-8) and the dragon too at the same hour, by Keresaspa (Y 9.11).

voice to the hotar, his mind to the brahman, etc., as if he were the primal Purusha.[802] After the evening pressing, the sacrificer and his wife undergo a final bath, the avabhrtha. They then adore the sun saying "By contemplating the radiant light, the god Sūrya, ... we have moved from darkness to the radiant light" and add "we have drunk Soma, have become immortal, we have contemplated the light and found the gods" (*TB* III,2,5).

The seminal power symbolised by the soma is clear from the section of the sacrifice which adores King Soma in the following manner: "Swell, O Soma, may the male power join you from all sides".[803] This power is also the source of immortality: "by swelling, O Soma, place your supreme glories in the heavens in order to become the liquor of immortality."[804] The soma is prepared primarily for the consumption of Indra, since this is the power with which he conquers the serpent Vrtra: "[Having drunk this soma] may Indra massacre the Vrtras, conquer [their] race".[805] At one stage are chanted the verses from *RV* VIII,17, 1-13:

4. Come unto us who bring the juice, come unto this our eulogy, Fair-visored! drink thou of the juice.

5. I pour it down within thee, so through all thy members let it spread: Take with thy tongue the pleasant drink.

6. Sweet to thy body let it be, delicious be the savoury juice: Sweet be the Soma to thine heart.

7. Like women, let this Soma-draught, invested with its robe,

---

[802] This action reveals the important difference between the Indo-European rituals and those of what Schroeder calls "primitive peoples" (p.65 above) since, whereas the latter may consider that they are eating their gods, the former are themselves divinised in the course of their rituals. The Pravargya sacrifice too is conducted to strengthen the developing sun and not to obtain its light just as the soma sacrifice is not designed to obtain rain but to acquire the immortality of the gods.

[803] See W. Caland and V. Henry, *L'Agnistoma*, p.44, cf. p.48.

[804] *Ibid.*, p.112.

[805] *Ibid.*, p.145.

approach, O active Indra, close to thee.

8. Indra, transported with the juice, vast in his bulk, strong in his neck and stout arms, smites the Vṛtras down.

9. O Indra, go thou forward, thou who rulest over all by might: Thou Vrtra-slayer slay the fiends.

The solar significance of this act is clear from the fact that Indra represents the force that manifests itself in our universe as the sun. The priests too elevate themselves through the soma sacrifice. At one stage, for instance, the priests chant the Rigvedic verses *RV* VIII,48,3-4:

We have drunk the soma, we have become immortal, we are allied to the light, we have found the gods, what can the demon do to us at the moment, what, immortal one, can the malice of a mortal do to us?

This is to be observed again in *TS* III,2,5, a-g:

O drink, come, penetrate into me, for long life, the health of the body, the prosperity of wealth, splendour, the good prosperity ... for energy, the pious address, the prosperity of wealth, the good virility ... for male force, life and splendour.[806]

Since Schroeder places considerable importance on the Pravargya milk-sacrifice within the Agnishtoma soma-sacrifice, we may observe its significance more closely here. As Eggeling pointed out:

the main object of sacrificial performances generally is the reconstruction of Prajāpati, the personified universe and (the divine body) of the sacrificer ... [the Pravargya] ceremony is thus performed in order to complete the universe and sacrifice as well as the divine body of the sacrificer by supplying them with their head.[807]

---

[806] *Ibid.*, p.216.

[807] *SBE* 44, pp.xlvii-xlviii.

Houben discerns two main constituents in the Pravargya ritual.[808] They are 1. (as described in the Brāhmanas, the Āranyakas and the Shrauta Sūtras) the gharma offering to the Ashvins, and 2. (as described in the *TĀ* V, *KĀ* II and III, *SB* XIV) the ceremonial preparation, sacrificial use and solemn disposal of a special vessel, which has several names: Head of Makha, Pravargya, Gharma, Mahāvïra. This is mainly performed by the Adhvaryu priest.

Clay is used to form one **main vessel**, two spare vessels and several minor clay implements. They are dried, baked in fire-pit, bathed in goat's milk. As Hillebrandt explained, the vessels constitute **the head of Makha**,

> The three Mahāvīra pots form the head over which a veda cluster rises as a tuft. [809] The milk tubs represent the ears, two gold chips or butter ladles the eyes, the two rohina cooking bowls the heels. The remnant flour signifies the marrow, a mixture of sour milk and honey blood, etc.[810]

Indeed, according to *TĀ* 5, the Agnishtoma sacrifice is, as it were, the body and the Pravargya the head. Thus, whereas the soma throne is only a "King's throne", the Pravargya throne is called the "Emperor's throne".[811] According to Hillebrandt,

> The glowing Mahāvīra pot, which is the central point of the sacrifice, is a symbol of the sun, as the juice-filled soma plant of the soma sacrifice is a symbol of the moon, and its stool should, according to some (*Āpasthamba* XV,5,7), be bigger than the soma stool. The ceremony is mentioned in the *RV*, apart from in other verses, also in the hymn of the frogs VII,103, verse 8 as well as 9.[812]

---

[808] See J. Houben, *The Pravargya Brahmana*.

[809] The tuft of hair on the top or back of the shaven head of an orthodox Hindu.

[810] See A. Hillebrandt, *Ritualiteratur*, p.135.

[811] *Ibid.*, p.16.

[812] *Ibid.*, p.136.

The head of Makha is, according to *SB* XIV,1,1,9, that of **Vishnu**, which was cut and turned into the sun (*JB* 3,126). It is Indra who reassembles Vishnu (*SB* XIV,1,1,13). In *TĀ*, Anuvāka 1, **the sacrifice** personified as Makha Vaishnava is beheaded and it is its trunk that is divided threefold into the morning, midday and evening pressing. This threefold sacrifice is however not sufficiently effective and needs to be completed with a fourth element: its head. The Ashvins, the physicians of the gods, know how to do this (*SB* XIV,1,4,12). This head is the Pravargya ceremony, which has to make the regular Soma sacrifice complete. The identification of the head of the phallic Mahāvīra with Vishnu and the three pressings of the sacrifice (also regularly called Vishnu) with the trunk of the Mahāvīra is significant since it suggests that Vishnu is indeed the solar force coursing through the phallus. When it reaches the head its potency is strongest since it is now ready to emerge as the sun, Sūrya. The references to the highest step of Vishnu confirms that the phallic Mahāvīra is an analog of the Tree of Life and that **Vishnu's three steps** are executed first in the underworld, where the roots of the Tree lie, and then in Earth, represented by the trunk of the Tree (or the shaft of the phallus) and, finally, in the Mid-region represented by the branches of the Tree (or the head of the phallus).[813] The Latvian song that Schroeder cites running: "Uhsing brews beer/In the footstep of the horse" also clearly refers to the phallus, which, in Shamanistic rituals, regularly represents as a horse, a charger.[814]

It must be noted however that, in the Pravargya Brāhmana of the *Kathāranyaka*, it is not Makha Vaishnava that is beheaded by his own bowstring but **Rudra** (*KĀ* 3,207) or the sacrifice (*KĀ* 2,115). Thus, while *SB* XIV,1,1,27 points to the (sun) as the Pravargya, the Kathas say "yonder Āditya (the sun) is actually Rudra Mahāvīra". In the Darshapūrnamāsaishti (New-moon and Full-moon) sacrifice described in *SB* I, Rudra is depicted as assaulting Prajāpati with a dart (I,7,4) which shows that Rudra and Prajāpati are the same deity

---

[813] In shamanism, the shaman climbs the Tree of Life, called Tuuru.

[814] This phallic symbolism is equally the source of the pagan English tradition of a hobby-horse (cf. M. Eliade, *Shamanism*, p.469).

and the sacrifice a self-sacrifice. This sacrifice of Rudra is however the second sacrifice, of Brahman-Prajāpati, rather than the third that precedes the manifestation of the sun in our system.

As Houben describes the ritual, the main vessel is first held with tongs over the Āhavaniya (or Gārhapatya) fire and anointed with clarified butter. The vessel is placed on a gold (or silver) disk lying on a special mound. The vessel is covered with the disk and the fire makes it red-hot. A cow and a goat are milked. **Milk** is poured into the Pravargya vessel. At the pouring of goat's milk on the Mahāvïra, the Adhvaryu says: "Heat the heat of the sun". According to *SB* XIV,1,4,4, Mahāvïra unites with the sun when the gharma glows. The Mahāvïra is then taken to the Āhavaniya fire where a gharma offering to the Ashvins is made. The gharma milk boils and the vessel overflows in all directions. This betokens the setting of the sun in the heavens. The principal participants in the sacrifice now partake of the milk. After the last Pravargya performance, the implements are disposed of at the Uttaravedi. The vessels and other implements are laid down in the form of a man or in the shape of the orb of the sun.

The singing of "Gandharva mantras", praising the Pravargya as the celestial Gandharva, are most probably introduced into the rite because of the connection and sometimes even identification of the Gandharva with the sun. However, Houben points out, many mantras that are connected with the sun can only be interpreted in the context of the well-known imagery of the sun as the 'light of inner vision'".[815]

A popular continuation of the Pravargya ritual is seen in the Dravidian **Pongal** feast that is celebrated at the winter solstice at the start of the Tamil month of Thai (around January 14-15) and is dedicated to the sun-god Sūrya. The main ritual, undertaken at sunrise, consists in the boiling of rice, along with milk and jaggery, in a clay pot called *kollam*. When the milk boils over, the sacrificers shout "Pongalo Pongal!" (Hail to the boiling over!), offer the newly cooked rice to the sun-god and then distribute it to those present. Although the same feast is celebrated in the rest of the Indian regions as a harvest festival called Makara Sankrānti (the transition of the sun

---

[815] Houben, *op.cit.*, p.13.

into Capricorn/*makara*), it is only in Dravidian Tamilnādu that the ritual most closely resembles the Vedic Pravargya.

Among the Germanic and Baltic peoples, the same celebration of the intensifying solar force is recorded not in religious rituals, since these have been mostly forgotten, but in folkloric form in the several fairy-tales that recount the operation of a wonder-mill that produces food inexhaustibly. Thus the tale found in Grimm of the "sweet porridge" that, like the pongal "kollam", overflows from a magical pot until it engulfs an entire village. In Latvian folklore the original solar association of such stories is made clearer since, as we have seen, it is the sun-god Uhsing who is said to brew beer in the "footstep of the horse".[816] From our study of the Indo-European cosmogony, we will realise that the significance of this brewing is the fermentation of the seeds of life (soma) that are borne by the invigorated solar deity in the divine phallus.

Similarly, in the Germanic mythology, we have noted the reference in the Edda to the renewed brewing of beer by the (actually ailing) sea-god Aegir after his "cauldron" has been regained by Thor. This event may be considered in tandem with the account of Mimir drinking mead at his well with Heimdallr's "horn". For both these scenes correspond to the episode of the consumption of Soma by Indra in the original Aryan mythology where the (equally ailing) Varuna is sexually resuscitated in the form of Indra and the solar force is finally propelled to the heavens as the sun.

---

[816] For the phallic significance of the horse, see above p.245.

IV. THE GRAIL

Before we turn to the Celto-Germanic cult of the Grail itself, we may briefly consider here Julius Evola's study of the Grail, *The Mystery of the Grail*, since it contains many interesting elucidations of the various symbols associated with this mysterious object. For instance, in Ch.14 Evola rightly notices the "supernatural light" it bears and the identification of this light with enlightenment in Borron's *Joseph d'Arimathie*. Following Guenon,[817] Evola also points (Ch.17) to the similarity of the stone to the frontal stone that symbolises Shiva's third eye, although he does not elaborate on its significance much. Further, he notes that this stone is

> the foundation, or center of the world, hidden in the "primordial depths, near God's temple." It is put in relation with the body of the primordial man (Adam) and, interestingly enough, with an inaccessible mountain place, the access to which must not be revealed to other people; here Melchizedek,[818] "in divine and eternal service,' watches over Adam's body. In Melchizedek we find again the representation of the supreme function of the Universal Ruler, which is simultaneously regal and priestly; here this representation is associated with some kind of guardian of

---

[817] In his work *Le roi du monde*, Ch.5.

[818] Melchizedek is a priest-king mentioned in *Genesis* 14. In the NT Epistle to the Hebrews, Christ is identified with this primal priesthood of Melchizedek.

Adam's body who originally possessed the Grail and who, after losing it, no longer lives.

The true solar significance of the Grail is more clearly revealed in the Hermetic texts that emphasise the *ars regia* or the royal art. For example, Cesare della Riviera, in his *Il mondo magico degli heroi*, (1605) characterises the "heroes" as those who succeed in conquering the "second Tree of Life" and in introducing a second "earthly paradise" as an image of the primordial center which

> does not appear to base and impure souls, but remains hidden in the celestial spheres of the inaccessible light of the heavenly Sun. It shows itself only to the 'happy' magical hero, who alone gloriously possesses it, enjoying the salvific Tree of Life, located in the middle of this universe.[819]

This glorious vision was, in ancient India as well as in Egypt and Sumer and as late as in Mithraism, originally reserved for the king, as we have noted above. It is not, as Evola suggests (Chs.23,24), the sole prerogative of the Ghibellines who sought to oppose the Christian Church through anti-Christian Knights Templar. In fact, Eschenbach's association of the bearer of the grail stone with Anjou, whose count Charles (1226-1285) supported the Guelph or Papal party against the Ghibellines,[820] suggests that the authors of the Grail romances may indeed have supported the Guelphs rather than the Ghibellines.

Evola further points to the fact that in *Perceval li Gallois*, Perceval's father travelled to the west to die there and that Arthur in the Arthurian legends is also to be found in the "western island" of Avalon. Evola does not seem to understand that this is simply a common reference to the west as the place of the setting sun so that the dying Osiris is commonly called the god of the "westerners".[821] Saturn's location in the Hyperborean regions is likewise a cosmic and not a terrestrial one.

---

[819] *Il mondo magico degli heroi*, 14, cited in Evola, *op.cit.*, Ch.27.

[820] The Ghibellines were the party of the Swabian Hohenstaufens chief of whom was Frederick Barabarossa (1122-1190), while the Guelphs were Bavarians dukes.

[821] See above p.200.

To return to the Grail itself, we find that the mysterious object is described in Wolfram's *Parzival*, Bk.IX, by the hermit Trevrizent as a **stone** called "lapis exilis", that is, the stone of the banishment [of Lucifer]". It was apparently brought to earth from heaven by a host of angels during Lucifer's battle against God and given over to the purest knights of Anjou,[822] of whom Titurel was the first Lord of the Grail. From our knowledge of the Indo-European cosmology, we may understand the stone as a symbol of the divine phallus castrated by the storm-god, who is, in the Christian context, called "Lucifer", the bearer (or robber) of the light. Trevrizent continues to recount that God created Adam (Brahman/Helios) in place of Lucifer and from Adam Eve, who represents Earth. Of the two sons of Adam, Cain and Abel, the former violates his mother and thereby plunges mankind into sin. Cain is thus similar to Zeus/Seth, just as Lucifer is similar to Chronos. In this context, it is interesting to note that the wound of Amfortas, who represents Osiris/Varuna becomes more painful with the advent of Saturn (Chronos, who castrated Ouranos/Horus the Elder):

In this wise did he learn the tidings that Saturn drew near again,
And the star with a sharp frost cometh, and it helpeth no whit to lay
The spear on the sore as aforetime, in the wound must it plunge alway
When that star standeth high in heaven the wound shall its coming know
Afore, tho' the earth shall heed not, nor token of frost shall show.

Trevrizent further adds that the manifestation of Christ as a son of man was in order to redeem sinful mankind, so that Christ is a counterpart of the solar brother of the storm-god Seth/Ganesha, that is, Horus the Younger/Muruga/Marduk.[823]

---

[822] These guardians of the Grail are also called Templars (*Parzival*, Bk IX, 'Trevrezent'). Cf. p.112n above.

[823] See above p.227f.

The Grail stone is also described by Trevrizent as possessing the power of reviving even the burnt Phoenix and of rendering deathless and ageless all those who look upon it. Its productive power is renewed annually on Good Friday by a heavenly **dove** that blesses the stone with a **host**. The dove represents the Holy Spirit and the host (from Lt. *hostia*, sacrificial victim) represents the body of the resurrected Christ. The dove thus not only transforms the bread and wine of the eucharist into those of Christ but is also the agent of the revivification of the dead Christ just as Re is the force whereby the moribund Osiris is revived and made ithyphallic.[824] The host is also the symbolic counterpart of the new immaterial body that the sacrificer acquires in the Agnishtoma sacrifice.[825] More significant is the corresponding moment in the Rājasūya sacrifice where the king, upon his consecration, stands on his throne with arms raised to represent the phallic cosmic pillar and he is asked by the priests to fertilise the earth with "ghee".[826] We see therefore that the representation of the grail in Wolfram's *Parzival* retains the original phallic significance of the solar mystery of the resurrection since the resurrected body of Christ that the host represents is indeed one that rises through the Soma-filled Tree of Life as the sun. This is also clearly why Trevrizent refers to the burnt Phoenix, or the moribund sun.

The Welsh stories of the grail are also of crucial importance for a proper understanding of the grail not only because the story of Perceval is one that is set in Wales but also because the extraordinary story of Bran is indispensable for a proper identification of the Fisher King and the Grail itself. As we have seen, the first Fisher King in *Joseph d'Arimathie* is called Bron. And, like Chrétien's Fisher King, who is wounded in the leg, Bran too is wounded in his foot. This is

---

[824] In the Roman Rite, the host is raised aloft by the priest to reveal to the congregation the transsubstantiation of the consecrated bread. This practice, adopted in the 12th century by Eudes de Sully, Bishop of Paris, is indeed symbolic in more than one way.

[825] See above p.258.

[826] See above p.250.

an euphemistic reference to the actual wounding of the Fisher King in his genitals, as we have noted from the supplementary information provided by Wolfram's *Parzival*. While the Fisher King is sustained by the Grail, Bran's **head** is sustained by its own life. Bran as the Fisher King is identical to Aegir/Hymir who are associated with the Midgard serpent or "fish" that they are surrounded by. We have also noted the account of Mimir's decapitated head as a depiction of a castration that is revived by the drinking of solar "mead".[827] Bran's decapitated head, like the head of Makha in the Pravargya ritual, is thus the head of the divine phallus that the Fisher King is deprived of.

The continuation of the legends concerning Joseph in Britain are also to be noted carefully in this context. John of Glastonbury, who composed a chronicle of Glastonbury Abbey in the 14th century, for instance, claimed that Joseph brought with him a wooden cup used in the Last Supper along with two cruets containing the blood and sweat of the crucified Christ respectively. A later 16th century metrical *Lyfe of Joseph of Arimathea* however maintains that when Joseph visited Glastonbury he planted his staff in the ground and it forthwith sprouted into a **thorn tree** that unusually flowered twice a year, first in the winter and then again in the spring. The phallic symbolism of the object borne by Joseph is clear enough.

We note that the grail has the property of supplying abundant food and drink and of sustaining a guardian who is wounded. Thus its essential characteristic is a life-sustaining one. This particular property it derives in Chrétien's *Perceval* and Wolfram's *Parzival* from the holy host, which is the Christian equivalent of the rebirth of the sacrificer in an immortal body in the Indic sacrifices. The description of the Grail as a stone, and its appearance at the moment when Lucifer revolts against God makes clear its identity as the divine phallus which finally formed the universe and its sun. The association of the Grail in the original Celtic stories first with a head that is akin to the head of Makha, the phallic pot of the Indic Pravargya ritual, and then with a tree in the *Lyfe of Joseph of Arimathea* confirms this identification.[828]

---

[827] See p.211 above.

[828] For evidence of phallic worship in Celtic Ireland see J. Bonwick, *Irish Druids*

For the pre-Christian prevalence of phallic worship in Scandinavia until the 11th century we have evidence in the account of phallic worship recorded in the 'Völsa Þáttr'[829] where the penis of a dead horse is ritually preserved and worshipped by a pagan family. First the woman of the house wraps the penis in linen with herbs and prays to it as to a god, after which the penis grows strong and stands erect. It is then worshipped every evening in a ritualistic manner whereby the woman first holds the penis chanting sacred verses and then passes it on to the other members of the family who do likewise.[830] Finally King Olaf II of Norway enters and, preaching to the family about Christianity, succeeds in converting them to the new religion.

In light of our survey of the cosmological underpinnings of the mythology of the ancient Indo-Europeans, we may now recognise some errors in Leopold von Schroeder's interpretation of the significance of the Grail vessel. For example, Schroeder maintains in his work that the prototype of the grail beaker or bowl was **the sun and moon** considered in Vedic literature **as vessels** (Ch.II). Schroeder adduces especially the fact that the grail is represented as a dish or bowl freely floating in the air while dispensing food as evidence that it is a symbol of a heavenly body, the moon or the sun. But this ignores the passage in Eschenbach's *Parzival* where Trevrizent clearly describes the Grail as a "stone".[831] And while Schroeder rightly points to the Germanic Eddas as precedents of the Grail story, he does not understand that the cauldron that Thor gets from Hymir and gifts to Aegir is indeed nothing but the phallus that Seth/Ganesh/Zeus get from Osiris the Elder/Brahman-Prajāpati/Phanes and bestow upon the same solar force now moribund in the "underworld" as Osiris/Varuna. Indra does not thus steal the "sun" but rather the solar force and that, first, from Brahman, the manifest cosmic form of the Ideal

---

and Old Irish Religions, Part II, 'Stone-worship'.

[829] This is a short story included in the *Flateyjarbók* (Ólafs saga helga).

[830] One is reminded of the knights' meal in Wolfram's *Parzival*, Bk.V (Amfortas), where the Grail is brought in to provide food and drink magically to those assembled in the castle.

[831] See above p.266.

Man, Purusha/Hymir, and, then, from Vrtra, the serpent in the depths of the underworld that must be dompted before the solar force can emerge in our system as the sun. Another reference that Schroeder makes, to the "shaking"of this bowl (caru) in the Vedas (p.75), is further evidence that what is indeed sometimes called a "bowl" in the Vedas is in fact a phallic symbol since we have here clearly a reference to the stroking of the phallus that stimulates the ejaculation of the divine semen.

Neither are the "**odana**" or "**odana vishtarin**" (the sacrificial porridge offering) that Schroeder points[832] to references to the moon and the sun at the zenith, but rather descriptions of Indra's developing solar force which liberates the solar energy or rays from the frigid Panis that constrain them and allows them to be manifest first as the moon and then as the sun at its zenith. Schroeder's reference to German folk-songs that describe the sun as standing in the Milky Way at noon (p.51) are, in this context, useful in suggesting the force of the sun in this astronomical situation.

Schroeder also tends to confuse **soma** with **madhu** (mead) and thinks that at the zenith the solar force merely enjoys the bliss associated with Soma. Thus, according to him, the mead in the highest step of Vishnu, or at the red zenith (of the sun) is the same as soma. But, as we have noted above, the soma-sacrifice is indeed different from the milk-sacrifice of the Pravargya,[833] and milk representing "mead" is indeed more potent than soma. Soma is indeed the sap that Indra imbibes in the company of his mother from his father Tvashtar (who is represented, as Schroeder points out, as an old man "rich in seed" (p.72)). This is the life-force of the universe that is stored in the moon. It is not the same as the essence of the solar force that is manifest at the zenith of the sun's heavenly circuit, when the sun is indeed represented as Indra/Re.[834] Schroeder's comment that Indra cannot be imagined as a milk-drinker (p.54) is plainly wrong since the "mead" that is drunk by Indra after the incident wherein the sun-

---

[832] See above p.39.

[833] See above p.255.

[834] See above p.239.

falcon[835] protects Indra from the attack of Krishanu is indeed milk, as Griffith rightly translated v.5 of *RV* IV,27.

Schroeder's comparison of the **thunderbolt** of Thor to the vajra of Indra and the **lance** of Peronnik and Longinus in Parzival is accurate. It is with this instrument that the heroic god destroys the serpent which occludes the solar force. Hence the account of Thor catching the Midgard serpent in *Hymisqvidha*. However, Schroeder's references to the **thunder-drum** are misleading in that they suggest that it was used mainly as an instrument of rain-magic. In fact, from our study of Indra's drum, we note that the drum is related to Indra's vajra with which Vrtra the serpent and the Panis are destroyed in order to release the solar rays from these agents of constraint.[836] The drum represents the roar of the flood that issues from "Indra's arm", which, as we have seen, is itself a phallic term. In this context, we may also observe that the drum of the shamans is also considered as a "spirit **horse**" and its rim is made of larch wood, the larch being considered a sacred tree.[837] We have already noted the phallic significance of the "horse" in shamanism.[838] Significantly too, beer (representing soma) is spilled on the Altaic shaman's drum to vivify it.[839] So it is clear that the drum, as a thunder-instrument, is indeed a symbol of Indra's phallic force.

Schroeder's conjecture that soma and milk sacrifices are basically designed to produce rain and sustain the light of the sun (Ch.III) is, in general, unconvincing. As we have seen, it is clearly indicated that the Pravargya sacrifice follows on the Agnishtoma soma-sacrifice. This is because the soma-pressings produce the life of the universe that is stored in the moon whereas the boiling of the milk produces the sun. And the "vessel" that Schroeder associates with the soma is

---

[835] The sun-falcon itself, which is a symbol of the Egyptian Horus the Younger, is indeed Vishnu, the expansive force of Indra.

[836] See above p.231.

[837] See Joseph Campbell, *Primitive Mythology*, cf. M. Eliade, Shamanism, pp.168,171,173.

[838] See above p.260. The horse is indeed used in shamanism "to fly through the air, to reach the heaven" (see M. Eliade, *Shamanism*, p.467).

[839] See M. Eliade, *Shamanism*, p.170.

not interchangeable with that which he associates equally with the sun (Ch.II). The Grail is indeed not a vessel at all but more accurately a stone, a phallic stone whose activation produces first the moon and then the sun.

Another mistake that Schroeder makes is in his identification of **Hymir** with the Fisher King because he takes Thor out on a fishing trip in "Hymisqvidha". The Fisher King is one that suffers from a dreadful wound and he is rather Aegir who bemoans the lack of a "cauldron", whereas Hymir is the Cosmic Man Ymir before he is castrated by his impetuous son. The Edda has no clear awareness of the different re-enactments of the sacrifice of the Purusha/Ymir/Hymir/Gymir in the ideal realm, the cosmos and in the "underworld".

However, the castration of the solar deity in the underworld does result in a **desolation** that recurs in the Grail stories, where not only the Lord of the Grail Castle but also his entire domain suffers from a fearful decay. But Schroeder's theory that the land will be revivified by renewed rainfall produced by the Moon/Soma and that the Vedic sacrifices are rain-magic is a superficial one in that soma in general represents the life-force that is stored in the moon and is not really just a rain-producing agent.

Schroeder is right in pointing to the importance of **abstinence** in ensuring the efficacy of the sacrificial ritual. In the soma sacrifices of the Shrauta Sūtras too the abstinence of the sacrificer before and after the ritual is insisted upon.[840]

Schroeder's identification of the moon as a realm inhabited by **souls** of good men who are not yet freed from the cycle of the transmigration of souls (p.107) is an interesting one. The moon is indeed ruled by Manu's twin brother, Yama, the king of the dead.[841] The Soma is said to be guarded by the Gandharvas, whose female companions are called Apsaras. According to Hillebrandt, the **Gandharvas** are mainly wind-gods and, in the *Vishnupurāna*, their prince is said to be the major wind-god Vāyu (Wata/Wotan).[842]

---

[840] Cf. A. Jacob, *Brahman*.

[841] See *RV* IX,113.

[842] See A. Hillebrandt, *Vedische Mythologie*, Bd. I: *Soma und verwandte Götter*,

Their female companions, the Apsaras, are water-goddesses. At this juncture, we may recall Schroeder's reference to Indra being shot at by an archer called Kriçânu (whom he assumes to be a Gandharva) and being borne by a falcon in *RV* IV,27 (p.114). Schroeder explains this as an incident where the falcon steals Soma from the sun for Indra. This is hard to understand when Indra is indeed the bearer of the sun and is already invigorated with Soma that he has drunk in the house of his father, Tvashtr. Even the falcon, the typical form of Horus the Younger/Vishnu, is only an aspect of Indra and indeed both the previous and the following Rigvedic hymns are about Indra. However, it is possible that Indra, before becoming the sun at the zenith, had to obtain the Soma also from the falcon at the head of the Tree of Life[843] and was for this reason, like Prometheus, considered to have "robbed" the solar force for mankind.

Schroeder perceptively reminds us of the Buddhist doctrine that relates the Gandharvas to the **jīvas** or the personal souls that enter the embryos formed from the union of the male and the female seed.[844] The entry of the Jīva into the embryo is described in the (Hindu) *Garbha Upanishad* as taking place in the seventh month of pregnancy. This Upanishad further explains that, when the embryo has fully formed sense and intellectual organs, the Jīva is reminded of its previous births and pledges to repent of its former sins. However, on emerging from the womb at birth

> it is inflicted with the illusory force of Māya created by Vishnu and immediately forgets all its previous births and the deeds performed therein. Its memory is cleansed of all its history the very moment it first inhales the air on coming to the earth.[845]

This may indeed explain the curious feature of the Lohengrin myth that Lohengrin, who is, like the Gandharvas, a protector of the Grail/

---

p.442.

[843] See above p.209.

[844] See above p.109.

[845] See *Thirty Minor Upanishads*.

Soma is forced to prohibit all questions regarding his spiritual identity, for the recognition of the latter would preclude any association with an earthly woman, such as Elsa.[846]

It is interesting, in this context, to note that Lohengrin is, in the French romance *Naissance du Chevalier au Cygne*, called Elias, which is a mediaeval French form of the Latin Aelius and Greek Helios, equivalents of the solar force Brahman.[847] In this romance, unlike in Eschenbach's *Parzival*, Lohengrin is not forced to leave his wife and has a daughter Ida, who is said to be the mother of Godfrey[848] de Bouillon (ca.1061-1100), the Crusader knight in whose honour the romance was written. The association of Godfrey's grandmother and Ida's mother to a legendary swan-knight was in order to give Godfrey de Bouillon a divine ancestry. It is interesting that Ida is also the name of the daughter of Manu, who, as we have seen, is the ancestress of the Aila lunar dynasty of kings. In Greek mythology, Idaea is also the name of the nymph (the Greek equivalent of the Indic Apsara) who married the river-god Scamander and gave birth to Teucer, the ancestor of the Trojans. Even though it is difficult to substantiate, it is possible that the composer of the romance was aware of the Greek and Indic myths related to the nymph Idaea and the daughter of the First Man, Ida, and that this was what prompted him to compose the the legend of the swan-knight Lohengrin as a means of glorifying Godfrey as the scion of a semi-divine race. Lohengrin thus is not only a Gandharva-type figure but also a solar one since the swan is the vehicle of Brahman, the primal solar light of the cosmos,[849] and Lohengrin's name Elias is the French form of Helios, the Greek equivalent of Brahman. As the father of Ida he is also like the First Man, Manu Vaivasvata, or Manu of the sun.

---

[846] The *Rigveda* (X,95) refers to an occasion where an Apsara named Urvashi falls in love with an earthly prince, Pururuvas.

[847] See above p.190. While Helios is the same as Brahman, Apollo is the Greek counterpart of Sūrya.

[848] Godfrey's mother was Ida, daughter of Godfrey III, Duke of Lower Lorraine (ca.997-1069).

[849] See above p.203.

A final observation should be made regarding Schroeder's equation of the **secret question** that Parsifal must ask of the Fisher King in order to save him with the catechisms of the Vedic literature that relate to the secret signifance of the rituals[850] and with those of the exegetical Upanishads. This is somewhat inaccurate since the question that Parsifal has to ask is one that reveals his sympathy with the Fisher King's suffering. For the suffering of Amfortas is essentially akin to the suffering that Parsifal himself has been subject to ever since he, like Lucifer once, became estranged from God:

> For I against God bear hatred, and my wrath ever waxeth strong.
> For my sorrow and shame hath He cherished, and He watched them greater grow
> Till too high they waxed, and my gladness, yet living, He buried low
> And I think were God fain to help me other anchor my joy had found
> Than this, which so deep hath sunk it, and with sorrow hath closed it round.
> A man's heart is mine, and sore wounded, it acheth, and acheth still.
> Yet once was it glad and joyous, and free from all thought of ill !
> Ere sorrow her crown of sorrow, thorn-woven, with stem hand pressed
> On the honour my hand had won me o'er many a foeman's crest
> And I do well to lay it on Him, the burden of this my shame,
> Who can help if He will, nor withholdeth the aid that men fain would claim,
> But me alone, hath He helped not, whatever men of Him may speak,
> But ever He turneth from me, and His wrath on my head doth wreak![851]

---

[850] See, for instance, *SB* XIII,5,2.

[851] Tr. J.L. Weston, *Parzival*, a knightly epic.

The physical suffering that Amfortas experiences can only be removed through an infusion of divine life into his wound with the lance and Parsifal's spiritual suffering can likewise be removed only through an understanding of the cause of the original revolt of Lucifer against God that caused the "stone" to fall from heaven.

This motif of compassionate understanding of the pain of human desire informs the entire opera of Richard Wagner on the Grail based on Wolfram's *Parzival*, for Parsifal is described continually as a pure fool who understands through compassion, "durch Mitleid wissend". The importance of the innocence of Parsifal in Wolfram and Wagner is thus not exactly related to that in the Indic story of Rishyaçringa, as Schroeder's reference would suggest.[852] In the Indic story, the sexual union of the chaste Rishyaçringa and the princess brings about the revivification of the land, just as the abstinence of the sacrificer in the Indic sacrifices we have studied only increases the potency of the solar force that they are intended to stimulate. In Wolfram the emphasis is more on the essentially monastic virtue of adherence to God, even though Parsifal himself as the Lord of the Grail may be married to Kondwiramur. In Wagner, Kundry, the only female character in the opera, dies soon after her baptism by Parsifal. Amfortas' suffering itself has not only been brought about by sexual desire in the castle of Klingsor but continues to manifest itself as an unquenchable emission of sinful "blood" from the wound:

> ... aus der nun mir, an heiligster Stelle,
> dem Pfleger göttlischer Güter,
> des Erlösungsbalsams Hüter,
> das heisse Sündenblut entquillt,
> ewig erneut aus des Sehnens Quelle,
> das, ach! keine Büssung je mir stillt![853]

This wound can only be healed by the pure blood that issued from the wound of Christ on the cross:

---

[852] See above p.99.

[853] Richard Wagner, *Parsifal*, Act I.

aus der mit blut'gen Tränen
der Göttliche weint' ob der Menschheit Schmach,
in Mitleids heiligem Sehnen.[854]

What Wagner brought to the Indo-European conception of the life-giving Grail (or divine Phallus) is thus a Schopenhauerian emphasis on the essentially painful nature of all desire, which has to be dompted just as it was in the divine Passion of Osiris/Varuna/Aegir in the Ocean and the underworld and that of Wotan/Christ on Yggdrasil and the Cross respectively. It is this abjuration of the world that gives Wagner's opera its extraordinarily tragic atmosphere. We see therefore that the most ancient Indo-European myths concerning the creation of the cosmos are continued and even deepened within a human context in the Christian Grail stories of the Celts, French and Germans from Chrétien to Wagner. As Schroeder remarked of Wagner's *Parsifal* in his next work, *Die Vollendung des arischen Myteriums in Bayreuth* (p.144),

> We call [*Parsifal*] rather ... Aryan-Christian, for it represents indeed the most powerful synthesis of Aryanhood and Christianity. The roots are Aryan, but the crown of this mighty tree is Christian. However, the whole is a completely uniform organism, the most perfect creation of the greatest artistic genius of our age.

---

[854] Richard Wagner, *Parsifal*, Act I.

BIBLIOGRAPHY

I. REFERENCE WORKS

The Hindu World: An Encyclopedic Survey of Hindusim, 2 vols., ed. B. Walker, London: Allen and Unwin, 1968.
Encyclopedia of Indo-European Culture, ed. J. Mallory and D.Q. Adams, London: Fitzroy Dearborn, 1997.

II. PRIMARY LITERATURE

Ancient Near Eastern

A. Annus, *The Standard Babylonian Epic of Anzu*, Helsinki: The Neo-Assyrian Text Corpus Project, 2001.
H.W. Attridge and R.A. Oden Jr. (tr.), Philo of Byblos, *The Phoenician History*, Washington, D.C.: The Catholic Biblical Association of America, 1981.
H.W. Attridge and R.A. Oden (tr.), Lucian, *De Dea Syria, The Syrian Goddess*, Missoula, MT: The Society of Biblical Literature, n.d.

A. Barucq and F. Daumas, *Hymnes et Prières de l'Egypte ancienne*, Paris: Cerf, 1980.

E.A.W. Budge, *The Alexander Book in Ethiopia*, London: Oxford University Press, 1933.

L. Cagni (tr.), *The Poem of Erra*, Malibu, CA: Undena Publications, 1977.

CT = *The Ancient Egyptian Coffin Texts*, tr. R.O. Faulkner.

CT = Cuneiform Texts from Babylonian Tablets in the British Museum.

F.H. Colson and GH. Whitaker (tr.), Philo Judaeus, *De Mutatione nominum*, in Philo, Vol.V, London: Heinemann, 1934.

E. Ebeling (ed.), *Keilschrift aus Assur religösen Inhalts* [=KAR], Leipzig, 1915-23.

A. Falkenstein, "*Sumerische religiöse Texte*", ZA 55 (1962), 11-67.

R.O. Faulkner (tr.), *The Egyptian Book of the Dead*, San Francisco: Chronicle Books, 1994.

C.J. Gadd and L. Legrain, *Ur Excavations: Texts*, Vol. I: Royal Inscriptions, London, 1928.

J.G. Griffiths (tr.), Plutarch, *De Iside et Osiride*, University of Wales Press, 1970.

E. Hornung, *Das Amduat: Die Schrift des verborgenen Raumes*, 3 vols., Wiesbaden: O. Harrassowitz, 1977-78.

E. Hornung, *The Ancient Egyptian Books of the Afterlife*, tr. D. Lorton, Ithaca: Cornell University Press, 1999.

T. Jacobsen, *Sumerian King-List*, Chicago: University of Chicago Press, 1939.

L. King (ed.), *Enuma Elish: The Seven Tablets of Creation* (=EE), London: Luzac and Co., 1902.

M.G. Kovacs (tr.), *The Epic of Gilgamesh*, Stanford: Stanford University Press, 1985.

S. N. Kramer, *Enmerkar and the Lord of Aratta*, Philadelphia: University Museum, 1952.

W. Lambert and A.R. Millard, *Atrahasis: The Babylonian Story of the Flood*, Oxford: Clarendon Press, 1969.

R. Litke, *A Reconstruction of the Assyro-Babylonian God-list An:dA-*

nu-um and An: anu šá amēli, New Haven, CT: Yale Babylonian Collection, 1998.

J.B. Pritchard, *Ancient Near Eastern Texts relating to the Old Testament*, Princeton, NJ: Princeton University Press,1969.

M.-J. Seux, *Hymnes et Prières aux Dieux de Babylonie et d'Assyrie*, Paris: Editions du Cerf, 1976.

H. St. J. Thackeray (tr.), Josephus, *Jewish Antiquities, in Josephus, with an English translation*, London: Heinemann, 1926-65.

J. Van Dijk, *Lugal ud me-lam-bi Nir-gal*, Leiden: E.J. Brill, 1983.

G.P. Verbrugghe and J.M. Wickersham (tr.), *Berossus and Manetho, introduced and translated: Native Traditions in ancient Mesopotamia and Egypt, Ann Arbor*, MI: University of Michigan Press, 1996.

Indo-Iranian

RV = Rgveda
KYV = Krishna Yajurveda
TS = Taittirīya Samhita
Katha Upanishad
Thirty Minor Upanishads, tr. K.N. Aiyar, Madras: Vasanta Press, 1914.
SB = Shatapatha Brāhmana
KB = Kaushītiki Brāhmana
Taittriyopanishad Brāhmana
The Pravargya Brāhmana of the Taittirīya Āranyaka: An ancient commentary on the Pravargya ritual, tr. J.E.M. Houben, New Delhi: Motilal Banarsidass, 1991.
BrdP = Brahmānda Purāna
PP = Padma Purāna
BP = Bhāgavata Purāna
SP = Shiva Purāna
VP = Vishnu Purāna
Mbh = Mahābhārata
Gautama Dharmasūtra in *The Dharmasūtras: The law-codes of Āpastamba, Gautama, Baudhāyana and Vasistha*, tr. P. Olivelle, N.Y.: Oxford University Press, 1999.

W. Caland and V. Henry, *L'Agnistoma: Description complète de la forme normale de sacrifice de soma dans le culte védique*, Paris: E. Leroux, 1906.

H.W. Bodewitz, *The Jyotistoma Ritual, Jaiminiya Brahmana I,66-364* (Orientalia Rhenotraiectina Vol.34).

Translation of the Surya-Siddhanta, tr. E. Burgess, New Haven, CT: American Oriental Society, 1860

R.C. Majumdar, *The Classical Accounts of India*, Calcutta: Firma K.L. Mukhopadhyay, 1960.

Bundahishn, in *Pahlavai Texts*, Part I, tr. E.W. West (Sacred Books of the East, Vol.5), Oxford: Clarendon Press, 1880.

R.C. Zaehner, *The Teachings of the Magi*, London: George Allen and Unwin Ltd., 1956.

European

Caesar, *Gallic Wars*, tr. H.J. Edwards, London: Heinemann, 1917.

H. Diels, *Doxographi Graeci*, Berlin, 1879.

The Poetic Edda, tr. H.A. Bellows, Princeton, NJ: Princeton University Press, 1936.

The Prose Edda of Snorri Sturlusson, tr. J.I. Young, Cambridge: Bowes and Bowes, 1954.

Geoffrey of Monmouth, *History of the Kings of Britain*, tr. L.Thorpe, Harmondsworth: Penguin, 1966.

Herodotus, *Histories*, 4 vols., tr. A.D. Godley, London: Heinemann, 1924-28.

Hesiod, *The Shield, Catalogue of Women and other fragments*, tr. G.W. Most, Cambridge, MA: Harvard University Press, 2007.

Hesiod, *Theogony, Works and Days, Testimonia*, tr. G.W. Most, Cambridge, MA: Harvard University Press, 2007.

Tacitus, Agricola, *Germania, Dialogus*, tr. M. Hutton, London: Heinemann, 1914.

Wolfram von Eschenbach, *Parzival*, a knightly epic. tr. J.L. Weston, London: D. Nutt, 1894.

Richard Wagner, *Parsifal*, 1882.

III. SECONDARY LITERATURE

G.W. Ahlström, *Ancient Palestine: A historical Introduction*, Minneapolis: Fortress Press, 2002.

G.W. Ahlström, *The History of Ancient Palestine from the paleolithic period to Alexander's conquest*, Minneapolis, MN: Fortress Press, 1993.

G. Algaze, *The Uruk World-System: The Dynamics of Expansion of early Mesopotamian Civilization*, Chicago: Chicago University Press, 1993.

R. and B. Allchin, *The rise of civilization in India and Pakistan*, Cambridge: Cambridge University Press, 1982.

K. Al-Nashef, "The Deities of Dilmun", in A. Al Khalifa, M. Rice, T. Almoayed (ed.), *Bahrain through the Ages*, London: Routledge and Kegan Paul, 1993.

C. Autran, *Sumérien et Indo-Européen*, Paris: Librairie Orientaliste Paul Geuthner, 1925.

M. Biardeau, *Le sacrifice dans l'inde ancienne*, Paris: Presses universitaires de France, 1976.

S. Bickel, *La Cosmogonie egyptienne avant le nouvel empire*, Fribourg: Éditions universitaires, 1994.

K. Bittel, *Les Hittites*, Paris: Gallimard, 1976.

J. Bonwick, *Irish Druids and Old Irish Religions*, London: Griffith, Farran and Co., 1894.

J. Bottero, *Mesopotamia: Writing, Reasoning and the Gods*, tr. Z. Bahrani and M. van de Mieroop, Chicago: University of Chicago Press, 1992.

E.A.W. Budge, *The Gods of the Egyptians, or Studies in Egyptian Mythology*, 2 vols., London: Methuen and Co., 1904.

E. Bryant, *The Quest for the Origins of Vedic Culture: The Indo-Aryan Migration Debate*, Oxford: Oxford University Press, 2001.

Joseph Campbell, *Primitive Mythology*, N.Y., NY: Viking, 1959.

J. Cauvin, *Religions néolithiques de Syro-Palestine*, Paris: J. Maisonneuve,1972.

D. K. Chakrabarti, "The archaeology of Hinduism", in T. Insoll (ed.), *Archaeology and World Religion*, London: Routledge, 2001.

J. Charpentier, "The Date of Zoroaster", *BSOS* 3 (1923-25), 747-55.

P. Charvat, *Mesopotamia before History*, London: Routledge, 2002.

G. Childe, *The Dawn of European Civilization*, London: Routledge and Kegan Paul Ltd., 1961.

U. Chouduri, *Indra and Varuna in Indian Mythology*, Delhi: Nag Publishers, 1981.

A.B. Cook, *Zeus: A Study in Ancient Religion*, 2 vols. in 3, New York: Biblo and Tannen, 1964-5.

R. Cook, *The Tree of Life: Symbol of the Centre*, London: Thames and Hudson, 1974.

S.A. Cook, *The Religion of ancient Palestine in the Light of Archaeology*, London: Oxford University Press, 1930.

F. Cornelius, "Erin-Manda", *Iraq* 25 (1963), pp.167-70.

A. Daniélou, *Shiva and Dionysus, the omnipresent gods of transcendence and ecstasy*, New York: Inner Tradition International, 1984.

A. Deimel, *Pantheon Babylonicum: Nomina deorum e textibus cuneiformibus excerpta et ordine alphabetico distributa*, Rome: Pontifical Biblical Institute, 1914.

G. Dumezil, *Dieux cassites et védiques à propos d'un bronze du Louristan*, RHA 52 (1950), 16-37.

M. Eliade, *Shamanism: Archaic Techniques of Ecstasy*, N.Y.: Pantheon Books, 1964.

J. Evola, *The Mystery of the Grail: Initiation and Magic in the Quest for the Spirit*, Rochester, VT: Inner Traditions, 1996.

G. Erdosy, (ed.) *The Indo-Aryans of Ancient South Asia*, Berlin: Walter de Gruyter, 1995.

J. Finegan, *Archaeological History of the Ancient Middle East*, Boulder, CO: Westview Press, 1979.

E. Forrer, "Stratification des langues et des peuples dans le Proche-Orient préhistorique", *JA* 217 (1930), pp.227-52.

H. Frankfort, *Archaeology and the Sumerian Problem*, Chicago: Chicago University Press, 1932.

D. Frayne, "Indo-Europeans and Sumerians: Evidence for their linguistic Contact", *CSMS Bulletin* 25 (1993), 19-42.

H.D. Galter, *Der Gott Ea/Enki in der akkadischen Überlieferung*, Graz, 1983.

I. Gelb, *Hurrians and Subarians*, Chicago: University of Chicago Press, 1944.

K. Gerhardt, *Die Glockenbecherleute in Mittel- und Westdeutschland*, Stuttgart: Schweizerbart'sche Verlag, 1953.

A. Ghose, "The Origins of Aryan Speech", *Sri Aurobindo Birth Centenary Library*, vol.10, Pondicherry: Sri Aurobindo Ashram, 1971.

G.S. Ghurye, *Indian Acculturation: Agasthya and Skandha*, Bombay: Popular Prakashan, 1977.

J. Gonda, *Die Religionen Indiens*, II: Der jüngere Hinduismus, Stuttgart: Kohlhammer, 1963.

J. Gonda, *Prajāpati's rise to higher rank*, Leiden: E.J. Brill, 1986.

C.H. Gordon, "Canaanite Mythology", in S. Kramer (ed.), *Mythologies of the Ancient World*, Garden City, NY: Doubleday, 1961 , pp.181-215.

A.R.W. Green, *Storm-God in the Ancient Near East*, Winona Lake, IN: Eisenbrauns, 2003.

H.G. Güterbock, *Kumarbi, Istanbuler Schriften* 16, 1946.

H.G. Güterbock, "*Hittite Mythology*" in S. Kramer, *op.cit.*, 139-79.

H.G. Güterbock, "*The god Suwalliyat reconsidered*", RHA 19 (1961), 1-18.

V. Haas, *Geschichte der hethitischen Religion*, Leiden: E.J. Brill, 1994.

D. Handelman, "Myths of Murugan: Asymmetry and Hierarchy in a South Indian Puranic Cosmology", *History of Religions*, 27, no.2.

T. Harpur, *The Pagan Christ: Recovering the lost light*, Toronto: Thomas Allen, 2004.

R.J. Harrison, *The Beaker Folk*, London: Thames and Hudson, 1980.

J.E. Hartley, *The Book of Job*, Grand Rapids, MI: W.E. Eerdmans Publishing Co., 1988.

A. Heidel, "*The meaning of Mummu in Akkadian literature*", JNES, 7, no.2, April 1948.

J.C. Heesterman, *The ancient Indian royal consecration: the Rājasūya described according to the Yajus texts and annotated*, 's-Gravenhage: Mouton, 1957.

J.C. Heesterman, *The broken world of sacrifice: An essay on ancient*

Indian ritual, Chicago: University of Chicago Press, 1993.

A. Hillebrandt, *Vedische Mythologie*, 3 vols., Breslau: Wilhelm Koebner, 1891-1902.

A. Hillebrandt, *Ritualiteratur. Vedische Opfer und Zauber*, Strassburg: Karl J. Trübner, 1897.

W. Hinz, *Lost World of Elam*, tr. J. Barnes, London: Sidgwick and Jackson, 1972.

S. Hood, *The Minoans: Crete in the Bronze Age*, London: Thames and Hudson, 1971.

E. Hornung, *Conceptions of God*, tr. J. Baines, Ithaca: Cornell University Press, 1982.

A. Jacob, "Cosmology and Ethics in the Religions of the Peoples of the Ancient Near East", *Mankind Quarterly* 140, no.1 (Fall 1999), 95-119.

A. Jacob, *Ātman: A Reconstruction of the Solar Cosmology of the Indo-Europeans*, Hildesheim, Georg Olms Verlag, 2005.

A. Jacob, *Brahman: A Study of the Solar Rituals of the Indo-Europeans*, Hildesheim, Georg Olms Verlag, 2012.

T. Jacobsen, *Treasures of Darkness: A History of Mesopotamian Religion*, New Haven: Yale University Press, 1976.

E.O. James, *The Tree of Life: An Archaeological Study*, Leiden: E.J. Brill, 1966.

S.W. Jamison and M. Witzel, "Vedic Hinduism", 1992,
 http://www.people.fas.harvard.edu/~witzel/vedica.pdf

P. Jensen, "Assyrio-Hebraïca", *ZA* IV (1889), 268-80.

P. Jensen, "Adad-Mythus", *RLA*, I:126.

A. Kaliff, *Fire, Water, Heaven and Earth: Ritual practice and cosmology in ancient Scandinavia: an Indo-European perspective*, Stockholm: Riksantikvarieämbetet, 2007.

K.A.R. Kennedy, "Have Aryans been identified in the prehistoric skeletal record from South Asia?" in G. Erdosy (ed.), *op.cit.*

K.M. Kenyon, *Digging up Jericho*, London: E. Benn, 1957.

J.V. Kinnier Wilson, *The Rebel Lands: An Investigation into the Origins of early Mesopotamian Mythology*, Cambridge: Cambridge University Press, 1979.

S. Kramer, *Sumerian Mythology: A Study of spiritual and literary acievement in the third millennium B.C.*, Philadelphia: American

Philosophical Society, 1944.

S. Kramer, "Review of A. Hendel, *The Babylonian Genesis: The Story of Creation*", *JAOS*, 63 (1943), 69-73.

P. Kretschmer, Kuhns Zeitschrift 55.

A.K. Lahiri, *Vedic Vrtra*, Delhi: Motilal Banarsidass, 1984.

N. Lahovary, tr. K.A. Nilakantan, *Dravidian origins and the West: Newly discovered ties with the ancient culture and languages, including Basque, of the pre-Indo-European Mediterranean world*, Bombay: Orient Longmans, 1963.

W.G. Lambert, "Ninurta Mythology in the Babylonian Epic of Creation" in *Keilschriftliche Literaturen, Ausgewählte Vorträge der XXXII RAI*, Berlin: D. Reimer, 1985, 55-60.

B. Landsberger, "The Beginnings of Civilization in Mesopotamia" [1944], in *Three Essays on the Sumerians*, tr. M. DeJ. Ellis, Los Angeles: Undena Publications, n.d.

B. Landsberger and T. Bauer, "Zu neueröffentlichen Geschichtsquellen", *ZA* 37 (1927), 61-98.

D. Lang, *Armenia: Cradle of Civilization*, London: George Allen and Unwin, 1980.

S. Langdon, *Tammuz and Ishtar: A monograph upon Babylonian Religion and Theology*, Oxford: Clarendon Press, 1914.

S. Langdon and A.H. Gardiner, "The treaty of alliance between Hattusili, king of the Hittites, and the pharaoh Rameses II of Egypt", *JEA* 6 (1920).

E. Laroche, *Recherches sur les noms divins hittites*, RHA VII, 45 (1946-47).

G. Leick, *Mesopotamia: The Invention of the City*, London: Penguin Books, 2000.

B. Lincoln, *Myth, Cosmos and Society: Indo-European Themes of Creation and Destruction*, Cambridge, MA: Harvard University Press, 1986.

A. Livingstone, *Mystical and Mythological Explanatory Texts of Assyrian and Babylonian Scholars*, Oxford: Clarendon, 1986.

R. Loomis, *The Grail: From Celtic Myth to Christian Symbol*, Cardiff: University of Wales Press, 1963.

A.A. Macdonell, *A History of Sanskrit Literature*, Delhi: Munshiram Manoharlal, 1961.

A.A. Macdonell, *Vedic Mythology*, Strassburg: K.J. Trübner, 1897.

J.P. Mallory and V. H. Mair, *The Tarim Mummies: Ancient China and the mystery of the earliest peoples from the West*, London: Thames and Hudson, 2008.

J. Mellaart, *Çatal Hüyük: A Neolithic Town in Anatolia*, London: Thames and Hudson, 1967.

S. Mercer, *Horus Royal God of Egypt*, Grafton, MA: Society of Oriental Research, 1942.

A. Michaels, *Hinduism past and present*, Princeton, NJ: Princeton University Press, 2004.

A. Miles, *Land of the Lingam*, London, 1933.

J.Miller, *The Vision of Cosmic Order in the Vedas*, London: Routledge and Kegan Paul, 1985.

S.L. Nagar, *The Cult of Vinayaka*, N.Delhi: Intellectual Publishing House, 1992.

H. Nissen, *The Early History of the Ancient ear East 9000-2000 B.C.*, tr. E. Lutzeier and K.J. Northcott, Chicago: University of Chicago Press, 1988.

H. Nissen, P. Damerow, R.K. Englund, *Archaic Bookkeeping*, Chicago: University of Chicago Press, 1993.

J. Oates, "Ur and Eridu: the Prehistory", *Iraq* 22 (1960), 32-50.

W. O'Flaherty, *Asceticism and Eroticism in the Mythology of Śiva*, London: Oxford University Press, 1973.

F.E. Pargiter, *Ancient Indian Historical Tradition*, London: Milford, 1922.

A. Parpola, "The Problem of the Aryans and the Soma", in G. Erdosy (ed.), *op.cit.*

A. Parrot, *Sumer*, Paris: Gallimard, 1960.

J.A. Philip, *Pythagoras and early Pythagoreanism*, Toronto: University of Toronto Press, 1966.

S. Piggott, *The Druids*, London: Thames and Hudson, 1975.

D.T. Potts, *The Archaeology of Elam*, Cambridge: Cambridge University Press, 1999.

A.D. Pusalkar, *"Pre-Harappan, Harappan and post-Harappan culture and the Aryan problem"*, Quarterly Review of Historical Studies, 7,4 (1967-8).

C.K. Raja, *Survey of Sanskrit Literature*, Bombay: Bharatiya Vidya Bhavan, 1962.

V.G. Rele, *The Vedic Gods as Figures of Biology*, Bombay: D.B. Taraporevala Sons, 1931.

K. Rönnow, "Zur Erklärung des Pravargya, des Agnicayana, und der Sautrāmani", *Le monde orientale*, 23 (1929), 113-73.

G. Rubio, *"On the alleged 'Pre-Sumerian Substratum'"*, JCS 51 (1999), 1-16.

R.T. Rundle Clark, *Myth and Symbol in ancient Egypt*, London: Thames and Hudson, 1959.

M. Rutten, "Les Religions Asianiques", in M. Brillant and R. Aigrain, *Histoire des religions IV*, Paris, 1956, 1-117.

M.Sandman-Holmberg, *The God Ptah*, Lund: C.W.K. Gleerup, 1946.

H.-P. Schmidt, *Brhaspati und Indra*, Wiesbaden: Otto Harrassowitz, 1968.

Giovanni Semerano, *Le Origini della Cultura Europea: Rivelazioni della linguistica storica*, Firenze: Leo Olschki,

G. Sergi, *The Mediterranean Race: A Study of the Origin of European Peoples*, London: W. Scott, 1909.

K. Sethe, *Amun und die acht Urgötter von Hermopolis* ('Abhandlungen der preussischen Akademie der Wissenschaften', 1929, Nr.4).

M. Sharma, *Fire-worship in ancient India*, Jaipur: Publication Scheme, 2002.

S. Sharma, *Scientific Basis of Yajnas along with its wisdom aspect*, ed. A.N. Rawal and tr. H.A. Kapadia, E-book: www.shriramsharma.com.

D. Shulman, "Murukan, the Mango and Ekambaresvara-Siva Fragments of a Tamil Creation Myth", *Indo-Iranian Journal* 21 (1979).

P.O. Skjaervo, "The Avesta as source for the early history of the Iranians", in G. Erdosy (ed.), *op.cit.*

G.E. Smith, *The Ancient Egytians and the Origin of Civilization*, London: Harper, 1923.

E. A. Speiser, *Mesopotamian Origins*, Philadelphia: University of

Pennsylvania Press, 1930.

E.A. Speiser, *Introduction to Hurrian*, AASOR 20, New Haven,CT, 1941.

P. Steinkeller, "Early Political Development in Mesopotamia and the Origins of the Sargonic Empire", in *Akkad, the First World Empire*, ed. M. Leverani, Padua: Sargon srl, 1993.

G.G. Stroumsa, *Another Seed: Studies in Gnostic Mythology*, Leiden: E.J. Brill, 1984.

K. Tallquist, *Akkadische Götterepitheta* ('Studia Orientalia' 7), Helsinki, 1938.

H. te Velde, *Seth God of Confusion: A Study of his Role in Egyptian Mythology and Religion*, Leiden: E.J. Brill, 1967.

F. Thureau-Dangin, "An acte de donation de Marduk-Zâkir-Šumi", *RA* 16 (1919).

H.W. Tull, *The Vedic origins of Karma*, Albany: State University of New York Press, 1989.

S. Tyler, "Dravidian and Uralian: the lexical Evidence", *Language*, 44, pp.1 98-212.

A. Ungnad, *Subartu: Beiträge zur Kulturgeschichte und Völkerkunde Vorderasiens*, Berlin: de Gruyter, 1936.

H. Usener, *Die Sintfluthsagen*, Bonn: Friedrich Cohen, 1899.

J. van Buitenen, *The Pravargya: An ancient Indian iconic ritual*, Poona: Deccan College Post-graduate and Research Institute, 1968.

N. Veldhuis, *A Cow of Sin*, Groningen: Styx Publications, 1991.

A.E. Waite, *The Hidden Church of the Holy Graal: Its Legends and Symbolism considered in their Affinity with certain Mysteries of Initiation and other Traces of a secret Tradition in Christian Times*, London: Rebman, 1909.

A.J. Wensinck, "Tree and Bird as Cosmological Symbols in Western Asia", *Verhandelingen der Koninklijke Akademie van Wetenschappen*, XXII (1921), no.1.

M.L. West, *The East Face of Helicon*, Oxford: Clarendon Press, 1997.

M.L. West, *Orphic Poems*, Oxford: Clarendon Press, 1983.

G. Wilhelm, *Grundzüge der Geschichte und Kultur der Hurriter*, Darmstadt: Wissenschaftliche Buchgesellschaft, 1982.

G. Wilhelm, *Hurrians*, tr. J. Barnes, Warminster: Aris and Phillips Ltd., 1989.

R.H. Wilkinson, *Symbol and Magic in Egyptian Art*, London: Thames and Hudson, 1994.

T. Wilkinson, *Genesis of the Pharoahs*, London: Thames and Hudson, 2003.

H. Wohlstein, *The Sky-god An-Anu*, Jericho, NY: Paul A. Stroock, 1976.

D. Wolkstein and S. Kramer, *Inanna, Queen of Heaven and Earth: Her Stories and Hymns from Sumer*, N.Y.: Harper and Row, 1983.

H. Zimmern, "Religion und Sprache" in E. Schrader, *Die Keilinschriften und das Alte Testament*, Berlin: Reuther und Reichard, 1903, 343-653.

K. Zvelebil, *Tamil Traditions on Subrahmanya-Murugan*, Madras: Institute of Asian Studies, 1991.

CPSIA information can be obtained
at www.ICGtesting.com
Printed in the USA
LVHW101700211122
733710LV00002B/250